TREASURY OF LITERATURE

EMERALD FOREST

SENIOR AUTHORS
ROGER C. FARR
DOROTHY S. STRICKLAND

AUTHORS
RICHARD F. ABRAHAMSON
ELLEN BOOTH CHURCH
BARBARA BOWEN COULTER
BERNICE E. CULLINAN
MARGARET A. GALLEGO
W. DORSEY HAMMOND
JUDITH L. IRVIN
KAREN KUTIPER
DONNA M. OGLE
TIMOTHY SHANAHAN
PATRICIA SMITH
JUNKO YOKOTA
HALLIE KAY YOPP

SENIOR CONSULTANTS
ASA G. HILLIARD III
JUDY M. WALLIS

CONSULTANTS
ALONZO A. CRIM
ROLANDO R. HINOJOSA-SMITH
LEE BENNETT HOPKINS
ROBERT J. STERNBERG

HARCOURT BRACE & COMPANY
Orlando Atlanta Austin Boston San Francisco Chicago Dallas New York
Toronto London

Acknowledgments continue on page 622, which constitutes an extension of this copyright page.

Acknowledgments

For permission to reprint copyrighted material, grateful acknowledgment is made to the following sources:

Atheneum Publishers, an imprint of Macmillan Publishing Company: *The Gold Coin* by Alma Flor Ada, illustrated by Neil Waldman. Text copyright © 1991 by Alma Flor Ada; illustrations copyright © 1991 by Neil Waldman. "Why Frog and Snake Never Play Together" and cover illustration from *Beat the Story-Drum, Pum-Pum* by Ashley Bryan. Copyright © 1980 by Ashley Bryan. Illustration from *Lion and the Ostrich Chicks*, retold and illustrated by Ashley Bryan. Copyright © 1986 by Ashley Bryan.

Avon Books: Text and cover illustration from *The Plant That Ate Dirty Socks* by Nancy McArthur. Text and cover illustration copyright © 1988 by Nancy McArthur.

Barron's Educational Series, Inc.: Cover illustration from *Aesop's Fables*, illustrated by Fulvio Testa. Illustration copyright © 1989 by Fulvio Testa. Original edition published in Italy under the title *Favole di Esopo*. Copyright © 1989 by Edizioni Scolastiche Walk Over, Bergamo, Italy.

Beautiful America Publishing Company: Cover illustration by Carol Johnson from *A Journey of Hope/Una Jornada de Esperanza*, text and photographs by Bob Harvey and Diane Kelsay Harvey. Copyright 1991 by Little America Publishing Co.

David Boxley: Illustrations by David Boxley from *Totem Pole* by Diane Hoyt-Goldsmith. Copyright © 1990 by David Boxley.

Bradbury Press, an Affiliate of Macmillan, Inc.: *Dream Wolf* by Paul Goble. Copyright © 1990 by Paul Goble.

Curtis Brown, Ltd.: "Last Laugh" by Lee Bennett Hopkins. Text copyright © 1974 by Lee Bennett Hopkins. Photographs by James B. and Martin Scheiner and Ann McGovern from *Down Under, Down Under: Diving Adventures on the Great Barrier Reef* by Ann McGovern. Photographs copyright © 1989 by Martin Scheiner, James B. Scheiner and Ann McGovern. Published by Macmillan Publishing Company.

Carolrhoda Books, Inc., Minneapolis, MN: Cover illustration by Karen Ritz from *The Country Artist: A Story about Beatrix Potter* by David R. Collins. Illustration copyright © 1989 by Carolrhoda Books, Inc.

CPP/Belwin, Inc., Miami, FL: Lyrics from "Talk To The Animals," music and lyrics by Leslie Bricusse. Copyright © 1967 by Twentieth Century Music Corporation, c/o EMI Hastings Catalog Inc.

Dial Books for Young Readers, a division of Penguin Books USA Inc.: *Daydreamers* by Eloise Greenfield, illustrated by Tom Feelings. Text copyright © 1981 by Eloise Greenfield; illustrations copyright © 1981 by Tom Feelings.

Doubleday, a division of Bantam Doubleday Dell Publishing Group, Inc.: "Sun Dancers" by Patricia Irving from *Whispering Wind* by Terry Allen. Text copyright © 1972 by the Institute of American Indian Arts.

Eakin Press, an imprint of Sunbelt Media, Inc.: Cover illustration by Karl Shefelman from *A Paradise Called Texas* by Janice Jordan Shefelman. Illustration © 1985 by Karl Shefelman.

Farrar, Straus & Giroux, Inc.: Cover illustration from *Kneeknock Rise* by Natalie Babbitt. Copyright © 1970 by Natalie Babbitt. "The Song of a Dream" from *In the Trail of the Wind* by John Bierhorst. Text copyright © 1971 by John Bierhorst. "The Drum" from *Spin a Soft Black Sun* by Nikki Giovanni. Text copyright © 1971, 1985 by Nikki Giovanni.

Sid Fleischman, Inc.: *McBroom Tells the Truth* by Sid Fleischman. Text copyright © 1966 by Sid Fleischman.

Greenwillow Books, a division of William Morrow & Company, Inc.: Cover illustration by Noela Young from *Finders Keepers* by Emily Rodda. Illustration copyright © 1990 by Noela Young.

Harcourt Brace & Company: From *A Guide Dog Puppy Grows Up* by Caroline Arnold, photographs by Richard Hewett. Text copyright © 1991 by Caroline Arnold; photographs copyright © 1991 by Richard Hewett. *A River Ran Wild* by Lynne Cherry. Copyright © 1992 by Lynne Cherry. *The Great Kapok Tree* by Lynne Cherry. Copyright © 1990 by Lynne Cherry. Cover illustration by Jerry Pinkney from *Drylongso* by Virginia Hamilton. Illustration copyright © 1992 by Jerry Pinkney. *Finding the Green Stone* by Alice Walker, illustrated by Catherine Deeter. Text copyright © 1991 by Alice Walker; illustrations copyright © 1991 by Catherine Deeter. "The Marmalade Man Makes a Dance to Mend Us" from *A Visit to William Blake's Inn* by Nancy Willard, illustrated by Alice and Martin Provensen. Text copyright © 1981 by Nancy Willard; illustrations copyright © 1981 by Alice and Martin Provensen. Pronunciation Key from *HBJ School Dictionary*, Third Edition. Text copyright © 1990 by Harcourt Brace & Company.

HarperCollins Publishers: "Pearls" from *Hey World, Here I Am!* by Jean Little. Text copyright © 1986 by Jean Little. "Is It Waiting Just for Me" from *Flower Moon Snow: A Book of Haiku* (Retitled: "Wildflower") by Kazue Mizumura. Text copyright © 1977 by Kazue Mizumura. Cover illustration by Vladimir Vagin from *The King's Equal* by Katherine Paterson. Illustration copyright © 1992 by Vladimir Vagin. From *Charlotte's Web* by E. B. White, illustrated by Garth Williams. Copyright 1952 by E. B. White. Text copyright renewed © 1980 by E. B. White; illustrations copyright renewed © 1980 by Garth Williams. From *On the Banks of Plum Creek* by Laura Ingalls Wilder, illustrated by Garth Williams. Text copyright 1937 by Laura Ingalls Wilder, renewed © 1963 by Roger L. MacBride; illustrations copyright 1953 by Garth Williams, renewed © 1981 by Garth Williams.

continued on page 622

TREASURY OF LITERATURE

Dear Reader,

An emerald, a deeply shining green jewel, is a treasure in itself. It can also be a symbol for other treasures that shine like jewels. The animals of the rain forest are like jewels among its leaves. A friend is a person to treasure, shining like an emerald among people. In the same way, a funny story or a moving poem is like a jewel that can brighten your day. You will discover many jewels in *Emerald Forest* as the literature takes you to amazing new places.

As part of your discoveries, you will celebrate the value of many different people and cultures. You will travel from the rooftops of nineteenth-century Paris to a studio on a Caribbean island, and onward to Australia's Great Barrier Reef and a ranch in Argentina. You'll learn about some traditions celebrated by Native Americans in the Northwest and be swept up in the current of a wild river in New Hampshire. Laugh and wonder with the characters as you read about the precious gift of friendship. These lines from an Aztec poem express how valuable that gift can be:

> To know that the hearts of our friends
> are true is to put around us
> a necklace of precious stones.

Venture into the *Emerald Forest* and make it an important part of a great school year. Discover the shining lights and deep shadows in these stories, poems, and articles. Maybe you'll find some sparkle in yourself that you didn't know was there.

Sincerely,
The Authors

UNIT ONE

CELEBRATIONS / 16

Unit Two

Animal Tales /134

UNIT THREE
NATURE'S GIFTS / 230

UNIT FOUR

DISCOVERIES / 328

UNIT FIVE

ACROSS AMERICA / 418

UNIT SIX

Dreamers / 514

UNIT ONE

CeLeBrAtions

Why do people celebrate? A holiday like Cinco de Mayo or the Fourth of July is a good reason, but there are others. For example, if you did something very well or found something you thought was lost, you might want to celebrate. In fact, just knowing that other people care about you can be a reason for special joy. Think about your own reasons to celebrate as you read these stories.

THEMES

BOOKSHELF

CLASS PRESIDENT

by Johanna Hurwitz

Julio Sanchez and his classmates are starting a
new school year. With the help of their teacher,
Mr. Flores, the students learn some fun and
valuable lessons.

Award-Winning Author

Harcourt Brace Library Book

THE SKATES OF UNCLE RICHARD

by Carol Fenner

Marsha dreams of performing on the ice in
shining white skates, looking like the champion
skaters she watches on television. She feels her
dream fading when she receives Uncle Richard's
old skates for Christmas.

Harcourt Brace Library Book

GETTING ELECTED: THE DIARY OF A CAMPAIGN

by Joan Hewett

Gloria Molina wants to be elected to the California State Assembly. Read to see whether her hard work and campaigning pay off.

Award-Winning Author

DRYLONGSO

by Virginia Hamilton
illustrated by Jerry Pinkney

Lindy and her family are hoping for a rainstorm. When a storm does come, it does not bring the much-needed rain. But the storm does bring Drylongso, someone Lindy and her family will never forget.

Award-Winning Author and Illustrator

THE KING'S EQUAL

by Katherine Paterson
illustrated by Vladimir Vagin

Prince Raphael's father, the king, has given him a strange blessing: Raphael will not become king until he marries a woman who is his equal in beauty, intelligence, and wealth. Will such a proud man find a woman he will admit is his equal?

Award-Winning Author and Illustrator

T H E M E

performances

Have you ever accomplished something even though you weren't sure you could? The characters in the following stories show that wonderful things can happen when you believe in yourself.

C O N T E N T S

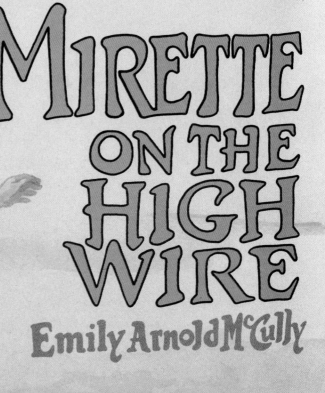

MIRETTE
ON THE
HIGH
WIRE

Emily Arnold McCully

One hundred years ago in Paris, when theaters and music halls drew traveling players from all over the world, the best place to stay was at the widow Gâteau's, a boardinghouse on English Street.

Acrobats, jugglers, actors, and mimes from as far away as Moscow and New York reclined on the widow's feather mattresses and devoured her kidney stews.

Madame Gâteau worked hard to make her guests comfortable, and so did her daughter, Mirette. The girl was an expert at washing linens, chopping leeks, paring potatoes, and mopping floors. She was a good listener too. Nothing pleased her more than to overhear the vagabond players tell of their adventures in this town and that along the road.

One evening a tall, sad-faced stranger arrived. He told
Madame Gâteau he was Bellini, a retired high-wire walker.

"I am here for a rest," he said.

"I have just the room for you, Monsieur Bellini: in the
back, where it's quiet," she said. "But it's on the ground floor,
with no view."

"Perfect," said the stranger. "I will take my meals alone."

The next afternoon, when Mirette came for the sheets, there was the stranger, crossing the courtyard on air! Mirette was enchanted. Of all the things a person could do, this must be the most magical. Her feet tingled, as if they wanted to jump up on the wire beside Bellini.

29

Mirette worked up the courage to speak. "Excuse me, Monsieur Bellini, *I* want to learn to do that!" she cried.

Bellini sighed. "That would not be a good idea," he said. "Once you start, your feet are never happy again on the ground."

"Oh, please teach me!" Mirette begged. "My feet are already unhappy on the ground." But he shook his head.

Mirette watched him every day. He would slide his feet onto the wire, cast his eyes ahead, and cross without ever looking down, as if in a trance.

Finally she couldn't resist any longer. When Bellini was gone, she jumped up on the wire to try it herself. Her arms flailed like windmills. In a moment she was back on the ground. Bellini made it look so easy. Surely she could do it too if she kept trying.

In ten tries she balanced on one foot for a few seconds. In a day, she managed three steps without wavering. Finally, after a week of many, many falls, she walked the length of the wire. She couldn't wait to show Bellini.

He was silent for a long time. Then he said, "In the beginning everyone falls. Most give up. But you kept trying. Perhaps you have talent as well."

"Oh, thank you," said Mirette.

She got up two hours earlier every day to finish her chores before the sun shone in the courtyard. The rest of the day was for lessons and practice.

Bellini was a strict master. "Never let your eyes stray," he told her day after day. "Think only of the wire, and of crossing to the end."

When she could cross dozens of times without falling, he taught her the wire-walker's salute. Then she learned to run, to lie down, and to turn a somersault.

"I will never ever fall again!" Mirette shouted.

"Do not boast," Bellini said, so sharply that Mirette lost her balance and had to jump down.

One night an agent from Astley's Hippodrome in London rented a room. He noticed Bellini on his way to dinner.

"What a shock to see him here!" he exclaimed.

"See who?" asked a mime.

"Why, the great Bellini! Didn't you know he was in the room at the back?"

"Bellini . . . the one who crossed Niagara Falls on a thousand-foot wire in ten minutes?" asked the mime.

"And on the way back stopped in the middle to cook an omelette on a stove full of live coals. Then he opened a bottle of champagne and toasted the crowd," the agent recalled.

"My uncle used to talk about that," said a juggler.

"Bellini crossed the Alps with baskets tied to his feet,
fired a cannon over the bullring in Barcelona, walked a
flaming wire wearing a blindfold in Naples—the man had
the nerves of an iceberg," the agent said.

Mirette raced to Bellini's room.

"Is it true?" she cried. "You did all those things? Why didn't you tell me? I want to do them too! I want to go with you!"

"I can't take you," said Bellini.

"But why not?" asked Mirette.

Bellini hesitated a long time. "Because I am afraid," he said at last.

Mirette was astonished. "*Afraid*?" she said. "But *why*?"

"Once you have fear on the wire, it never leaves," Bellini said.

"But you must *make* it leave!" Mirette insisted.

"I cannot," said Bellini.

Mirette turned and ran to the kitchen as tears sprang to her eyes. She had felt such joy on the wire. Now Bellini's fear was like a cloud casting its black shadow on all she had learned from him.

Bellini paced his room for hours. It was terrible to disappoint Mirette! By dawn he knew that if he didn't face his fear at last, he could not face Mirette. He knew what he must do. The question was, could he succeed?

That night, when the agent returned, Bellini was waiting for him. The agent listened to Bellini's plan with mounting excitement. "I'll take care of it," he promised. To himself he added, "A big crowd will make me a tidy profit. What luck I just happened to be in Paris now."

Bellini went out to find a length of hemp with a steel core. He borrowed a winch and worked until daylight securing the wire.

The next evening, Mirette heard the commotion in the street.

"Go and see what it is," her mother said. "Maybe it will cheer you up."

In the square was a hubbub. The crowd was so thick she couldn't see, at first, that the agent was aiming a spotlight at the sky.

". . . return of the great Bellini!" he was yelling. Could it be? Mirette's heart hammered in her chest.

47

Bellini stepped out onto the wire and saluted the crowd. He took a step and then froze. The crowd cheered wildly. But something was wrong. Mirette knew at once what it was. For a moment she was as frozen as Bellini was.

Then she threw herself at the door behind her, ran inside, up flight after flight of stairs, and out through a skylight to the roof.

She stretched her hands to Bellini. He smiled and began to walk toward her. She stepped onto the wire, and with the most intense pleasure, as she had always imagined it might be, she started to cross the sky.

"Brava! Bravo!" roared the crowd.

"Protégée of the Great Bellini!" shouted the agent. He was beside himself, already planning the world tour of Bellini and Mirette.

As for the master and his pupil, they were thinking only of the wire, and of crossing to the end.

How does the author seem to think people should
handle their fears? Use details from the story to
support your answer. Then tell whether you agree,
giving your reasons.

What kind of person is Mirette? What words tell what
she is like?

Could this story take place in real life? Explain why
you think as you do.

WRITE   When do you think people learn more
about themselves—when times are difficult or when
things are going well? Write a paragraph explaining
your opinion.

Words About the Author and Illustrator:

Emily Arnold McCully

Emily McCully had several reasons for writing *Mirette on the High Wire*. She had traveled and studied in Europe, and she especially loved Paris. She had also been a writer of children's books for nearly thirty years and was feeling a little discouraged. She wanted to write a book that would make her soar, and she decided that a nineteenth-century daredevil was just the heroine she needed.

Emily McCully had to be a bit of a daredevil herself as she painted this book. The style was new for her, much looser and with no lines: "I kept trying to make pictures that were like paintings, asking more of my little watercolor set, certainly more of my brushes than ever before, adding pastel for the first time, then failing less and finally getting to the point where I was comfortable enough to go on with the book." Emily McCully won the Caldecott Medal, perhaps the highest honor a children's book illustrator can earn, for *Mirette on the High Wire*.

▲ Emily (left) and her sister, Becky

53

PHILIPPE
and the Blue Parrot

by Nancy White Carlstrom
illustrated by Cristine Mortensen

When Philippe was a young boy, his mother told him a story about a beautiful blue parrot who stole a golden earring from the sun.

"Watch for it, Philippe, my boy," she said. "And when you find that golden earring, we will never go hungry again."

And so Philippe kept his head down as he walked to school through the streets of Port-au-Prince, always looking for a glint of gold.

Years passed. Philippe did well in his studies. He was especially good at art. When Philippe was thirteen, he decided to make a birthday gift for his mother.

He took his art supplies to the park, and there, leaning the canvas against a bench, he painted *Blue Parrot and the Sun.* As he waited for the paint to dry, he studied the blue smudges between his fingers and a drop of yellow shining on his black wrist.

"Is that for sale?"

Philippe was startled by the question. He had not heard the tourist walk up to him. The woman squinted her eyes at the bright colors and asked again.

"Is that for sale?" Before Philippe could answer, she added, "I'll pay twenty-five dollars for it."

Twenty-five dollars! That was more than Philippe had earned in his whole life. It would take a long time to make that much money, even if he could get a job. What wonderful things he could buy his mother.

And so Philippe sold *Blue Parrot and the Sun.*

Years passed. Philippe's paintings were sold in a Port-au-Prince gallery. Many tourists liked his work and bought the canvases.

Every time Philippe painted a *Blue Parrot and the Sun* for his mother, the gallery owner had a buyer. The price went up and Philippe could not resist. But every time he sold a *Blue Parrot*, he put aside some money for his mother.

Many years passed. Now Philippe's paintings could not be afforded by most tourists. His work hung in galleries and museums in Europe and the United States.

One day, he sat in his fine studio, ready to begin work on another *Blue Parrot and the Sun*. A journalist who had come to interview him stood nearby.

"Monsieur, your *Blue Parrot and the Sun* paintings are now very famous. Some critics say that they have a life and power that your other works lack. Why is that? Do you know?"

"Oh yes, I know," Philippe replied slowly. "It is because I paint each *Blue Parrot* for my mother."

"And how much will this new one sell for?" the journalist asked. "Thousands, I suppose?"

"Oh, this painting will not be for sale," Philippe answered. He knew he had said that before, but this time, he really meant it.

And he added: "I found the golden earring many years ago. Now it's time to give it back."

There is a story the art collectors tell about a famous painting called *Blue Parrot and the Sun*. Oh, there are many, but the one to hunt for has a small golden earring hidden in the picture. Yes, that is the one worth a fortune. Some say it hangs on the wall of a simple house in the Haitian countryside. Others are not so sure. It could be anywhere.

What part of the story did you like the best? What made it your favorite part?

How does Philippe change from the beginning of the story to the end of the story?

WRITE Philippe is a talented artist. Write a short description of a talent you possess.

Performances

Think about why Mirette walks the high wire and why Philippe paints. How are their reasons for performing the same? How are their reasons different?

WRITER'S WORKSHOP

Think about something you had to practice doing in order to do it well. Write a personal narrative about how you practiced and how you felt when you reached your goal.

Writer's Choice Mirette and Philippe perform for others. You might want to write about something you have done for someone else. You might want to respond in some other way. Choose your own way to respond, and share your work.

THEME

Celebrating Ourselves

Sometimes people forget what is important to them. Read the following selections to see how the gentleness of friends can help them remember.

CONTENTS

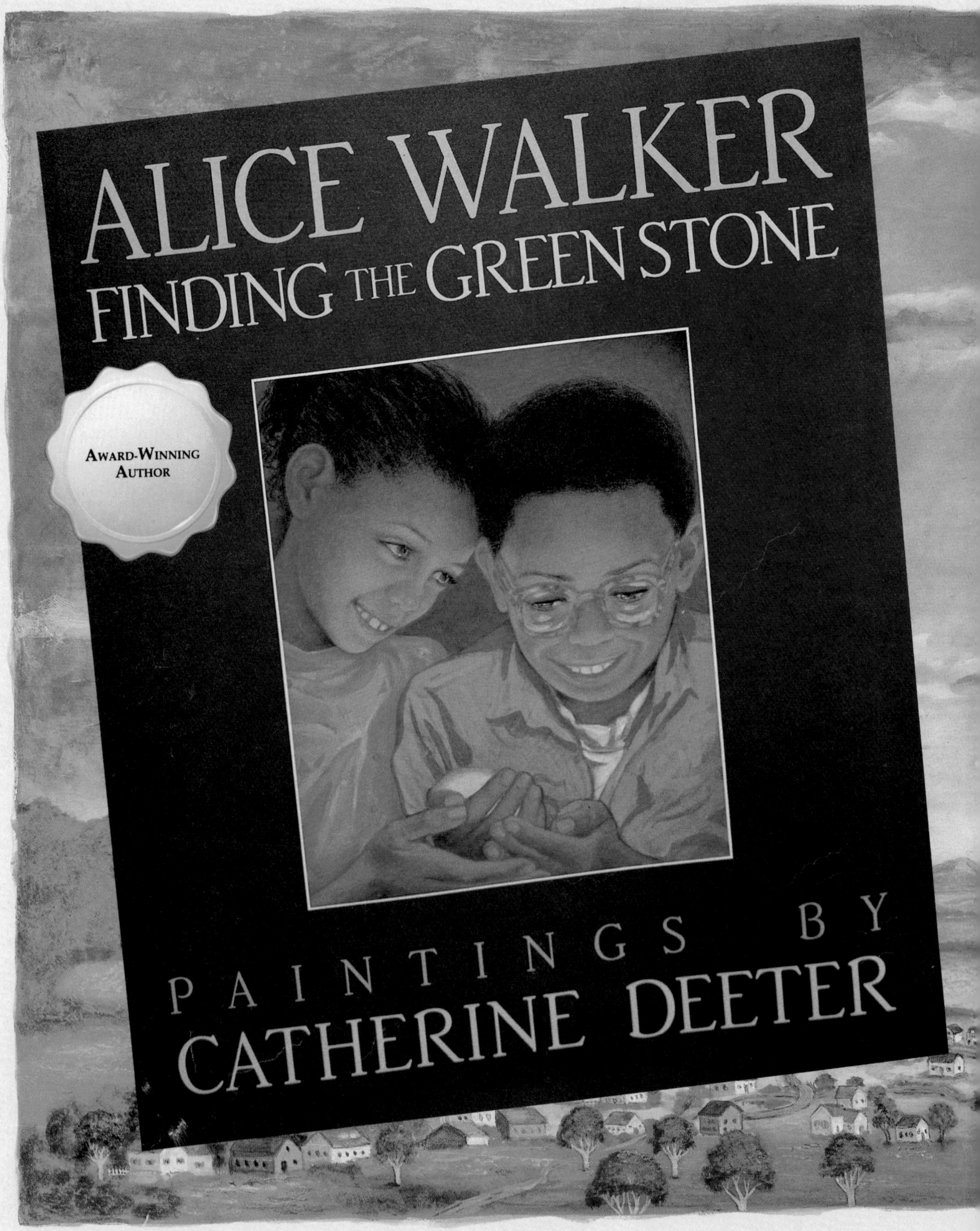

ALICE WALKER
FINDING THE GREEN STONE

AWARD-WINNING
AUTHOR

PAINTINGS BY
CATHERINE DEETER

Right at this very time, in a small community on the Earth, live a brother and sister who have identical, iridescent green stones. The stones shine brightly and are small enough to fit into their hands.

The children prize their stones and often play with them, taking them out of their pockets and holding them up to the sun, putting them in the clear water of the seaside among the rocks and plucking them out again, and so on. They are very happy with their stones.

But one day Johnny, the brother, lost his green stone. He looked everywhere for it.

Then he looked at his sister Katie's green stone, and, because his own stone was missing, he imagined that hers looked bigger and shinier than ever. He thought maybe his green stone had disappeared into hers.

"You've stolen my green stone!" he said.

"No way!" said Katie.

Johnny frowned at her and tried to grab her green stone—and even the memory of his own stone vanished.

As the days passed, Johnny became very dull and sat for hours under the big tree in the center of the community.

But Katie never forgot that Johnny had once possessed his very own brightly glowing green stone, exactly like hers. And every day, while he sat under the tree fuming and casting mean looks at everybody who passed and sometimes muttering nasty things as well, she brought him her green stone to hold and reminded him that he had once had one too.

At first, Johnny liked to play with Katie's stone, because whenever he did so he felt much better. But then he would remember that it was hers and that he did not have one of his own, and he would become angry.

One day, when Johnny was feeling this way, he tried to steal Katie's stone by pretending it was his.

"This is my green stone," he cried, clutching it in his fist, not intending to give it back, "not yours!"

But as soon as he did that, the stone turned gray in his hand, just like the rocks by the ocean, and when he looked over at Katie again she had her green stone, as bright and shining as ever!

Johnny felt sad. He realized that stealing somebody else's green stone would never make it his. Besides, it was lonely under the big tree, and trying to look mean all day was boring.

One day he mustered the courage to talk about his change of heart to Katie, who rarely talked to him now because she was afraid.

"I will never try to steal your green stone again," he said to her. "But I miss my own stone *so* much. Will you help me find it?"

At first Katie didn't know what to do. How could she believe Johnny meant what he said? That he would not try to grab her green stone?

"No," she said, after a long pause. "I can't help you at all."

Johnny's eyes were bright with unshed tears. Katie

could see he meant her no harm, but something inside her liked being the powerful one for a change.

"No," she said again, sticking out her chest just as she'd seen Johnny do. But when she said "No" the second time, with a new coldness in her heart, her own green stone began to flicker and almost stopped shining!

Katie glanced at Johnny's sweet, sad face, so like her own, and then at her flickering green stone. Being spiteful to her brother would never work.

"I love you, Johnny," she said quietly. "I'm happiest when you have your very own green stone. I will do everything I can to help you find it."

The radiance of her stone, when she said this and reached for Johnny's hand, dazzled them both.

Johnny and Katie set out on their search, hearts pounding, hand in hand.

They looked first near Old Mr. Roseharp's house.

"I'm afraid to go up to the porch," said Johnny. "Last week, when Mr. Roseharp came by the big tree on his way to the store, I called him a bad name."

But old Mr. Roseharp had seen them coming and stood on his porch in his long red nightshirt, a big yellow broom in his hand. He lived alone in a little wooden house painted blue, and all over it there were painted flowers. In some places you almost couldn't tell where his flower garden ended and his house began.

Old Mr. Roseharp looked down at Johnny and Katie expectantly.

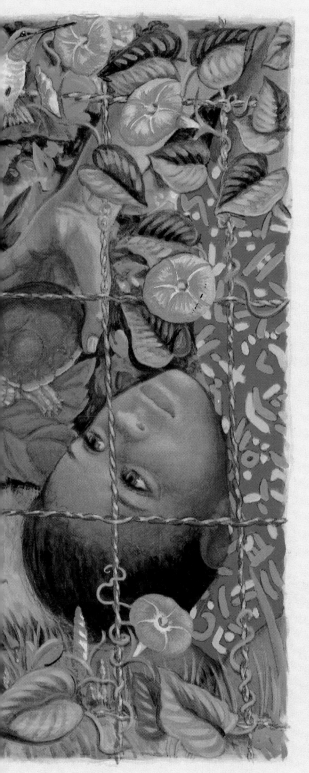

Katie gave Johnny a nudge in the ribs to help him speak up. She could see that Mr. Roseharp was more sad than angry because of what Johnny had said.

"Since I called you a bad name," said Johnny, "I lost my green stone."

"Oh, no!" said old Mr. Roseharp, who knew what a tragedy that was.

He immediately tucked his nightshirt into his pants and put down his broom. Shaking his head with concern and saying, "Uh, uh, uh," he came down to where Katie and Johnny stood and began, right there in his own yard, to help them look.

Next they went to the woods where Johnny and Katie's father was busy loading a big pulpwood truck, using a noisy machine to lift the cut-up pieces of the trees. He turned it off when he saw them coming.

Again Johnny hung back, and this time he kicked the ground with his toe.

"What's the matter?" asked Katie.

"Last week I told Daddy I was ashamed of him for being the driver of a stupid pulpwood truck. I hurt his feelings and I don't know how to tell him I'm sorry."

But Johnny's father, Mr. Oaks, looked into Johnny's eyes and saw how sad they were.

"What's wrong, son?" he asked gently, folding Johnny in his large arms.

For some reason, being held in his father's arms made Johnny cry and cry. "I'm so sorry for what I said about you driving the pulpwood truck," he said through his tears. "I know it's the only way you can make a living. The only way you can help Mama feed and clothe us all."

"Hey, I knew you didn't mean it," said his father. "I knew you only said it because you hate what pulpwooding does to the trees. I hate it, too."

"And since I said it," said Johnny, "I've lost my green stone."

Mr. Oaks whistled in dismay. He'd lost his own stone many times in his life and each time he had felt terrible. He hugged Johnny and kissed him firmly on the forehead.

When Johnny and Katie and old Mr. Roseharp turned away, Mr. Oaks followed them in his truck.

Mr. Oaks wore his stone on a thong around his neck, Katie had made an earring of hers, and old Mr. Roseharp wore his on his hat. As they moved along, the stones sparkled and shone.

Soon Katie and Johnny saw their mother coming. Since she was the only doctor in their little community, she was always dressed for work and moving very fast. She was wearing a white pantsuit and carrying her black doctor's bag. Her green stone was an especially beautiful one, and because she was always in a hurry and changed clothes so often, she carried it, for safekeeping, in her cheek, which made her look like a mother squirrel carrying a large nut. When she saw everyone coming she took it out of her cheek and closed her hand around it. It shone so brightly that her fist seemed to have a green light in it.

"What's the matter? What's the matter?" their mother asked, kissing Mr. Oaks and Katie and Johnny. She stood tapping her foot as she waited for their reply.

Both Katie and Johnny wondered if they should tell her. Their mother was always in such a hurry that telling her things of importance sometimes felt like throwing your heart against the wind. She would cluck over you for about a minute, then she'd run off to tend to somebody who really needed attention.

Johnny had complained to her about this just last week. How she was never around like the other children's mothers and how he never got hugs and cookies and milk when he came home from school. He wanted another mother entirely from the one he had, he had said.

Still, with Katie's warm little fingers urging him on, Johnny said:

"It's nothing much." He thought: She's probably on her way to deliver a baby, for heaven's sake! "It's just that I lost my green stone."

"You what?" said his mother, dropping her bag—something he'd never seen her do.

Johnny thought that his mother knew almost everything, even if she was usually too busy to say so.

"Do you know where it might be?" he asked. "Do you have it?"

"I can't keep up with every single thing, Johnny," said his mother, in a voice that sounded like she was tired of trying. "Maybe if you'd do a better job of cleaning up your room you wouldn't need help finding your stuff. And no, I do not have your green stone. I have my own."

She picked up her bag, looked at her watch, and placed her own green stone back in her cheek. It tasted like copper. She spat it out and looked at it. It was like a small, sickly olive.

"Oh-oh," she said.

Then she put her arm around Johnny's shoulder. "Listen, son, everybody has his or her own green stone. You ought to know that by now. Nobody can give it to you and nobody can take it away. Only you can misplace or lose it. If you've lost it, it's your own fault."

Johnny felt sadder than he'd ever felt in his life. He thought about his beautiful green stone and how he would probably never see it again. And about how his mother, whom he loved and would never wish to replace with another, always spoke so impatiently. He knew she would not have time to help them look. Without his mother's help, they had no chance at all, Johnny felt.

To his surprise, however, his mother took his hand and said, in her fast leaping-over-the-gatepost voice: "We will get everybody in the community to help look for your green stone anyway!" She smiled over at Mr. Oaks, as if seeing him for the first time, even though she'd already kissed him, and he smiled back at her. And they all set off down the road.

Before Johnny knew it, he and Katie, Mr. and Dr. Oaks, and old Mr. Roseharp were being followed by Miss Rivers, Johnny and Katie's teacher, Mr. Skies, the minister, and Mr. Birdfield, the shoeshine man. Sunny, the paperboy, and all their classmates and friends also came along. There was even a baby crawling after them. Its glowing green stone was the handle of its pacifier. The dog that was its guardian walked beside it, a green stone glistening in its collar.

Johnny felt embarrassed that all these people knew he had lost his green stone, but Katie went back and picked up the baby, who was almost as large as she was, and then held on to her brother's hand. Johnny looked at his sister's hopeful face, and at the baby who seemed so happy to be out strolling with the big people, and tried to keep his chin up for their sakes.

Finally, after hours and hours of searching—under
doorsteps, in orchards, in flowerbeds, and even on the cliff—
everyone was tired and so they stopped to rest under the big
tree. The tree's green stone was one of its millions of fat green
leaves. Sometimes it was hard to see, but not today. Today it
sparkled brightly, way up high above everybody's head, and
this made Johnny sadder still.

Tears came again to his eyes. He was not crying just because he'd lost the green stone; he knew that because of his hurtful behavior, he deserved to lose it. He was crying because all these people, and especially Katie, loved him and were trying to help him find his green stone, even though they knew perfectly well he could only find it for himself!

Idly, Johnny picked up a small rock and fondled it.

He was puzzled that everyone in his community wanted to help him do something he could only do himself, and in his puzzlement, he began to feel as if a giant bee were buzzing in his chest. It felt exactly as if all the warmth inside himself was trying to rush out to people around him. He noticed that as soon as the warmth that was inside him touched them, they began to shine.

"You should all go home," he said to Katie, ashamed to have taken up so much of everyone's time. "You've wasted a whole afternoon. There's no point in helping me look for something that you can't actually help me find."

"We wanted to be with you when you found it!" said Katie, softly, wiping Johnny's tears away with her sleeve.

And sure enough, when Johnny followed Katie's gaze and looked down at his hand, what did he see? Not the dull and lifeless rock that he'd thought he was holding, but his very own bright green stone!

83

Johnny jumped up and began to dance around the tree. And all the people—his mother and father, old Mr. Roseharp, his teacher and minister and the shoeshine man and the paperboy, and Katie—returned the smile he gave them.

They welcomed the rising of a bright green sun in his heart, which they knew was Johnny's love for them, its warm light overflowing the small brown fingers clutched close to his chest.

The characters' green stones help them know when they are being kind or unkind. Would you like to have an object like the green stone? Tell why you feel as you do.

How does Johnny feel about losing his green stone? Use details from the story to support your answer.

What do you think Alice Walker wants readers to learn from this story?

WRITE   Imagine that you have just been given a green stone. Write a few sentences telling how you plan to keep your stone shining brightly.

Words About the Author:

Alice Walker

Alice Walker was born in Eatonton, Georgia, in 1944, the youngest of eight children. Her interest in books and writing began when she was very young: "My mother says that when I was crawling she would look for me and I would have crawled to the back of the house, having snatched the Sears Roebuck catalog. I would quietly sit scribbling in the catalog with a twig."

Some of Alice's best memories from her childhood are of the gardens that her mother planted. She loved the beautiful flowers and plants, and even today she looks to the beauty of nature for inspiration.

Alice Walker now lives in northern California. In addition to her children's books, she also writes books for adults. Alice Walker has become one of the most famous writers of our time. She has won many awards, including the Pulitzer Prize.

The Song of a Dream

an Aztec poem
translated by John Bierhorst
illustrated by Lorraine Silvestri

Now, my friends, please hear:
it is the song of a dream:
each spring the gold young corn
gives us life;
the ripened corn gives us refreshment;
to know that the hearts of our friends
are true is to put around us
a necklace of precious stones.

Celebrating Ourselves

How is the necklace in the poem like the green stone in the story?

WRITER'S WORKSHOP

List some times when you feel close to your family or your friends. Choose one special time, such as a holiday, and write a paragraph about it. Be sure to give information that answers the questions *Who? What? When? Where? Why?* and *How?*

Writer's Choice
If you wish, write about some other topic. You might want to write about a special time you spend alone.

THEME

contests

Have you ever entered a contest, hoping more than anything else to win? The main characters in the next two selections are both winners—proving to themselves and to the world that they are special.

CONTENTS

Class President
by Johanna Hurwitz

Supergrandpa
by David M. Schwartz

A Note from the Author: David M. Schwartz

CLASS PRESIDENT

by Johanna Hurwitz

illustrated by Ruben DeAnda

On the first day of school, Julio Sanchez's new teacher, Mr. Flores, tells the class about some interesting things he has planned for the school year. In math class, the students are going to decide how they would spend a million dollars! They are also going to elect a class president, something that has Julio and the other students very excited.

The next morning in Mr. Flores's class, everyone was kept busy discussing how he or she was going to spend a million dollars. Just before lunchtime, Cricket raised her hand. "Can't we vote for a class president today?" she asked. She was probably going to nag the teacher about it every day, thought Julio.

"What's the rush?" asked Mr. Flores. "This is only the second day of school. We have a whole year ahead of us."

"Don't remind me," Julio groaned under his breath, but loudly enough for Lucas and others nearby to hear.

"You said we should wait to know each other better," Cricket pointed out. "But we already know each other."

"Yeah," several of the fifth graders chorused.

"It's true you know each other better than I know you," said Mr. Flores. "But since you've never voted for a class president before, you may not have thought about what qualities a president should have."

"It's got to be somebody that everyone likes," said Arthur.

"True," Mr. Flores said. "However, is an election just a popularity contest? Does the most popular person make the best president?"

"It's the most popular person who always wins an election," said Zoe.

"Yes. Nevertheless, a person should be popular for the right reasons," said Mr. Flores. "What other qualities should a good president have?"

No one answered. Even Cricket, who always had the right answers to even the hardest questions, didn't know what to say.

"What about leadership ability?" asked Mr. Flores.

"But the teacher is the leader," said Cricket.

"Of course," said Mr. Flores. "But the student you elect must have the *potential* to be a leader, even though the teacher is still in charge."

"Sometimes teachers are absent," Lucas pointed out.

"Yeah, but then we get a substitute," said Julio.

Just then the bell rang for lunch. "We'll have an election on the second Friday in September," said Mr. Flores. "I want you to think hard about the best candidate for the job. Look for a good leader, someone who is fair and who stands up for what he or she thinks is right. Think about someone who is concerned about the whole class and not just a few special friends."

Julio looked at Cricket. She was very smart and she spoke out a lot in class. Probably she would make an okay president, but he didn't think she thought about anyone except herself and a few of the girls who were her friends. Mr. Flores was right, Julio thought as the class headed down to the lunchroom. He wondered if he himself had what it took to be a good leader.

Lunch that day was another of Julio's favorites—hot diggity dog, a fancy name for a hot dog on a bun, with potato puffs, coleslaw, and oatmeal-raisin cookies.

Cricket looked around the table. "If you vote for me," she told everyone, "you *know* you'll get a *smart* president."

"Zoe is smart, too," said Sara Jane.

"I don't want to be president," said Zoe. "I'm voting for Cricket."

"Lucas is going to run for president," Julio announced.

"You are?" Cricket asked him.

"I might," said Lucas.

"I'm going to be his campaign manager," Julio said.

"Then he'll never win," said Cricket.

"Aren't you finished yet?" Lucas asked Julio. "Let's go out and play soccer. We're not having the election yet."

Julio licked the mustard off his fingers and gathered up his lunch tray. "I'm coming," he said. Soccer was a lot more important than the election.

Outside, the boys quickly formed teams. Some days the girls played soccer, too. Or sometimes they jumped rope together. Julio was the best player and he was chosen captain of one team. Everyone wanted to be on Julio's team. At recess, Julio was a leader, but not in the classroom.

Arthur Lewis stood watching. He didn't move very quickly and he had never scored a goal in his life. He was surprised and grateful when Julio picked him for his team.

Julio kicked the ball and immediately scored a goal. "Yeaaa, Julio!" Zoe Mitchell called out from the sidelines.

Julio heard a noise behind him. He turned and saw that Arthur Lewis had fallen down. The other kids kept on playing, running around Arthur as he slowly got up.

"Where are my glasses?" asked Arthur. Julio saw Arthur's glasses on the ground. Just then, the soccer ball landed on top of them, breaking the frame right in half. One of the lenses was cracked, too.

The soccer game stopped and everyone gathered around Arthur to see what had happened.

"They're not looking too good," said Julio, picking up the glasses and handing them to their owner.

"My new glasses! They cost a lot of money and they're

supposed to be unbreakable." Arthur's eyes filled with tears. "My mother is going to have a fit."

"Crybaby. Crybaby!" someone called out.

"He's not crying," said Julio. "His eyes are tearing because he's straining to see without his glasses."

Julio put his arm around Arthur's shoulders. "Don't worry," he said. "We'll all chip in and help you pay for them."

"Hey, no way," said one of the boys. "Just because he falls over his own feet doesn't mean we have to pay for his glasses."

"Who kicked the ball that landed on the glasses?" asked another boy.

"That doesn't matter," said Julio. "We were all playing,

so we should all chip in. It's only fair."

"It's an awful lot of money," said Arthur. "I don't think you'll be able to pay for them."

"Don't worry," said Julio. "We'll figure out a way." He stuck his hands into his pockets. He had a quarter and two pennies. He handed them to Arthur. "This is just for a start," he said. "Who else has some money?"

"I spent my allowance already," said Sara Jane Cushman. "Besides, the girls weren't even playing soccer today."

"That's not the point," said Julio. "Arthur's in our class and I think we should all help him out."

Lucas handed over a dime and two quarters. Even without his glasses on, Arthur could figure out that he had only eighty-seven cents. It wasn't even enough for the tiny screws on the frames.

The teacher who was supervising recess came over to see what was wrong. "Is anyone hurt?" she asked.

"Just his glasses," said Julio as the bell rang for the students to return to the building. Julio kept his arm around Arthur's shoulders as they went inside. "It's okay," he said. "We'll get

96

the money. Tell your mother not to worry. It will just take a little more time."

"I hope it doesn't take too long. I can hardly see anything without my glasses," complained Arthur.

"I'll be your Seeing Eye boy," Julio said, and he guided Arthur right to his seat.

"Arthur broke his glasses," Cricket announced when they were all seated.

"Kevin Shea did it," said Sara Jane. "He kicked the soccer ball that landed on Arthur's glasses."

Everyone spoke at once, trying to explain the accident. Finally, Mr. Flores had the whole picture.

"We should all chip in and help pay for the new glasses," said Julio. "We could earn the money."

Mr. Flores looked at Julio. "That's a good idea," he said. "Any suggestions on how we could do it?"

"We could put on a play and charge admission," said Lucas.

"A project like that would take a long time," said Mr. Flores. "If we're going to pay for Arthur's glasses, we have to do something quickly."

"I know," said Cricket. "We could have a bake sale. My mother taught me how to make chocolate-chip cookies. If everyone baked one thing, we could have a big sale. We could do it tomorrow!"

"I can make cupcakes," said Sara Jane.

"My mother makes great peanut-butter cookies," said Lucas. "I bet she'd help me make some for the sale."

Soon everyone had suggestions for what they could bake. Julio had never baked anything in his life and he knew his mother would be too tired to start making cakes or cookies when she got home from work.

"What about you, Julio?" asked Cricket. She was making a list of what everyone could bring. "We already have cupcakes and two kinds of cookies. We can't have too many people making the same things."

Julio thought fast. "Brownies," he said. "With lots of nuts."

"Good," said Cricket, and she wrote that down on her list.

"Tomorrow seems too soon," said Mr. Flores as the students went on with their planning. "Let's have this sale on Friday. We'll put up signs around the school so everyone will know about it and then they'll bring a little extra money."

Arthur Lewis spent the rest of the afternoon in a haze. He couldn't concentrate because he was worrying about what his mother would say when she saw the glasses.

Julio Sanchez spent the rest of the afternoon in a daze.

Somehow, he had to figure out how to make brownies between now and Friday. Brownies with lots of nuts! He must have been *nuts* himself.

After school, Julio walked home with Lucas until they reached the street where they always parted. "See you tomorrow," Lucas called after him.

Julio shifted his backpack and kept walking. He wondered what things besides chocolate you needed to make brownies. Milk? Eggs? Sugar? Nuts.

When he reached the next corner, he saw a boy sitting on the curb. It was Arthur Lewis.

"Hey, Arthur," Julio called out. "What are you doing here? Don't you take the bus?"

"I couldn't see the numbers on the buses without my glasses," Arthur explained, "so I didn't get on any bus at all. Now I'm probably going to get run over before I get home." Arthur sighed. "I don't want to go home, anyhow. My mother is going to be furious."

"Don't worry," Julio said. "Tell her that our class is going to raise the money for new glasses."

"You tell her," said Arthur. "She won't yell at you."

"Why would she yell at you? You didn't break the glasses on purpose."

"Oh, you know how mothers are. They always yell," said Arthur.

Julio thought Arthur was exaggerating. His own mother hardly ever yelled, but when she told him he had to do his homework before he could watch TV, he knew she meant business.

"Please come home with me," said Arthur. "You said you'd be my Seeing Eye boy."

101

"All right," Julio agreed. In all the years they'd known each other, Arthur had never invited Julio to his house before. "Let's get going. If you usually take the bus, it's going to be a long walk," said Julio.

"You're a real pal," said Arthur.

The two boys set off. As they walked, Arthur told Julio all the things he was going to buy with his imaginary million dollars. He had thought of some things that Julio hadn't, like a ticket to all the football games and a swimming pool in his backyard.

"I don't have a backyard, so I can't get a swimming pool," said Julio. "Can I come and swim in yours?"

"Sure," said Arthur. "You can come to the football games with me, too."

It sounded great until Julio remembered it was all pretend.

He felt in his pockets and found a pack of gum. "You want a piece?" he asked Arthur.

Arthur shook his head. "My mother doesn't let me chew gum," he said. "It's bad for your teeth."

Julio felt around in his mouth with his tongue. His teeth felt okay to him, so he kept on chewing.

"You know what, Julio?" said Arthur. "I think you'd be a good president for our class."

"Me?" said Julio, amazed. How did Arthur guess that he secretly wanted to be class president? "That's crazy," he said.

"No, it's not," said Arthur. "I'd vote for you. I bet a lot of kids would. You're always fair, and you're nice to everyone. You always pick me to be on your team even though I'm rotten at sports."

Julio thought about what Arthur had said. He wondered if anyone else would agree with Arthur—not including his mother, of course. She didn't count because she couldn't vote.

When they reached Arthur's house, Mrs. Lewis was standing outside. "Where were you?" she called to her son. "The bus went by half an hour ago. I was getting very worried."

"Mom, this is my friend Julio—" Arthur began, but Mrs. Lewis interrupted.

"Arthur, where are your glasses? Were you in an accident?"

"Arthur fell when we were playing soccer during recess," Julio explained. "He didn't get hurt but his glasses fell off and the soccer ball bounced on top of them."

"I just bought those glasses a week ago," said Mrs. Lewis, "and they're broken already."

"It was an accident," said Julio.

"Why were you playing soccer?" asked Mrs. Lewis.

"Can't you find some quiet activity for after lunch? You could have gotten a stomachache, or broken your leg. I never played soccer once in my life. I don't see why you have to do something like that, either."

"Oh, Mom," said Arthur. "All the boys play soccer."

"Mrs. Lewis," said Julio, "Arthur didn't get a stomachache and he didn't break a leg. Our class is going to have a bake sale to earn money for a new pair of glasses. So you see, there's nothing to worry about."

Mrs. Lewis looked at Julio. "I don't think I heard your name," she said.

"I'm Julio. Julio Sanchez. I've been in Arthur's class a long time. I knew him even before he wore glasses."

"Well hello, Julio," said Mrs. Lewis. "It was nice of you to walk Arthur home. Come inside and I'll give you boys a snack."

Arthur's mother opened the door. There was a smell of something good cooking on the stove. Julio didn't recognize the smell but he liked it.

"Wash your hands," Mrs. Lewis told the boys.

Julio was about to say that his hands weren't dirty, but he thought better of it. He didn't want to upset Mrs. Lewis. Julio followed Arthur to the bathroom. It was all blue and white. Blue and white tiles, a blue basin, and even a blue toilet. The toilet paper was a blue and white pattern, the soap was blue, and the towels were blue-and-white striped. It was like a bathroom in a movie. He spit his piece of gum into the toilet and flushed it away.

Back in the kitchen, Mrs. Lewis had poured two glasses of milk and set out a plate of cookies. "Two each," she said. "I don't want to spoil your suppers."

Julio bit into one of the cookies, a soft oatmeal cookie with raisins in it. It was a hundred times better than the one he had eaten at school.

"These are great," Julio told Mrs. Lewis. "Maybe you could make some for the bake sale."

"When is this sale?" asked Mrs. Lewis.

"Friday," said Arthur. "I can wear my old glasses until then."

"And no soccer playing," said Mrs. Lewis.

Arthur nodded.

When they finished their snack, Arthur led the way to his bedroom. He had a big room lined with shelves that were filled with games and toys.

Arthur didn't really need a million dollars, Julio thought. He had a lot of neat stuff already.

"Look at this," said Arthur, showing Julio an old kitchen clock. The hands on the clock said 1:15. Julio didn't have a watch, but he knew it had to be after four.

"It's got the wrong time," said Julio.

"Look some more," said Arthur.

"The second hand is moving *backward*!" said Julio in amazement.

"Right," said Arthur. "Isn't it neat? It got broken and now it runs the wrong way. My mother was going to throw it out but I asked her to let me keep it. Every other clock in the world goes in a different direction from mine."

"Yours runs counterclockwise," said Julio.

"Right," said Arthur. "Sometimes I like things that are different."

Julio looked around at Arthur's bedroom. The bedspread matched the curtains. There was a carpet on the floor and many toys, but Arthur's favorite thing was the broken clock. Julio's grandmother always said that it took all kinds of people to make up the world. She said it in Spanish, but it was true in English, too.

Julio stayed at Arthur's until the counterclockwise clock said it was quarter to one. Then he walked home slowly. Arthur sure was a funny kid. That's probably why he thought Julio should run for president.

What qualities do you think a class president should have? Explain why you think each quality you mention is important.

Think about how Julio treats his classmate Arthur. What do Julio's words and actions tell about his character?

Why do you think Mr. Flores wants his students to think carefully about the election?

WRITE   Julio is kind to people in many different ways. Record on a chart some ways you could be kind to people you know.

Supergrandpa

DAVID M. SCHWARTZ

ILLUSTRATED BY
BERT DODSON

AWARD-WINNING
AUTHOR

G ustaf Håkansson was sixty-six years old. His hair was snow white. His beard was a white bush. His face rippled with wrinkles whenever he smiled. Gustaf Håkansson looked like an old man, but he didn't feel old, and he certainly didn't act old.

Everyone for miles around knew Gustaf. People saw him on his bicycle, rain or shine, riding through the crooked streets of Grantofta—past the baker's and the butcher's and the wooden-toy maker's, over the stone bridge leading out of town, up steep hills scattered with farms, down narrow lanes bordered by stones, then home again to his morning paper and a bowl of sour milk and lingonberries.

One morning Gustaf read something very interesting in the paper. There was going to be a bicycle race called the Tour of Sweden. It would be more than one thousand miles long, and it would last many days.

"This Tour of Sweden is for me!" exclaimed Gustaf.

"But you're too old for a bicycle race," said Gustaf's wife.

"You'll keel over," said his son. "It would be the end of you."

Even his grandchildren laughed at the idea. "You can't ride your bike a thousand miles, Grandpa," they scoffed.

"*Struntprat!*" Gustaf answered. "Silly talk!" And he hopped onto his bike and rode off to see the judges of the race. He would tell them that he planned to enter the Tour of Sweden.

"But this race is for young people," said the first judge. "You're too old, Gustaf."

"You would never make it to the finish," said the second judge.

"We can only admit racers who are strong and fit," said the third judge. "What if you collapsed in the middle of the race?"

"*Struntprat!*" protested Gustaf. "I have no intention of collapsing, because I *am* strong and fit!"

But the judges were not to be moved. "We're sorry, Gustaf," they grumbled. "Go home. Go home to your rocking chair."

Gustaf went home, but he did not go to his rocking chair. "They can keep me out of the race," he muttered, "but they can't keep me off the road."

The next morning, Gustaf began to prepare for the long ride ahead. He arose with the sun, packed some fruit and rye bread, and cycled far out of town—over rolling hills dotted with ancient castles, across valleys dimpled with lakes, through forests thick with birches and pines. It was midafternoon before he returned. The next day he biked even farther. Each day he added more miles to his ride.

A few days before the race, all the young cyclists boarded a special train to Haparanda, in the far north of Sweden, where the race was to begin. But Gustaf was not an official racer. He had no train ticket.

There was only one way for Gustaf to ride in the Tour of Sweden. He would have to pedal six hundred miles to the starting line!

It took him several days to bike there. He arrived just as the Tour of Sweden was about to begin.

All the racers wore numbers, but of course there was no number for Gustaf. So he found a bright red scrap of fabric and made his own.

What number should he be? He had an idea. He wasn't supposed to be in the race at all, so he would be Number Zero!

He chuckled as he cut out a big red zero and pinned it to his shirt. Then he wheeled his bicycle to the starting line.

The starting gun went off and all the young cyclists took off in a spurt. Their legs pumped furiously and their bikes sprinted ahead. They soon left Gustaf far behind.

That night, the racers stopped at an inn. They were treated to dinner and a bed.

Hours later, Gustaf reached the inn too. But there was no bed for him, so he just kept riding. While the others snoozed the night away, Gustaf pedaled into the dawn.

Early the next day, the other cyclists passed Gustaf. But he kept up his steady pace, and late that evening he again overtook the young racers as they rested. In the middle of the night, he napped for three hours on a park bench.

On the third morning, Gustaf was the first to arrive in the little town of Lulea. A small crowd of people waited, hoping to catch a glimpse of the racers zooming by. Instead they saw Gustaf. His white beard fluttered in the breeze. His red cheeks were puffed out with breath.

"Look!" cried a little girl. "Look! There goes Supergrandpa!"

"Supergrandpa?" Everyone craned to see.

"Yes, yes, he does look like a Supergrandpa!" A few clapped. Others shouted friendly greetings. Some of the children held out their hands and Gustaf brushed their palms as he rode by. "Thank you, Supergrandpa! Good luck to you."

A photographer snapped Gustaf's picture. It appeared the next day in the newspaper. The headline read: *Supergrandpa Takes a Ride.*

Now all of Sweden knew about Supergrandpa Gustaf Håkansson.

When he got hungry or thirsty, people gave him sour milk with lingonberries, tea and cake, fruit juice, rye bread, or any other snack he wanted.

Newspaper reporters rushed up to talk with him. Radio interviewers broadcast every word he spoke. Everyone wanted to know how he felt.

"I have never felt better in my whole life," he told them.

"But aren't you tired?" they asked.

"How can I be tired when I am surrounded by so much kindness?" And with a push on the pedal and a wave of his hand, Gustaf was rolling down the road again.

Once again Gustaf rode through the night, passing the other racers while they slept. When his muscles felt stiff, he remembered his cheering fans. He pedaled harder.

And so it went, day after night, night after day. By the light of the moon, Gustaf quietly passed the young racers in their beds, then slept outside, but only for a few hours. Under the long rays of the morning sun, they overtook him and left him struggling to keep up his spirits and his pace. But each day it took them a little longer to catch up with Gustaf.

On the sixth morning of the race, thousands lined the road. As Gustaf rode by, their joyful cheers travelled with him like a wave through the crowd.

"You're almost there, Supergrandpa!"

"A few more miles!"

"Don't look back."

"You're going to win!"

Win? Gustaf hadn't thought about winning. He had simply wanted to ride in the Tour of Sweden and reach the finish line. But win?

"You're out in front, Supergrandpa."

"A few more miles, Supergrandpa, and you'll be the winner!"

The winner? Gustaf glanced over his shoulder. The pack of racers was catching up. Their heads and shoulders were hunched low over their handlebars. Their backs were raised high above their seats.

Gustaf decided not to think about them. Instead he thought about his many fans. He thought about how they wanted him to win. And suddenly, he wanted to win too!

Gustaf looked ahead. In the distance he could see a bright banner stretched all the way across the road. The finish line!

Gustaf lowered his head. He raised his back. He whipped his legs around with all their might and all their motion.

The next time he looked up he was bursting through
the banner and rolling over the finish line—just before
another racer thundered past.

The crowd roared. People lifted Gustaf onto their shoulders. They showered him with flowers. They sang victory songs. The police band played patriotic marches.

The three judges, however, said that Gustaf could not be the winner, because he was never actually in the race. Besides, it was against the rules to ride at night. No, the big gold trophy would go to another racer, not to Gustaf.

But no one seemed to care what the judges said. Even the king stepped up to hug Gustaf and invite him to the palace. And to nearly everyone in Sweden, Gustaf Håkansson—sixty-six years old, his hair as white as snow, his beard a great white bush, his smiling face an orb of wrinkles—to them, Supergrandpa Gustaf Håkansson had won the Tour of Sweden.

When the judges said that Supergrandpa could not enter the race, how did you feel? Explain why.

If you met Supergrandpa, what would you ask him?

What do you think David M. Schwartz wants readers to learn from this story?

WRITE Imagine that you were part of the cheering crowd that saw Supergrandpa win the race. Write him a letter to congratulate him on his victory.

A NOTE FROM THE AUTHOR:
David M. Schwartz

There really was a sixty-six-year-old Gustaf Håkansson who, in 1951, defied the judges and rode 1,761 kilometers (1,094 miles) in the Tour of Sweden. Cycling day and night, Gustaf did indeed finish first. A little girl who saw the old man on his bike called him *Stålfarfar*. It means "Steel Grandfather," but since Swedish children call "Superman" *Stålman*, we can loosely translate *Stålfarfar* as "Supergrandpa."

The tale of Gustaf Håkansson lives on in Sweden, where he is a folk hero. Parents who want their children to eat well, to get plenty of exercise, and to try hard at whatever they do, tell them "Va' som Stålfarfar"—"Be like Supergrandpa." In fact, Gustaf lived to the age of 102 and was still riding in races at the age of 85!

130

Contests

Julio is not sure he wants to enter the class election, but Supergrandpa is eager to enter the bicycle race. Why do you think each character feels as he does?

WRITER'S WORKSHOP

Think of a time when you entered a contest. Write a descriptive paragraph about the contest itself and about how you felt before, during, and after it.

Writer's Choice
What do you think about contests, now that you've read "Class President" and "Supergrandpa"? Choose and plan your own way to respond. Then carry out your plan.

CONNECTIONS

Multicultural Connection

Celebrating America's Great Athletes

"When I'm skating, I just feel I can express myself. I feel free," says Kristi Yamaguchi, an Asian American figure skater and Olympic Gold Medalist. Kristi has spent years of hard work and discipline to become one of the best skaters in the world. She began skating at age six, to help overcome a childhood disability. She grew to love the sport so much that she would practice five hours a day, every day, while keeping up her good grades.

The practice paid off. Kristi Yamaguchi won the World Figure Skating Championship in 1991 and 1992. She represented the United States at the Olympic Games in 1992 and won the Gold Medal for Women's Figure Skating, the first American woman to do so in sixteen years.

Many other Americans, such as Jackie Joyner-Kersee and Jim Abbott, have become Olympic champions even though they have had medical difficulties. Find out more about one of these great athletes. Share what you learn with others, perhaps by creating a poster about the person.

Entrance to ancient Olympic Stadium

Kristi Yamaguchi

Social Studies Connection

Olympic History

The Olympic Games began over 2,700 years ago in Greece. Find out how the original games were similar to and different from the games today. What events were included? Who competed? Where were the games held? Find the answers to these questions, or think of your own questions. Share your answers with your classmates.

Jim Abbott

Health Connection

Personal Best

Even if you don't want to be an Olympic champion, you can help yourself feel better and even think better by staying healthy. With a group of classmates, make a list of ten healthy things that everyone can do every day. Then do them!

Jackie
Joyner-Kersee

UNIT TWO

ANIMAL TALES

All cultures tell stories about animals. Some of these stories are true, and others are make-believe. Some are about wolves that roam the plains of North America, and others are about graceful cats that rule the forests and plains of Africa. Each culture's tales can help you understand and appreciate the animals of your world. As you read about the animals in this unit, think about what a remarkable creature each one is.

THEMES

BOOKSHELF

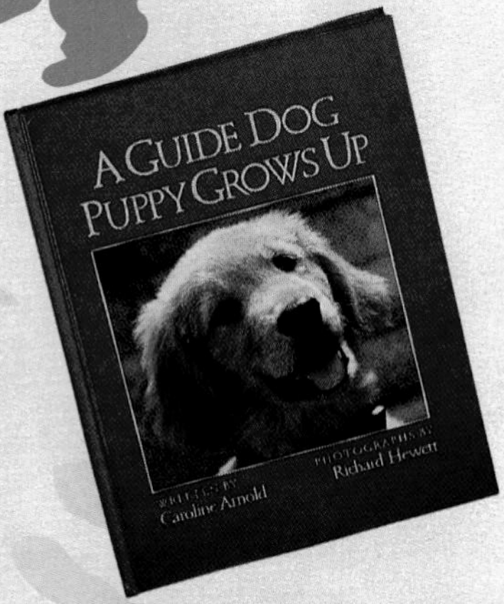

A GUIDE DOG PUPPY GROWS UP

by Caroline Arnold

Honey is a golden retriever puppy *and* a student. She is learning to become a Guide Dog with the help of some special people.

Award-Winning Author

Harcourt Brace Library Book

TURTLE IN JULY

by Marilyn Singer

The changing of the seasons affects not only trees and flowers, but also animals. Each poem, beautifully illustrated by Jerry Pinkney, focuses on an animal in one season or month of the year.

Award-Winning Illustrator

Harcourt Brace Library Book

AESOP'S FABLES

by Aesop

Aesop's fables are some of the oldest and most popular stories in the world. The animals in the fables are a lot like people—some are clever and some are foolish—and they make us laugh while they make us think.

TWO OF A KIND

by Beatriz Doumerc and Ricardo Alcántara

When an important-looking hen arrives at the barnyard, the farm animals gather around to hear her lively story.

Award-Winning Author

THE COUNTRY ARTIST: A STORY ABOUT BEATRIX POTTER

by David R. Collins

This is a biography of Beatrix Potter, author and illustrator of some of the most famous children's stories ever published.

T H E M E

Clever Creatures

Would you like to get to know some extraordinary animals? The animals in the selections that follow have a talent for helping others.

C O N T E N T S

139

Charlotte's Web

by E. B. White
illustrated by Garth Williams

Fern sold her favorite pig, Wilbur, to her uncle, Homer Zuckerman. Fern knew that her uncle and his hired hand, Lurvy, would take good care of Wilbur. They did their best to keep Wilbur well fed.

When the other animals in Zuckerman's barnyard informed Wilbur that he was to be the main course at the Christmas feast, only Charlotte, the beautiful spider, had a plan to save Wilbur.

On foggy mornings, Charlotte's web was truly a thing of beauty. This morning each thin strand was decorated with dozens of tiny beads of water. The web glistened in the light and made a pattern of loveliness and mystery, like a delicate veil. Even Lurvy, who wasn't particularly interested in beauty, noticed the web when he came with the pig's breakfast. He noted how clearly it showed up and he noted how big and carefully built it was. And then he took another look and he saw something that made him set his pail down. There, in the center of the web, neatly woven in block letters, was a message. It said:

SOME PIG!

Lurvy felt weak. He brushed his hand across his eyes and stared harder at Charlotte's web.

"I'm seeing things," he whispered. He dropped to his knees and uttered a short prayer. Then, forgetting all about Wilbur's breakfast, he walked back to the house and called Mr. Zuckerman.

"I think you'd better come down to the pigpen," he said.

"What's the trouble?" asked Mr. Zuckerman. "Anything wrong with the pig?"

"N-not exactly," said Lurvy. "Come and see for yourself."

The two men walked silently down to Wilbur's yard. Lurvy pointed to the spider's web. "Do you see what I see?" he asked.

Zuckerman stared at the writing on the web. Then he murmured the words "Some Pig." Then he looked at

Lurvy. Then they both began to tremble. Charlotte, sleepy after her night's exertions, smiled as she watched. Wilbur came and stood directly under the web.

"Some pig!" muttered Lurvy in a low voice.

"Some pig!" whispered Mr. Zuckerman. They stared and stared for a long time at Wilbur. Then they stared at Charlotte.

"You don't suppose that that spider . . ." began Mr. Zuckerman—but he shook his head and didn't finish the sentence. Instead, he walked solemnly back up to the house and spoke to his wife. "Edith, something has happened," he said, in a weak voice. He went into the living room and sat down, and Mrs. Zuckerman followed.

"I've got something to tell you, Edith," he said. "You better sit down."

Mrs. Zuckerman sank into a chair. She looked pale and frightened.

"Edith," he said, trying to keep his voice steady, "I think you had best be told that we have a very unusual pig."

A look of complete bewilderment came over Mrs. Zuckerman's face. "Homer Zuckerman, what in the world are you talking about?" she said.

"This is a very serious thing, Edith," he replied. "Our pig is completely out of the ordinary."

"What's unusual about the pig?" asked Mrs. Zuckerman, who was beginning to recover from her scare.

"Well, I don't really know yet," said Mr. Zuckerman. "But we have received a sign, Edith—a mysterious sign. A miracle has happened on this farm. There is a large spider's web in the doorway of the barn cellar, right over the pigpen, and when Lurvy went to feed the pig this morning, he noticed the web because it was foggy, and you know how a spider's web looks very distinct in a fog. And right spang in the middle of the web there were the words 'Some Pig.' The words were woven right into the web. They were actually part of the web, Edith. I know, because I have been down there and seen them. It says, 'Some Pig,' just as clear as clear can be. There can be no mistake about it. A miracle has happened and a sign has occurred here on earth, right on our farm, and we have no ordinary pig."

"Well," said Mrs. Zuckerman, "it seems to me you're a little off. It seems to me we have no ordinary *spider*."

"Oh, no," said Zuckerman. "It's the pig that's unusual. It says so, right there in the middle of the web."

"Maybe so," said Mrs. Zuckerman. "Just the same, I intend to have a look at that spider."

"It's just a common grey spider," said Zuckerman.

They got up, and together they walked down to Wilbur's yard. "You see, Edith? It's just a common grey spider."

Wilbur was pleased to receive so much attention. Lurvy was still standing there, and Mr. and Mrs. Zuckerman, all three, stood for about an hour, reading the words on the web over and over, and watching Wilbur.

Charlotte was delighted with the way her trick was working. She sat without moving a muscle, and listened to the conversation of the people. When a small fly blundered into the web, just beyond the word "pig," Charlotte dropped quickly down, rolled the fly up, and carried it out of the way.

After a while the fog lifted. The web dried off and the words didn't show up so plainly. The Zuckermans and Lurvy walked back to the house. Just before they left the pigpen, Mr. Zuckerman took one last look at Wilbur.

"You know," he said, in an important voice, "I've thought all along that that pig of ours was an extra good one. He's a solid pig. That pig is as solid as they come. You notice how solid he is around the shoulders, Lurvy?"

"Sure. Sure I do," said Lurvy. "I've always noticed that pig. He's quite a pig."

"He's long, and he's smooth," said Zuckerman.

"That's right," agreed Lurvy. "He's as smooth as they come. He's some pig."

When Mr. Zuckerman got back to the house, he took off his work clothes and put on his best suit. Then he got into his car and drove to the minister's house. He stayed for an hour and explained to the minister that a miracle had happened on the farm.

"So far," said Zuckerman, "only four people on earth know about this miracle—myself, my wife Edith, my hired man Lurvy, and you."

"Don't tell anybody else," said the minister. "We don't know what it means yet, but perhaps if I give thought to it, I can explain it in my sermon next Sunday. There can be no doubt that you have a most unusual pig. I intend to speak about it in my sermon and point out the fact that this community has been visited with a wondrous animal. By the way, does the pig have a name?"

"Why, yes," said Mr. Zuckerman. "My little niece calls him Wilbur. She's a rather queer child—full of notions. She raised the pig on a bottle and I bought him from her when he was a month old."

He shook hands with the minister, and left.

Secrets are hard to keep. Long before Sunday came, the news spread all over the county.

Everybody knew that a sign had appeared in a spider's web on the Zuckerman place. Everybody knew that the Zuckermans had a wondrous pig. People came from miles around to look at Wilbur and to read the words on Charlotte's web. The Zuckermans' driveway was full of cars and trucks from morning till night—Fords and Chevvies and Buick roadmasters and GMC pickups and Plymouths and Studebakers and Packards and De Sotos with gyromatic transmissions and Oldsmobiles with rocket engines and Jeep station wagons and Pontiacs. The news of the wonderful pig spread clear up into the hills, and farmers came rattling down in buggies and buckboards, to stand hour after hour at Wilbur's pen admiring the miraculous animal. All said they had never seen such a pig before in their lives.

When Fern told her mother that Avery had tried to hit the Zuckermans' spider with a stick, Mrs. Arable was so shocked that she sent Avery to bed without any supper, as punishment.

In the days that followed, Mr. Zuckerman was so busy entertaining visitors that he neglected his farm work. He wore his good clothes all the time now—got right into them when he got up in the morning. Mrs. Zuckerman prepared special meals for Wilbur. Lurvy shaved and got a haircut; and his principal farm duty was to feed the pig while people looked on.

Mr. Zuckerman ordered Lurvy to increase Wilbur's feedings from three meals a day to four meals a day. The Zuckermans were so busy with visitors they forgot about other things on the farm. The blackberries got ripe, and Mrs. Zuckerman failed to put up any blackberry jam. The corn needed hoeing, and Lurvy didn't find time to hoe it.

On Sunday the church was full. The minister explained the miracle. He said that the words on the spider's web proved that human beings must always be on the watch for the coming of wonders.

All in all, the Zuckermans' pigpen was the center of attraction. Fern was happy, for she felt that Charlotte's trick was working and that Wilbur's life would be saved. But she found that the barn was not nearly as pleasant— too many people. She liked it better when she could be all alone with her friends the animals.

One evening, a few days after the writing had appeared in Charlotte's web, the spider called a meeting of all the animals in the barn cellar.

"I shall begin by calling the roll. Wilbur?"

"Here!" said the pig.

"Gander?"

"Here, here, here!" said the gander.

"You sound like three ganders," muttered Charlotte. "Why can't you just say 'here'? Why do you have to repeat everything?"

"It's my idio-idio-idiosyncrasy," replied the gander.

"Goose?" said Charlotte.

"Here, here, here!" said the goose. Charlotte glared at her.

"Goslings, one through seven?"

"Bee-bee-bee!" "Bee-bee-bee!" "Bee-bee-bee!" "Bee-bee-bee!" "Bee-bee-bee!" "Bee-bee-bee!" "Bee-bee-bee!" said the goslings.

"This is getting to be quite a meeting," said Charlotte. "Anybody would think we had three ganders, three geese, and twenty-one goslings. Sheep?"

"He-aa-aa!" answered the sheep all together.

"Lambs?"

"He-aa-aa!" answered the lambs all together.

"Templeton?"

No answer.

"Templeton?"

No answer.

"Well, we are all here except the rat," said Charlotte.

"I guess we can proceed without him. Now, all of you must have noticed what's been going on around here the last few days. The message I wrote in my web, praising Wilbur, has been received. The Zuckermans have fallen for it, and so has everybody else. Zuckerman thinks Wilbur is an unusual pig, and therefore he won't want to kill him and eat him. I dare say my trick will work and Wilbur's life can be saved."

"Hurray!" cried everybody.

"Thank you very much," said Charlotte. "Now I called this meeting in order to get suggestions. I need new ideas for the web. People are already getting sick of reading the words 'Some Pig!' If anybody can think of another message, or remark, I'll be glad to weave it into the web. Any suggestions for a new slogan?"

"How about 'Pig Supreme'?" asked one of the lambs.

"No good," said Charlotte. "It sounds like a rich dessert."

"How about 'Terrific, terrific, terrific'?" asked the goose.

"Cut that down to one 'terrific' and it will do very nicely," said Charlotte. "I think 'terrific' might impress Zuckerman."

"But Charlotte," said Wilbur, "I'm *not* terrific."

"That doesn't make a particle of difference," replied Charlotte. "Not a particle. People believe almost anything they see in print. Does anybody here know how to spell 'terrific'?"

"I think," said the gander, "it's tee double ee double rr double rr double eye double ff double eye double see see see see see."

"What kind of an acrobat do you think I am?" said Charlotte in disgust. "I would have to have St. Vitus's Dance to weave a word like that into my web."

"Sorry, sorry, sorry," said the gander.

Then the oldest sheep spoke up. "I agree that there should be something new written in the web if Wilbur's life is to be saved. And if Charlotte needs help in finding words, I think she can get it from our friend Templeton. The rat visits the dump regularly and has access to old magazines. He can tear out bits of advertisements and bring them up here to the barn cellar, so that Charlotte can have something to copy."

"Good idea," said Charlotte. "But I'm not sure Templeton will be willing to help. You know how he is— always looking out for himself, never thinking of the other fellow."

"I bet I can get him to help," said the old sheep. "I'll appeal to his baser instincts, of which he has plenty. Here he comes now. Everybody keep quiet while I put the matter up to him!"

The rat entered the barn the way he always did— creeping along close to the wall.

"What's up?" he asked, seeing the animals assembled.

"We're holding a directors' meeting," replied the old sheep.

"Well, break it up!" said Templeton. "Meetings bore me." And the rat began to climb a rope that hung against the wall.

"Look," said the old sheep, "next time you go to the dump, Templeton, bring back a clipping from a magazine. Charlotte needs new ideas so she can write messages in her web and save Wilbur's life."

"Let him die," said the rat. "I should worry."

"You'll worry all right when next winter comes," said the sheep. "You'll worry all right on a zero morning next January when Wilbur is dead and nobody comes down here with a nice pail of warm slops to pour into the trough. Wilbur's leftover food is your chief source of supply, Templeton. *You* know that. Wilbur's food is your food; therefore Wilbur's destiny and your destiny are closely linked. If Wilbur is killed and his trough stands empty day after day, you'll grow so thin we can look right through your stomach and see objects on the other side."

Templeton's whiskers quivered.

"Maybe you're right," he said gruffly. "I'm making a trip to the dump tomorrow afternoon. I'll bring back a magazine clipping if I can find one."

"Thanks," said Charlotte. "The meeting is now adjourned. I have a busy evening ahead of me. I've got to tear my web apart and write 'Terrific.'"

Wilbur blushed. "But I'm *not* terrific, Charlotte. I'm just about average for a pig."

"You're terrific as far as *I'm* concerned," replied Charlotte, sweetly, "and that's what counts. You're my best friend, and *I* think you're sensational. Now stop arguing and go get some sleep!"

If you heard about something as unusual as the message appearing in Charlotte's web, would you have to see it to believe it? Tell why you would or would not.

Why is it important that Mr. Zuckerman believe Charlotte's message?

How does the message in Charlotte's web change daily activities in the barnyard?

WRITE Wilbur is Charlotte's best friend. Write a postcard to your best friend, telling why his or her friendship makes you happy.

WORDS *About the* ILLUSTRATOR:
Garth Williams

Garth Williams's most famous illustrations can be seen in the *Little House* books by Laura Ingalls Wilder. Mr. Williams has also drawn pictures for many other classic books, such as E. B. White's *Charlotte's Web.*

After Garth Williams went to school in England to study painting and sculpting, he moved to New York and worked for *The New Yorker* magazine. Soon he began illustrating children's books. *Stuart Little*, also by E. B. White, was his first children's book. In over fifty years, Mr. Williams has illustrated more than fifty books.

Mr. Williams doesn't just draw things the way they look. He tries to draw the way things feel, too. He wants to see things the way the writer does. When Garth Williams was beginning to draw pictures for the *Little House* books, he visited with Laura Ingalls Wilder and took a trip to the same places that the Ingalls family had traveled to in their covered wagon. He worked on the illustrations for that series of books for almost ten years. Mr. Williams says his work is not "just making pictures." He wants his pictures to have a special feeling that goes with the story.

Turn to the illustrations in "On the Banks of Plum Creek" on page 452 to see more examples of Garth Williams's drawings.

Talk To The Animals

by Leslie Bricusse

illustrated by Sylvie Daigneault

If we could Talk To The Animals, just imagine it,
Chatting to a chimp in chimpanzee,
Imagine talking to a tiger,
chatting to a cheetah,
What a neat achievement it would be.

If we could Talk To The Animals,
learn their languages,
Maybe take an animal degree,
We'd study elephant and eagle,
buffalo and beagle,
Alligator, guinea pig and flea.
We would converse in polar bear and python,
And we would curse in fluent kangaroo.
If people asked us, "Can you speak rhinoceros?"
We'd say, "Of courseros! Can't you?"

If we conferred with our furry friends,
man to animal,
Think of all the things we could discuss.
If we could walk with the animals,
talk with the animals,
Grunt and squeak and squawk with the animals,
And they could talk to us.
If we consulted with quadrupeds, think what fun
we'd have,
Asking over crocodiles for tea,
Or maybe lunch with two or three lions,
walruses and sea lions,
What a lovely place the world would be.

If we spoke slang to orangutangs,
the advantages
Any fool on earth can plainly see.
Discussing eastern art and dramas
with intellectual llamas,
That's a big step forward, you'll agree.
We'd learn to speak in antelope and turtle,
Our Pekinese would be extremely good.
If we were asked to sing in hippopotamus,
We'd say, "Why notamus?" And would!

And we are sure ev'ry octopus,
Plaice and platypus
certainly would see it as a plus.
If we could walk with the animals,
talk with the animals,
Grunt and squeak and squawk with the animals,
And they could talk to us.

A GUIDE DOG
PUPPY GROWS UP

WRITTEN BY
Caroline Arnold

PHOTOGRAPHS BY
Richard Hewett

156

A GUIDE DOG PUPPY GROWS UP

Written by Caroline Arnold
Photographs by Richard Hewett

Puppies that grow up to be Guide Dogs spend the first twelve weeks of their lives at a training center. They are tested to make sure they are well-behaved and healthy. Then it is time for the next stage of Guide Dog training.

When a Guide Dog puppy is about three months old, it goes to live with a family. This family has volunteered to care for the puppy while it grows up. Honey's new home is with a nine-year-old girl named Amy and her family. Amy loves dogs and is eager to take care of one.

Like Amy, many puppy raisers are 4-H Club members. 4-H is a program that offers kids, usually in rural or suburban areas, the opportunity to do real-life projects in their homes, on farms, or in their communities. To become a puppy raiser, Amy filled out an application and had an interview with her 4-H project leader. The 4-H puppy placement department at Guide Dogs for the Blind gave Amy a pamphlet on puppy care and a chart to record Honey's growth and development.

157

They also provided a dog collar showing the telephone number of Guide Dogs for the Blind and Honey's identification number in case she ever got lost.

Puppy raisers are responsible for the complete care of their dogs during the fifteen months or so they have them. They must housetrain and feed the puppies and keep them clean and healthy. The dog is treated as a family pet and learns to live with people. One of the things Honey enjoys most is playing with Amy and her friends.

During the time Amy has Honey, she keeps track of all their activities. Once a month they go to puppy-club meetings where they learn about puppy care and exchange news with other club members. Amy also teaches Honey simple commands so she will behave when they go out.

An important part of being a puppy raiser is getting

the dog used to going out into the community, since this will be the dog's job when it is working with a blind person. So when Amy or her parents go to the supermarket, bank, or even sometimes to work or school, they often take Honey with them. Ordinarily, animals cannot go into most places of business unless they are helping a handicapped person. Honey's green jacket tells people she is a Guide Dog puppy. When Honey wears the jacket, people often stop Amy to ask her about being a puppy raiser.

By the time Honey is a year and a half old, she has grown from a bouncy young puppy to a well-mannered adult dog. Her soft puppy coat has grown dark and silky, and her body has filled out to its grown-up shape.

In every way, Honey has become a real member of Amy's family, but soon the time comes for Honey to go back to the Guide Dog campus and begin her formal training. Amy knows she has played an important part in getting Honey ready to help a blind person, but she wishes Honey didn't have to go.

Amy's mother drives them to the Guide Dog campus. A staff member greets them at the car and explains the next stage of Honey's training. Before they leave, Amy gives Honey an extra hug. "I'll be back for your graduation," she says.

159

On her arrival at the Guide Dog campus, Honey is given a new collar and put into the receiving kennel. First an instructor checks her over and measures her height and weight. The veterinarian then gives Honey a thorough examination and X-rays her hips. He wants to make sure she will not develop any problems that could prevent her from walking properly.

If Honey did not measure up exactly to Guide Dog standards either physically or later in training, she would be made available for adoption. Amy would have the first chance to adopt her, but if for some reason Amy didn't want Honey, she would be offered to someone else. Even though a dog may not be quite right for working with a blind person, it can still make an excellent pet. Only about half of the dogs successfully complete every stage of the training and become Guide Dogs.

Both male and female dogs can become guides. A few of the dogs with especially good characteristics are used as breeders. These dogs live with families in the community except when it is time for breeding or when the females are due to give birth to puppies. The rest of the dogs are spayed or neutered because a dog guide cannot leave its blind partner to mate or have puppies.

After completing her checkup, Honey is moved into her new training kennel.

"Hello, Honey," says Terry, as he snaps a leash onto her collar. "Today you and I are going to start working together. If all goes well, you will be ready to be a guide in five or six months."

Terry is Honey's instructor, and every day he spends some time working with her. At first, Terry teaches Honey to sit and stay and to obey other basic commands. When Honey follows his instructions, he pats her on the head and tells her she's a good dog. In all of her training, the only reward Honey needs is praise. Like most dogs, Honey is eager to please and learns quickly.

Each step of the training process helps Honey to learn skills she will need later when guiding a blind person. For instance, if a blind person drops something, the dog guide must know how to retrieve it. Early in her training, Honey learns to pick up an object and give it to Terry.

Each instructor is responsible for ten to fifteen dogs at a time. In the kennels next to hers, Honey can hear other dogs. She watches as instructors take these dogs out, one at a time, for their training sessions.

Three times a day, all the dogs in Honey's kennel are let out into a large fenced area where they can run freely and exercise. This is also a chance for the dogs

to get to know each other. Dog guides must be comfortable around other animals so they do not become afraid or aggressive.

After several weeks of working Honey on a leash, Terry is ready to add harness training to her workout. Although Honey's 4-H jacket has helped her get used to wearing something on her back, it will take a while before she feels completely at ease in the new harness.

Until now, Honey has just walked beside Terry, but during the harness training sessions he has to teach Honey to pull him. Honey listens to Terry's commands to know whether she should pull him forward, turn left or right, or stop. A dog guide is very intelligent, but it cannot know where a blind person wants to go without instructions. The dog and the person must work together to get safely to their destination.

Most of Honey's workouts are in downtown San Rafael. To get there, Terry takes her in a van along with several other dogs who are also being trained. When Honey's turn comes, she always jumps eagerly out of the van, ready to start working.

Six months go by quickly. In the final part of her training, Terry asks Honey to lead him on a walk as usual, but this time his eyes are covered by a blindfold. For safety, another trainer walks closely behind in case Honey makes a mistake. But the other trainer isn't needed this time because Honey guides Terry perfectly, just as she has been taught.

Honey has passed all her tests. Now she is ready to be placed with a blind person. Not all blind people want to have a dog guide. Some prefer to use a cane or to have

other people guide them. Some do not like animals or don't want the responsibility of taking care of a dog. However, any legally blind person over the age of sixteen can apply to Guide Dogs for the Blind for a dog. After an extensive interview, those people ready for the responsibility of learning to live and work with a dog guide come to the Guide Dogs for the Blind campus.

Usually there are sixteen students in a class. During the four weeks of training they live in the dormitory together, two to a room. The students are of all ages and come from a variety of backgrounds. Some have been blind all their lives, and others have lost their sight more recently. While there are many different kinds and causes of blindness, all the students share the problem of how to get around without being able to see.

When Anne Gelles arrives on campus to begin her Guide Dog training, Terry greets her. He will be one of the instructors for her class. During the school year, Anne works as a teacher of blind children. Like many of them, she has been blind all her life. She wants a dog to help her get to and from her job. Like the other new students at Guide Dogs for the Blind, she is excited about getting a dog and at the same time a little worried about everything she will have to learn.

During their first few days on campus, the students learn their way around and get used to the daily routine. Even though they do not have dogs yet, they are learning how to give the correct commands. Terry pretends to be a dog named Juno as he teaches each student how to move and speak to a Guide Dog.

"I feel a little silly," says Anne, "because I know you aren't a real dog."

"I know," says Terry. "But I can tell you when you make a mistake, and a real dog can't."

Finally, on their fourth day on campus, the students are ready to meet their dogs for the first time.

That morning a kennel worker gives Honey a bath. "Today is an important day," she says, "and I want you to look your best."

When Honey is clean and dry, Terry comes to get her. Together they walk across the campus to meet Anne, who will be Honey's new partner.

Over the last six months, Terry and the other instructors have gotten to know all their dogs very well. Like people, each dog has its own personality. After meeting the new students and reviewing their needs and desires, Terry and other staff members carefully matched each person with one of the dogs.

"Hello, Anne," says Terry. "Here's Honey. She's a beautiful russet-colored golden retriever. I picked her especially for you because you both have lively personalities."

Anne laughs and reaches out to scratch Honey under the chin. Honey stretches her neck with pleasure.

"Hello, Honey," Anne says. "I can't wait to get to know you better. We're going to have fun together."

If you had the opportunity to raise a Guide Dog puppy, would you want to accept the responsibility? Explain why or why not.

Why do only half of the dogs selected to be Guide Dogs complete the training?

What kind of person is Amy? Explain how you know.

WRITE   Think about how Amy might have felt on the day Honey went back to the Guide Dog campus. Write a diary entry she might have written that day, telling about her feelings.

166

Clever Creatures

You have read about a spider that weaves messages to help a friend and about a puppy that is training for an important career. How are Charlotte and Honey alike? How are they different?

WRITER'S WORKSHOP

Choose one of the animals mentioned in the selections or the song. Imagine that this animal has been your pet for a while. Write a story about a day in the life of your pet. Share your story with your classmates.

Writer's Choice
You have read about some very intelligent animals. You could tell about other smart animals, possibly one that shares your home. Choose an idea. Write about it, and share it.

THEME

Natural Friends

Think about a time when you had to make a decision. Was it easy to make? Did you have many choices? The following selection and poems tell about making decisions concerning animals and their treatment.

CONTENTS

ALA Notable
Book

THE MIDNIGHT

Fox

BY BETSY BYARS

illustrated by Jeffrey Terreson

Tom never expected that his boring summer on his aunt and uncle's farm would turn into an exciting game of chance. It started when Tom became entranced at the first sight of the beautiful midnight fox. He quickly developed a strong attachment to the graceful black fox and her playful cub. But when Aunt Millie's chickens started disappearing, Uncle Fred decided it was time to trap the fox. Tom reluctantly went with him to find her.

171

I heard the sound of Happ's barking coming closer. He had lost the fox in the woods but now he had a new scent, older, but still hot. He came crashing through the bushes, bellowing every few feet, his head to the ground. He flashed past me, not even seeing me in his intensity, his red eyes on the ground. Like a charging bull, he entered the thicket and he and Uncle Fred stepped into the small grassy clearing at the same moment.

"Here it is," Uncle Fred called. "Come here."

I wanted to turn and run. I did not want to see Uncle Fred and Happ standing in that lovely secluded clearing, but instead I walked through the trees and looked at the place I had avoided so carefully for weeks. There were the bones, some whitened by the sun, a dried turkey wing, feathers, and behind, the partially sheltered hole. Of course Uncle Fred had already seen that, and as I stepped from the trees he pointed to it with his gun.

"There's the den."

I nodded.

"The baby foxes will be in there."

This was the first time he had been wrong. There was only one baby fox in there, and I imagined him crouching now against the far wall of the den.

"Go back to the house and get me a shovel and sack," Uncle Fred said.

Without speaking, I turned and walked back to the house. Behind me the black fox barked again. It was a desperate high series of barks that seemed to last a long time, and Happ lunged after the fox for the third time. It was too late now for tricks, for Uncle Fred remained, leaning on his gun, waiting for the shovel and sack.

I went up the back steps and knocked. Usually I just went in the house like I did at my own home, but I waited there till Aunt Millie came and I said, "Uncle Fred wants me to bring him a sack and a shovel."

"Did you get the fox?"

"Uncle Fred found the den."

"If it's in the woods, he'll find it," she said, coming out the door, "but you ought to see that man try to find a pair of socks in his own drawer. Hazeline," she called up to her window, "you want to go see your dad dig out the baby foxes?"

"No."

"I declare that girl is in the worst mood." She walked with me to the shed, put the shovel in my hand, and then pressed a dusty grain sack against me. "Now, you don't be too late."

"I don't think it will take long."

"Are you all right? Your face is beet red."

"I'm all right."

"Because I can make Hazeline take that shovel to her dad."

"I feel fine."

I started toward the orchard with the shovel and sack and I felt like some fairy-tale character who has been sent on an impossible mission, like proving my worth by catching a thousand golden eagles in the sack and making a silver mountain for them with my shovel. Even that did not seem as difficult as what I was really doing.

It must have taken me longer to get back than I thought, for Uncle Fred said, "I thought you'd gotten lost."

"No, I wasn't lost. I've been here before."

I handed him the shovel and let the sack drop to the ground. As he began to dig, I closed my eyes and pressed my hands against my eyelids, and I saw a large golden sunburst, and in this sunburst the black fox came running toward me.

I opened my eyes and watched Uncle Fred. He dug as he did everything else—powerfully, slowly, and without stopping. His shovel hit a rock and he moved the shovel until he could bring the rock out with the dirt. At my feet the gravely pile of earth was growing.

I turned away and looked across the creek, and I saw for the fifteenth and last time the black fox. She moved anxiously toward the bushes and there was a tension to her steps, as if she were ready to spring or make some other quick, forceful movement. She barked. She had lost the dog again, and this bark was a high clear call for Uncle Fred and me to follow her.

There was a grunt of satisfaction from Uncle Fred and I turned to see him lift out, on the shovel, covered with sand and gravel, the baby fox.

He turned it onto the sack and the baby fox lay without moving.

"He's dead," I said.

Uncle Fred shook his head. "He's not dead. He's just play-acting. His ma taught him to do that."

We both looked down at the little fox without speaking. I knew that if I lived to be a hundred, I would never see anything that would make me feel any worse than the sight of that little fox pretending to be dead when his heart was beating so hard it looked like it was going to burst out of his chest.

I looked over my shoulder and the black fox was gone. I knew she was still watching us, but I could not see her. Uncle Fred was probing the den with his shovel. I said, "I don't think there are any more. She just had one."

He dug again, piled more earth on the pile, then said, "You're right. Usually a fox has five or six cubs."

"I think something happened to the others."

He bent, folded the ends of the sack, and lifted the baby fox. I took the shovel, he the gun, and we started home, the baby fox swinging between us. Happ joined us as we crossed the creek and began to leap excitedly at the sack until Uncle Fred had to hold it shoulder-high to keep it from him.

We walked back to the house without speaking. Uncle Fred went directly to some old rabbit hutches beside the garage. Bubba had once raised rabbits here, but now the cages were empty. Uncle Fred opened one, shook the baby fox out of the sack, and then closed the wire door.

The baby fox moved to the back of the hutch and looked at us. His fur was soft and woolly, but his eyes were sharp. Nervously he went to one corner.

Aunt Millie came out and looked. "Just like a baby lamb," she said. "It's a sweet little thing, isn't it?"

"That's not the way you were talking yesterday," Uncle Fred said.

"Well, I'm not going to have anything after my chickens," she said. "Not *anything*! I'd be after you with the broom if you bothered my chickens." They laughed. Her spirits seemed greatly improved now that the fox was doomed, and she called, "Hazeline, come on out here and look at this cute little baby fox."

"No."

Uncle Fred went into the shed, returned, and snapped a lock over the cage latch.

"You think somebody's going to steal your fox?" Aunt Millie laughed.

"I wouldn't put it past a fox to open up an unlocked cage to get her baby."

Aunt Millie shook her head in amazement, then said, "Well, you men have got to get washed up for supper."

We went into the house and I said to Uncle Fred, "What are you going to do with the baby fox?"

"That's my bait. Every hunter alive's got some way to get a fox. They got some special trap or something. Mr. Baynes down at the store makes up a special mixture that he says foxes can't resist. My way is to set up a trap, using the baby fox for bait. I'll sit out on the back porch tonight and watch for her."

"Oh."

"It never fails. That is one bait a fox can't resist."

ↄↄↄↄↄↄↄↄↄ

"Are you getting sick?" Aunt Millie asked at supper that night.

"I guess I'm a little tired."

"Well, I should think so! Helping with the pump out in the broiling sun all morning and then tracking that fox all afternoon. It's a wonder you don't have heat stroke. You eat something though, hear? You have to keep up your strength."

"I'm just not hungry."

"It's the heat. But, listen, you drink your tea. You will have heat stroke sure enough if you let your body get dried out."

I finished my tea and went up to my room. I did not even look out the window, because I knew I could see the rabbit hutch by the garage and I never again wanted to see that baby fox cowering against the wall.

Hazeline came out of her room and looked in at me on the bed. "You feeling better?"

I nodded. She was all dressed up now in a blue dress she had made for 4-H. Her face looked good, as if letting it get swollen had been beneficial. I knew she was going downstairs to sit on the porch and wait for Mikey. I knew he would come, too. One time Petie and I had the worst argument in the world. We were just sitting on the steps one afternoon and Petie had been thinking in silence for a while and then he said, "I wonder what I'll look like when I'm grown."

And I said, "Porky Pig." I don't know why I said that, because I wasn't mad at him or anything. And he said, "Well, that's better than looking like Daffy Duck." And I said, "Meaning I look like Daffy Duck?" And he said, "Yes, around the mouth." And then we both got angry and started screaming things and I thought our friendship was over, only two days later it was just like it had never happened.

"Mikey will come over," I said.

"Who cares? I don't care if I never see him again," she said, twisting her fingers in her pearls. He had given her those when she graduated from high school two months ago.

"I know, but I bet he comes anyway."

"Well, I can't stop him of course. It's a free country."

"Hazeline?"

"What?"

"You know that fox I was telling you about? The black one?"

"Sure."

"Well, your dad has her baby out in the rabbit hutch and he's going to shoot her."

"I know it. I heard. But, listen, don't let it upset you, hear?"

"Hazeline, I don't want anything to happen to that fox."

"Tommy, listen, all wild animals die in some violent way. It's their life. Wild animals just don't die of old age. They get killed by an enemy or by the weather or they have an accident or they get rabies or some other disease or they get shot. That's the way nature is."

"I know that," I said quickly, because I did not want to hear any more.

"You just forget the fox. Tomorrow maybe we can go to the picture show in Clinton or something."

"All right."

She went down the steps then and out onto the porch, and I could hear the swing begin to creak.

I got up and went down the steps and walked to the tree in front of the rabbit hutch. I could not explain why I did this. I didn't want to see the baby fox again, and yet here I was.

He did not see me. He was busy biting the wires of his cage with great fury and determination. I could hear the clicking of his sharp tiny teeth against the wire, but he was making no progress. Then he stopped. He still had not seen me, but he had heard or smelled something and he raised his head and let out a short cry. He waited, then after a moment he began biting the wires again.

I remained by the tree watching him, listening for the quavering cry that he uttered from time to time.

"Don't get your fingers in the cage," Uncle Fred warned behind me. "He may not be able to cut wire yet, but he sure could hurt a finger."

"All right."

"In a bit, when it starts getting dark, you can sit up here with me and watch for the fox."

A car came slowly up the drive, and I said to Uncle Fred, "It's Mikey."

Behind him in the doorway Aunt Millie said, "Did you say it's Mikey, Tom?"

I nodded.

"Praise be."

I walked around the front of the house and stood there for a minute. Mikey had not gotten out of the car but was sitting with one arm out the window, looking at Hazeline on the porch.

"What you doing?" he asked.

"Not much of anything," she said. "Just fighting the heat."

"You don't look hot—you look real good and cool."

"Sometimes looks are deceiving."

He ran his fingers over the steering wheel. There was a pause, then he said, "Do you want to ride up to the lake?"

"I don't know."

"When you going to make up your mind?"

"I just don't know whether I feel like looking at boats racing all over creation tonight."

"Do you want to go for a ride?"

"I don't know."

"I'll give you"—he looked at his watch—"one minute to make up your mind."

He started watching the seconds tick off, and I held up my watch too and counted, and only eleven seconds had gone by when Hazeline got up and said, "I'll go," and started laughing. "Tell Mom I'm going off with Mikey," she said over her shoulder and got in the car.

I went into the kitchen where Aunt Millie was standing in front of the electric fan and said, "Hazeline has gone off with Mikey."

I heard the cry of the baby fox again, and I thought I would be hearing that sound forever. One time Petie Burkis fell down and broke his leg on the school playground and he said, "Oh!" in this real terrible, painful way, and I never could forget it. Later I tried to make him say it again that same way, and one whole afternoon Petie did nothing but say the word *Oh* over and over—a thousand times maybe, and in all those thousand tries, he never sounded that same way again. I still remember it though, exactly, like I will always remember the way that baby fox sounded when he cried.

It seemed to get dark quickly that night. Uncle Fred was already out on the back porch. He had brought out a chair and was sitting with his gun beside him, pointing to the floor. I never saw anyone sit quieter. You wouldn't have noticed him at all he was so still.

I stood behind him inside the screen door. Through the screen I could see the tiny fox lift his black nose and cry again. Now, for the first time, there was an answer—the bark of his mother.

I looked toward the garden, because that's where the sound had come from, but Uncle Fred did not even turn his head. In a frenzy now that he had heard his mother, the baby fox moved about the cage, pulling at the wire and crying again and again.

Just then there was the sound of thunder from the west, a long rolling sound, and Aunt Millie came to the door beside me and said, "Bless me, is that thunder?" She looked out at the sky. "Was that thunder, Fred?"

"Could be," he said without moving.

"Look!" Aunt Millie said. "I swear I see black clouds. You see, Tom?"

"Yes'm."

"And feel that breeze. Honestly, when you think you have reached absolutely the end of your endurance, then the breeze comes. I could not have drawn one more breath of hot air, and now we are going to have a storm."

We stood in the doorway, feeling the breeze, forgetting for a moment the baby fox.

Then I saw Uncle Fred's gun rise ever so slightly in the direction of the fence behind the garage. I could not see any sign of the fox, but I knew that she must be there. Uncle Fred would not be wrong.

The breeze quickened, and abruptly the dishpan which Aunt Millie had left on the porch railing clattered to the floor. For the first time Uncle Fred turned his head and looked in annoyance at the pan and then at Aunt Millie.

"Did it scare your fox off?" she asked.

He nodded, then shifted in the chair and said, "She'll be back."

In just this short time the sky to the west had gotten black as ink. Low on the horizon forks of lightning streaked the sky.

"Now, Fred, don't you sit out here while it's thundering and lightning. I mean it. No fox is worth getting struck by lightning for."

He nodded and she turned to me and said, "You come on and help me shut the windows. Some of those upstairs are stuck wide open. Just hit them with the heel of your hand on the side till you can get them down."

I started up the stairs and she said again, "Fred, come on in when it starts storming. That fox'll be back tomorrow night too."

I went upstairs and started hitting the sides of the windows. I had just gotten one window to jerk down about two inches when I heard the gunshot. I had never heard any worse sound in my life. It was a very final sound, like the most enormous period in the world. Bam. Period. The end.

I ran out of my room and down the steps so fast I could not even tell you how many times my feet touched the stairs, none maybe. I went out the back door, opening it so fast I hit the back of Uncle Fred's chair. I looked toward the rabbit hutch, said, "Where?" then looked at the back fence. Then I looked down at Uncle Fred, who was doing something with his gun.

"Missed," he said.

Suddenly I felt weak. My legs were like two pieces of rope, like that trick that Hindu magicians do when they make rope come straight up out of a basket and then say a magic word and make the rope collapse. My legs felt like they were going to collapse at any second. I managed to force these two pieces of rope to carry me up the stairs and into the room.

I closed two windows, and the third one, in sympathy perhaps, just banged down all by itself. Then I sank to the bed.

☯☯☯☯☯☯☯☯☯

I had no intention of going to sleep when I lay down on the bed; I did not think I would ever be able to sleep again, but that is what I did. I fell right asleep and did not even move until four hours later when I awoke. It was one o'clock in the morning.

The storm was in full force, or perhaps it was a second storm, but the house was quiet. I got up and went out into the hall. I could not hear anything but the sound of the rain and Hazeline's transistor radio, which was sputtering with static beside her on the pillow.

I went down the stairs, one by one. I did not make a sound. I stepped on the part of the steps near the wall because Petie had told me that was how burglars got up stairs unheard. I was just stepping into the hall when without warning the hall light went on. Aunt Millie was standing there in her bathrobe squinting at me.

"What's wrong?" she asked.

"Nothing. I just didn't know what time it was."

"Well"—she looked closely at her watch—"it's just past one o'clock."

"I went to sleep in my clothes."

"Well, you get on your pajamas and get back to bed. This is the first good sleeping night we've had, and you mustn't let it go to waste."

"Sure."

"Well, go on back up the steps." She watched me go up two steps and then she said, "Goodness, we've gotten on so well all summer, I'd hate for anything to happen now right before your parents get home."

"Aunt Millie, did Uncle Fred get the fox?"

"No."

"Is he still out on the porch?"

"In this rain? No, he is fast asleep in his bed like you ought to be."

She waited until I was up the stairs and then she turned out the light. I went into my room and she called, "Are you getting in bed?"

I lay down. "Yes."

"And go to sleep."

I lay in bed for a long time, still in my clothes, and then I got up very carefully. I walked over to the window and looked out at the tree Bubba and Fred Jr. used to just run up and down all the time like monkeys. I could imagine them climbing up, laughing and brown, racing, going out on all sorts of perilous limbs just to be first at the window. I opened the window, pushed out the screen, reached out into the rain, and felt for the smooth spot Aunt Millie had told me was worn into the bark of the tree.

I took off my shoes and knelt on the window sill. There was an enormous flash of lightning that turned the whole world white for a moment, and then I climbed out onto the nearest branch and circled the trunk round with my arms.

I thought that I could never get one step farther. I thought that I could never move even one muscle or I would fall. I thought that in the morning when Aunt Millie came up to see why I wasn't at breakfast she would find me here, pressed into the tree, still frozen with fear.

The rain was hard and slanting directly into my face. Finally I got up just enough courage to turn my face out of the rain. Then the lightning flashed again and I saw the ground about a million miles below. I held the tree so tightly the bark was cutting into my cheek.

I don't know how long I stayed that way. If I had tried to look at my watch, just that little movement would have thrown me off balance. After a while, though, I began to sort of slip down the tree. I never let go of the main trunk for a second. I just moved my arms downward in very small movements. Then slowly, when I was practically kneeling on the first limb, I let my foot reach down for the next one.

If there were smooth spots on those branches, my feet never found them. They only touched one rough limb after another as, slowly, I kept inching down the tree, feeling my way, never looking down at the ground until, finally, my foot reached out for another limb and felt the cold wet grass. It shocked me for a moment and then I jumped down, landing on my hands and knees.

I got up and ran to the rabbit hutch. The baby fox was huddled in one corner of the pen where there was some shelter from the rain. The lightning flashed and I saw him watching me.

"I'm going to get you out," I said.

He crouched back farther in the hutch. In the next flash of lightning I looked on the ground for a rock and I saw at my feet a small dead frog. I knew that the black fox in all this rain had brought that frog here to her baby. She was right now watching me somewhere.

There were bricks stacked in a neat pile under the hutch and I took one and began to bang it against the lock. I was prepared to do this all night if necessary, but the lock was an old one and it opened right away.

The noise had scared the baby fox and he was now making a whimpering sound. I unhooked the broken lock, opened the cage, and stepped back against the tree.

The baby fox did not move for a moment. I could barely see him, a small dark ball in the back of the cage. He waited, alert and suspicious, and then, after a moment he moved in a crouch to the door of the cage. He cried sharply. From the bushes there was an answering bark.

He crouched lower. The lightning flashed again and in that second he jumped and ran in the direction of the bushes. He barked as he ran. There was an immediate answer, and then only the sound of the rain. I waited against the tree, thinking about them, and then I heard the black fox bark one more time as she ran through the orchard with her baby.

And I thought, Someday I will be in a famous museum, walking along on the marble floors, looking at paintings. There will be one called "Blue Flowers" and I will look at that for a while, and the next one will be "Woman on the Beach" and I will look at that for a while, and then I will glance at the name of the next painting and it will be "Fox with Baby at Midnight," and I will look up and my heart will stop beating because there it will be, just the way it was this night, the black fox and her baby running beneath the wet ghostly apple trees toward a patch of light in the distance. And I thought, leaning against that tree in the rain, if there is a picture like that, I hope sometime I will get to see it.

Suddenly the rain began to slacken and I walked around the house. I had never been so wet in my life and now that it was over I was cold too. And I was tired. I looked up at the tree and there didn't seem to be any point in climbing back up when in just a few hours everyone would know what I had done anyway. I went up on the porch and rang the doorbell.

In all my life I have never felt so dumb and foolish as I did barefooted, soaking wet on that slick porch at two o'clock in the morning, waiting for someone to come and answer the door.

It was Aunt Millie in her cotton robe who turned on the porch light and peered out through the side windows at me.

I must have been an awful sight, like the poor little match girl, for she flung open the door at once and drew me in.

"What are you doing out there? What are you doing?"

"Who is it?" Uncle Fred asked as he came into the hall. He was pulling his pants up over his pajamas.

"It's Tom," Aunt Millie said.

"I meant who's at the door."

"Tom," she said again.

"Tom?"

"Yes, he was just standing out there on the porch."

They both turned and looked at me, waiting for an explanation, and I cleared my throat and said, "Uncle Fred and Aunt Millie, I am awfully sorry but I have let the baby fox out of the rabbit hutch." I sounded very stiff and formal, and I thought the voice was a terrible thing to have to depend on, because I really did want them to know that I was sorry, and I didn't sound it the least bit. I knew how much Uncle Fred had looked forward to the hunt and how important getting rid of the fox was to Aunt Millie, and I hated for them to be disappointed now.

There was a moment of silence. Then Aunt Millie said, "Why, that's perfectly all right, isn't it, Fred? Don't you think another thing about that. You just come on to bed.

You're going to get pneumonia standing there in that puddle." She started for the linen closet. "I'll get you some towels."

Uncle Fred and I were left in the hall alone and I looked up at him and he looked like an enormous blue-eyed Indian.

"I'm sorry," I said again.

He looked at me and I knew he was seeing through all the very casual questions I had been asking all summer about foxes, and seeing through the long days I had spent in the woods. He was remembering the sorry way I had tried to keep him from finding the fox's den and the way I had looked when we did find it. I think all those pieces just snapped into place right then in Uncle Fred's mind and I knew that if there was one person in the world who understood me it was this man who had seemed such a stranger.

He cleared his throat. "I never liked to see wild things in a pen myself," he said.

Would you like to have Tom as a friend? Tell why you feel as you do.

Even though he knows Uncle Fred might be angry, Tom releases the baby fox. What does Tom believe that makes him do that?

Do you think Tom does the right thing? Explain your answer.

WRITE   Visualize the painting, "Fox with Baby at Midnight," that Tom imagines. Then write a poem with the same title.

WORDS FROM THE Author:
Betsy Byars

AWARD-WINNING
AUTHOR

When I started to write children's books, my own children were very helpful. They were never very excited about reading my manuscripts, but when they did, they would tell me, "No one talks like this," or "this would never happen." I also got many of my ideas from my children's lives. Sometimes I think I've used every single thing that ever happened to them. Now they're beginning to write their own books, and they say they've got nothing left to write about!

The Midnight Fox is my favorite book. It is one of the first ones I wrote that actually came out the way I thought it would. There can be such a gap between what you see in your mind's eye and what actually comes out on the page. The idea for *The Midnight Fox* came from a personal experience. We had a small cabin in West Virginia. We saw deer, raccoons, snakes, and beavers all the time, but I had never seen a fox. One day, I did. It was a stunning moment, and that's when the story came to me. Sometimes when I'm visiting schools, I read the beginning or the end of the book, and I like it more each time. I keep thinking I'm going to write something I like better, but I haven't yet.

THE MARMALADE MAN

from *A Visit to William Blake's Inn*

by Nancy Willard
illustrated by Alice and Martin Provensen

Tiger, Sunflowers, King of Cats,
Cow and Rabbit, mend your ways.
I the needle, you the thread—
follow me through mist and maze.

Fox and hound, go paw in paw.
Cat and rat, be best of friends.
Lamb and tiger, walk together.
Dancing starts where fighting ends.

MAKES A DANCE
TO MEND US

HURT NO LIVING THING

by Christina G. Rossetti

Hurt no living thing;
Ladybird, nor butterfly,
Nor moth with dusty wing,
Nor cricket chirping cheerily,
Nor grasshopper so light of leap,
Nor dancing gnat, nor beetle fat,
Nor harmless worms that creep.

ILLUSTRATED BY DUGALD STERMER

Theme Wrap-Up

Natural Friends

The selections in this theme deal with how people treat animals. Of course, it is not always possible to help every creature. What choices do people sometimes have to make about how they treat animals?

WRITER'S WORKSHOP

Think about a kind of animal that you know is endangered. Write a letter to a friend. Ask your friend to join you in a campaign to save the animal from extinction. Include details that tell why you want to save the animal. Mail or give the letter to your friend.

Writer's Choice

How do you feel about the way people share the world with animals? Write about your feelings, and plan how to share your writing with some classmates.

THEME

Wild Wonders

Imagine what it would be like to be a leopard or a wolf. Do you think you would want to change places with one of these animals for a day? The animals in the following selections face humorous, exciting, and dangerous problems.

CONTENTS

199

How Many Spots Does A Leopard Have?

from
*How Many Spots Does A Leopard Have?
And Other Tales*

by Julius Lester

illustrated by
David Shannon

ALA NOTABLE BOOK

One morning Leopard was doing what he enjoyed doing most. He was looking at his reflection in the lake. How handsome he was! How magnificent was his coat! And, ah! The spots on his coat! Was there anything in creation more superb?

Leopard's rapture was broken when the water in the lake began moving. Suddenly Crocodile's ugly head appeared above the surface.

Leopard jumped back. Not that he was afraid. Crocodile would not bother him. But then again, one could never be too sure about Crocodile.

"Good morning, Leopard," Crocodile said. "Looking at yourself again, I see. You are the most vain creature in all of creation."

Leopard was not embarrassed. "If you were as handsome as I am, if you had such beautiful spots, you, too, would be vain."

"Spots! Who needs spots? You're probably so in love with your spots that you spend all your time counting them."

Now there was an idea that had not occurred to Leopard. "What a wonderful idea!" he exclaimed. "I would very much like to know how many spots I have." He stopped. "But there are far too many for me to count myself."

The truth was that Leopard didn't know how to count. "Perhaps you will count them for me, Crocodile?"

"Not on your life!" answered Crocodile. "I have better things to do than count spots." He slapped his tail angrily and dove beneath the water.

Leopard chuckled. "Crocodile doesn't know how to count, either."

Leopard walked along the lakeshore until he met Weasel. "Good morning, Weasel. Would you count my spots for me?"

"Who? Me? Count? Sure. One-two-three-four."

"Great!" exclaimed Leopard. "You can count."

Weasel shook his head. "But I can't. What made you think that I could?"

"But you just did. You said, 'One-two-three-four.' That's counting."

Weasel shook his head again. "Counting is much more difficult than that. There is something that comes after four, but I don't know what it is."

"Oh," said Leopard. "I wonder who knows what comes after four."

"Well, if you ask at the lake when all the animals come to drink, you will find someone who can count."

"You are right, Weasel! And I will give a grand prize to the one who tells me how many spots I have."

"What a great idea!" Weasel agreed.

That afternoon all the animals were gathered at the lake to drink. Leopard announced that he would give a magnificent prize to the one who could count his spots.

Elephant said he should be first since he was the biggest and the oldest.

"One-two-three-four-five-six-seven-eight-nine-ten," Elephant said very loudly and with great speed. He took a deep breath and began again.
"One-two-three-four-five-si—"

"No! No! No!" the other animals interrupted. "You've already counted to ten once."

Elephant looked down his long trunk at the other animals. "I beg your pardon. I would appreciate it if you would not interrupt me when I am counting. You made me forget where I was. Now, where was I? I know I was somewhere in the second ten."

"The second ten?" asked Antelope. "What's that?"

"The numbers that come after the first ten, of course. I don't much care for those 'teen' things, thirteen, fourteen, and what have you. It is eminently more sensible to count ten twice and that makes twenty. That is multiplication."

None of the other animals knew what Elephant was talking about.

"Why don't you start over again?" suggested Cow.

Elephant began again and he counted ten twice and stopped. He frowned and looked very confused. Finally he said, "Leopard has more than twenty spots."

"How many more than twenty?" Leopard wanted to know.

Elephant frowned more. "A lot." Then he brightened. "In fact, you have so many more spots than twenty that I simply don't have time to count them now. I have an important engagement I mustn't be late for." Elephant started to walk away.

"Ha! Ha! Ha!" laughed Mule. "I bet Elephant doesn't know how to count higher than twenty."

Mule was right.

"Can *you* count above twenty?" Leopard asked Mule.

"Who? Me? I can only count to four because that's how many legs I have."

Leopard sighed. "Can *anyone* count above twenty?" he asked plaintively.

Bear said, "Well, once I counted up to fifty. Is that high enough?"

Leopard shrugged. "I don't know. It might be. Why don't you try and we will see."

Bear agreed. "I'll start at your tail. One-two-three-four-five-six. . . . Hm. Is that one spot or two spots?"

All the animals crowded around to get a close look. They argued for some time and finally agreed that it should only count as one.

"So, where was I?" asked Bear.

"Five," answered Turkey.

"It was six, you turkey," said Chicken.

"Better start again," suggested Crow.

Bear started again and got as far as eleven. "Eleven. That's a beautiful spot right there, Leopard."

"Which one?" Leopard wanted to know.

"Right there. Oh, dear. Or was it that spot there? They're both exquisite. My, my. I don't know where I left off counting. I must start again."

Bear counted as far as twenty-nine this time and then stopped suddenly. "Now, what comes after twenty-nine?"

"I believe thirty does," offered Turtle.

"That's right!" exclaimed Bear. "Now, where did I leave off?"

"You were still on the tail," offered Lion.

"Yes, but was that the twenty-ninth spot, or was it this one here?"

The animals started arguing again.

"You'd better start again," suggested Cow.

"Start what again?" asked Rabbit, who had just arrived.

The animals explained to Rabbit about the difficulty they were having in counting Leopard's spots.

"Is that all?" Rabbit said. "I know the answer to that."

"You do?" all the animals, including Leopard, exclaimed at once.

"Certainly. It's really quite simple." Rabbit pointed to one of Leopard's spots. "This one is dark." He pointed to another. "This one is light. Dark, light, dark, light, dark, light." Rabbit continued in this way until he had touched all of Leopard's spots.

"It's simple," he concluded. "Leopard has only two spots—dark ones and light ones."

All the animals remarked on how smart Rabbit was, all of them, that is, except Leopard. He knew something was wrong with how Rabbit counted, but unless he learned to count for himself, he would never know what it was.

Leopard had no choice but to give Rabbit the magnificent prize.

What was it?

What else except a picture of Leopard himself!

Which animal do you think is the most clever? Give reasons for your opinion.

What message do you think Julius Lester wants to give to readers? Support your answer with details from the selection.

WRITE Imagine that you are Leopard. Write a speech explaining why it is important to know how to count.

Indian people have wonderful stories of wolves (and other animals) who helped women and children when they were lost or in danger; stories of men who were wounded, far from home and help, whom the wolves fed until they recovered.

For centuries Indian people relied upon their dogs to help them. This close relationship extended to the wolves. We, too, love our dogs, and yet we seem unable to see the same expressions in the faces of wolves. We have driven them from nearly every part of North America, and where they still live they are fearful of us. Where the wolf no longer roams he is missed by everything in nature. We feel his loss; Creation is incomplete.

In the old days the people travelled over the plains. They followed the great herds of buffalo.

Every year when the berries were ripe, they would leave the plains and go up into the hills. They made camp in a valley where the berry bushes grow. Everyone picked great quantities. They mashed the berries into little cakes which they dried in the sun. These they stored in painted bags for the winter.

Tiblo (tee-blow) was too young to play with the older boys. He and his little sister, Tanksi (tawnk-she), had to go berry-picking with their mother and the other women and children.

Tiblo was soon tired of picking, and too full to eat any more. When nobody was looking he slipped away with Tanksi to climb the hills.

They climbed up and up among the rocks and cedar trees where bighorn sheep and bears live. Soon they could hardly hear the berry-pickers laughing and calling to each other far below. Tiblo wanted to reach the top. They climbed on.

They never noticed the sun starting to go down behind the hills.

It was getting dark when Tiblo knew they had to go back home. In the twilight every hill and valley looked the same. He did not know which way to go. He called out. . . . Only the echoes answered him.

They wandered on. Tiblo was lost. Darkness closed around them. It grew colder. They were tired and hungry, and Tanksi began to cry.

Speaking of happy things, Tiblo found a small cave among the rocks. They crawled inside to shelter for the night.

The children were tired, and in a little while they fell asleep. Tiblo had a dream.

He dreamed that a wolf with shining eyes entered the cave. In his dream he felt the wolf's hot breath and its rough tongue licking his face. The wolf lay down beside him. His shaggy fur was like a blanket which kept Tiblo and Tanksi warm.

The sun was already shining into the mouth of the cave when Tiblo opened his eyes again.

Tiblo woke up his sister. They crawled out of the cave into the warm sunshine. He took Tanksi by the hand, and they set off walking down the hill.

When the children came to a stream, they stopped to drink. Suddenly Tiblo saw that a wolf was sitting on some rocks close by, watching them. At once he remembered his dream.

"O Wolf," Tiblo said, "we are lost. Mother will be crying. Help us to find our way home again."

The wolf panted and smiled. "My children, do not worry. I will help you. Last night you slept in my den. Follow me now, and I will take you home."

The wolf trotted off. He looked back to see that the children were following. From time to time he trotted ahead out of sight, but he always returned.

At last the wolf led them to a hilltop. The children were filled with joy to see their home in the valley below. The wolf sat back on his haunches and smiled. And then he trotted off back toward the hills. The children begged him to come and live with them.

"No," the wolf called back, "I like to wander from place to place with my friends. Listen for me in the evenings! You will hear me calling, and you will know that I never forget you."

People in the camp saw the children coming down the hill. The men jumped onto their horses, and galloped out to bring them home. Everyone was happy that the children were safe.

Tiblo told how the wolf had brought them home. Everyone walked into the hills to thank the wolf. They spread a blanket for him to sit on. They gave him necklaces and other beautiful gifts.

There has been close kinship with the Wolf People for as long as anyone can remember. That is what they say.

The wolves are no longer heard calling in the evenings at berry-picking time. Hunters have killed and driven them away with guns and traps and poisons. People say that the wolves will return when we, like Tiblo and Tanksi, have the wolves in our hearts and dreams again.

Why do you think Tiblo dreams about a wolf?

Summarize how the wolf helps Tiblo and Tanksi.

How do the people in the camp thank the wolf after the children return?

WRITE   Other animals besides wolves need to be protected. Choose one, and make a poster that tells what can be done to help protect that animal.

RUNNING WITH THE

BY SHARON L. BARRY

PHOTOS BY
JIM BRANDENBURG
AND L. DAVID MECH

PACK

In a well-known fairy tale, the Big Bad Wolf tries to eat up Little Red Riding Hood. This story is one of many that have caused people to misunderstand and fear wolves. The truth is that healthy wolves do not attack people. Scientists say wolves tend to be intelligent and shy. They live in groups called packs, and cooperate to survive.

Wolves are the largest wild members of the dog family. Gray wolves, shown on these pages, live in parts of North America, Europe, and Asia—usually in packs with no more than eight members. A pack includes a head male and female, their young, and sometimes other adults. The head male usually decides when and what to hunt, and he settles fights. The head female leads the other females, the young, and sometimes the weaker males. The leaders and other pack members communicate by using facial expressions, body postures, and sounds. For example, by standing tall with its ears erect and tail held high, a leader says: "I'm boss." By crouching and lowering its ears and tail, a follower replies: "I know."

Usually only the head male and female have pups. But all pack members help raise the young. The mother gives birth to about six pups in a den underground, in a rock crevice, or under a fallen tree. She feeds them milk from her body. As the pups grow older, all the adults help feed them by bringing up meat they have swallowed. The whole pack plays with the pups and guards them against bears and other enemies.

Wolves will eat small mammals, lizards, and fruit, but they feed mainly on animals larger than themselves, such as deer and moose. Hunting large prey usually requires group efforts for success. However, even a group hunt may fail, and the wolves may have to go days without eating.

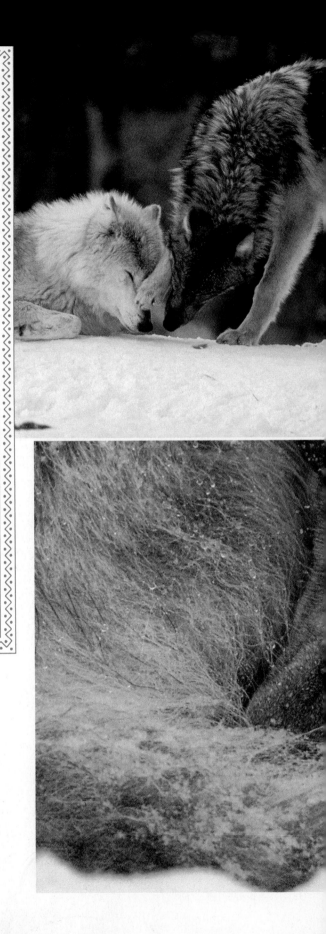

KEEPING IN TOUCH. A youngster nudges its mother's nose. Wolves show affection for other pack members by touching, nuzzling, and licking each other—and by wagging their tails. These gestures help keep the pack close together.

ASLEEP IN THE SNOW, a gray wolf lies curled in a ball with its nose tucked under its bushy tail. By pulling its legs, tail, and head close to its body, the wolf keeps warm. The animal's thick coat helps hold in body heat. Wolves spend most of their time in the open. They even sleep outside on winter days as cold as $-50°F$ ($-46°C$). Wolves dig dens or use other sheltered areas only when they have young.

Wolves once roamed most of North America. But as people settled the land the wolves occupied, many wolves were killed. Today, gray wolves still occupy much of Canada, but they are considered endangered in most of the United States. They can be found in Alaska, Minnesota, Michigan, Montana, and Wisconsin. Because wolves are shy, you probably won't see them if you visit these areas. But you may hear their howls echoing through the wilderness.

TIME-OUT. *A pack of gray wolves rests on a snowy hillside in Minnesota. Most gray wolves live in northern areas. In winter, a pack may travel 40 miles (64 km) a day across snow to find food.*

What have you learned about wolves that you didn't know before?

Describe how wolves cooperate to survive.

People have feared wolves for a long time. How has this affected the wolves?

WRITE   If you were a writer for a nature magazine, which animal would you choose to study as the subject of an article? Write the first paragraph for your article, describing that animal.

Wild Wonders

Wild animals are fascinating. Think about what you have learned about animals from reading the stories and the article in this theme. Which selection did you enjoy most? What did you like about the way the information was presented in that selection? Tell why you feel as you do.

WRITER'S WORKSHOP

Think about what you have just read about wolves. Do you think people should fear wolves? Write one or more persuasive paragraphs explaining your viewpoint. Share your writing with your classmates.

Writer's Choice

What do you think about the theme Wild Wonders, now that you've read the selections? Write about your ideas. Plan your own way to share them.

CONNECTIONS

◆ Multicultural Connection

African Storytellers

Long ago, African children listened to "why" tales, stories that explained such things as why a certain animal came to look or act as it does. These tales were told by a *griot*, who was the local storyteller and historian.

Augusta Baker

The art of storytelling is still alive today. Augusta Baker is known as one of America's greatest storytellers and teachers of the art of storytelling. Many other African Americans travel across the United States sharing stories, including "why" tales, that celebrate their culture.

Work with a group to find animal "why" stories from various cultures, and compare the tales. Select one to present as a play or a Readers Theatre production. Create masks for the actors and readers.

Social Studies Connection

Save the Species

In our country, early Native Americans told "why" stories about many animals that are in danger today. Choose a region of the United States, and find out what animals are endangered there and what is being done to save them. Share your findings in an oral report.

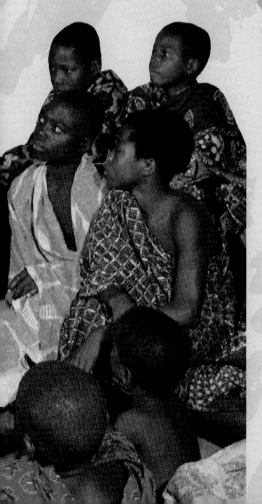

Endangered American bald eagle

Art/Language Arts Connection

Fantasy Creature

"Why" tales tell about animals that exist, but there are other tales that describe imaginary animals. Read a story about a fantasy animal, and make a clay or papier-mâché sculpture or a painting to show how you visualize it. Share the story through your art.

Children from a village in Africa listen to a storyteller.

229

Unit Three
3
Nature's Gifts

Come forth into the light of things,
Let Nature be your teacher.
William Wordsworth

Native Americans shared nature's gifts with the early European settlers. Since then, Americans have begun to better understand how nature provides food and other materials that are necessary for life. When we wonder at the beauty of nature around the world, we begin to see why we should save the rain forests of Brazil and take care of the land around our homes. Think about ways in which you appreciate nature's gifts as you read the selections in this unit.

THEMES

BOOKSHELF

THE PLANT THAT ATE DIRTY SOCKS

by Nancy McArthur

Two brothers, one neat and one messy, raise two fantastic plants. Each plant has its own personality, but both have very strange eating habits.

Harcourt Brace Library Book

IMAGINE LIVING HERE: THIS PLACE IS WET

by Vicki Cobb

Much can be learned from the Indian groups of Brazil. For years they have used their imagination to live in harmony with the creatures and plants of the rain forest.

Award-Winning Author

Harcourt Brace Library Book

232

THE PEOPLE WHO HUGGED THE TREES

by Deborah Lee Rose

As a young girl in India, Amrita loved the trees. Her love grew, and it inspired the people of her village to hug the trees in order to save them from being chopped down.

A JOURNEY OF HOPE/ UNA JORNADA DE ESPERANZA

by Bob Harvey and Diane Kelsay Harvey

Hope, a baby sea turtle, is making her way from the nest to the sea. Her journey is a tale of both danger and hope.

Outstanding Science Trade Book

THE GREEN SONG

by Doris Troutman Plenn

A tiny tree frog named Pepe Coqui decides to travel from the green fields to the big, colorful city.

THEME

Main Course

Did you ever plant a seed, water it, and wait for it to sprout? What did you feed your plant? The plants in the following selections grow and grow because they eat well!

CONTENTS

THE
PLANT
THAT ATE
DIRTY
SOCKS

BY NANCY McARTHUR
ILLUSTRATED BY KEN SPENGLER

*Michael was the world's messiest kid. He shared a
room with his brother, Norman, who was a neatness
nut. To keep Norman from complaining about their
messy room, Michael gave him an "Amazing Bean."
Michael had ordered the beans weeks before, and the
package had just arrived. Both boys planted the beans,
but Michael accidentally lost the instructions.*

Both plants were growing fast. The sprouts turned into strange vines and began crawling up the window.

As the days passed, little leaves spread out into long pointed shapes. Then they curled up like dark-green ice cream cones.

Norman said, "These plants look weird."

"You're right about something for once," Michael agreed.

Michael's friend Jason, who lived on the other side of town, had his mother drop him off one Saturday to see the plants. "You're right," he said. "These ARE weird."

Norman was using the bottled plant food, measuring carefully.

Michael sloshed some of that on his plant once in a while. He also slipped it a little dessert—a dab of peanut butter, chocolate chip cookie crumbs, a spoonful of pumpkin pie, and bits of Muncho Cruncho.

His vines got thicker than Norman's. Were they getting fat from all the goodies? He switched to bits of vegetables to see what would happen.

"Can I have a little broccoli, please?" he asked at dinner.

"Why this sudden urge for broccoli?" said Mom, passing it to him. "I usually have to tell you to eat it or else."

"I want to feed some to my plant."

"Aha!" said Norman. "No fair feeding your plant extra stuff!"

"I'm just experimenting."

Dad said, "Those plants are getting too big too fast. If they keep on like this, they'll fill up the whole room. So no more feeding them plant food. Not even broccoli. Just sun and water."

"But that will wreck my experiment," protested Michael.

"No, you've seen how it grows with feeding. Now see how it grows without it."

"But what if it collapses from no food?"

Dad smiled. "That plant looks as if it can take care of itself."

Mom added, "It looks as if it could take over the whole house. Now eat your broccoli or else."

"Or else what?" asked Michael with his mouth full of broccoli.

"Or else tomorrow we'll have those plants for dinner," joked Mom.

Both plants slowed down. Then Norman's seemed to stop growing while Michael's kept getting bigger.

"Are you sneaking food to yours," asked Norman, "when I'm asleep?"

"No, honest, I'm not," replied Michael. He was puzzled, too.

"Then why is yours still growing when mine isn't?"

"Maybe my messy growing methods work better than your neat ones."

Mom came in with a laundry basket. They handed over their dirty clothes. But Michael could find only five escaped socks.

"There must be more here somewhere," he said.

"They'll turn up," said Mom, "the next time you clean up."

But they didn't. The next time he found only three.

This mystery, he decided, was easy to solve.

"Norman, you're swiping my socks and hiding them when I'm asleep!"

"Nope, honest, I'm not. I wouldn't touch your yukky old socks!"

"OK, you guys," said Mom. "We're all going to look until we find them. Norman, why are you putting on your football helmet?"

"Because I'm going to look in the closet." He yanked the door open.

"Avalanche!" he yelled, but not much fell out. He was only up to his knees in junk. Norman looked disappointed. He high-stepped out of the pile and dived into the back of the closet.

Michael found one sock in his acorn collection box.

Mom found another one in a bulging book called *The Glob That Ate Outer Space*.

"Don't lose my place," said Michael, putting a blue jay feather between the pages where the sock had been.

"Aha!" exclaimed Norman from the closet. A rolled-up sock came flying out and bounced off Michael's head.

"Aha! Aha!" shouted Norman. Two more zoomed through the air and bonked Michael.

"Stop throwing socks!" yelled Michael.

"I can't stop throwing them."

"Why not?"

"Because I'm kicking them!" Another sock sailed overhead.

"If you don't stop that," Michael warned, "I'm going to drop-kick your football helmet with you in it."

"No fighting," said Mom. "And no more sock kicking."

Norman came out holding a sock with one hand and his nose with the other.

"Give me that," Mom said. "Now we're missing at least ten more."

They looked into and under everything. No more socks.

"Strange," said Mom, "that there were more in the closet than out here."

"Yeah," said Michael. "Mostly I drop my socks right around here by my bed."

That night when he took off his socks, he put them on top of his acorn box right next to the bed. That way they could not get lost among his junk.

In the morning they were gone.

"OK, Norman, very funny. Where are the socks I put right here last night?"

"I didn't touch your smelly old socks."

"Well, they couldn't walk away by themselves."

"Why not? Socks have feet in them."

"Come on, where did you hide them?"

"Maybe the monster in the closet took them."

"The only monster that's been in that closet is you."

"Honest, I didn't take them. Something very weird is going on."

They looked all over. They even used the magnifying glass from Norman's detective kit to search for clues.

But the socks had disappeared without a trace.

At bedtime Michael told Norman, "We're going to solve this mystery tonight."

"Good, I love to detect," said Norman.

Michael dug around in his stuff and found some black string he had known would come in handy some day.

He took off his socks, tied the strings to them, and put them where the others had vanished. Then he got into bed, lay there with his arms straight out, and told Norman to tie the strings to his wrists.

Norman got his Super Splasher Water Blaster and favorite disguise from his detective kit and climbed into bed.

"You don't need a disguise in the dark," said Michael.

"I always detect better when I'm wearing one," replied Norman. He turned out the light and put on his disguise.

"Ready?" asked Michael.

"Ready," said Norman.

They had left the door ajar so a little light came in from the hall. They could barely see the white socks on the floor.

They lay there in the dark waiting. Nothing happened. They waited some more. Norman was lying on his side staring at the socks.

Suddenly one moved!

"It's moving!" he shouted and began squirting wildly with his Water Blaster.

"Oh, no!" yelled Michael.

"I saw it!" Norman insisted excitedly. "It was creeping fast across the floor! Then it jumped up in the air and fell down! There it goes again!" he yelled, bouncing up and down on his bed and squirting more water in every direction.

"No," said Michael. "My nose started to itch. I forgot and reached up to scratch it."

Their parents ran in and turned on the light.

There was Michael with strings and socks dangling. Water was dripping off his hair and the end of his nose.

Norman was waving a giant water pistol and wearing glasses with an attached rubber nose and moustache.

Water was dripping off the plants, soaking into the rug and beds, and running down the walls.

"I know," said Mom, "that there has to be a logical explanation for all this, but it better be a good one, or else."

As they wiped up with towels, Michael explained.

Mom took the socks for safekeeping. Norman refilled his Water Blaster, but Dad took it away from him.

"But I need that," wailed Norman, "to water my plant!"

"No," said Dad. "Everything in this room has been watered enough already. I'll keep it next to my bed so there won't be any more midnight underwater adventures in here."

Since the beds were damp, Michael and Norman had to spend the rest of the night on the living room couch, one at each end with their feet kicking each other in the middle.

As they were falling asleep, Michael whispered, "Tomorrow I'll think of a new master plan."

But the next day he decided to try his original master plan once more. It might have worked if his nose hadn't itched.

"But what if your nose itches again?" asked Norman.

"I'm only going to use one sock so I'll have one hand to scratch."

Norman said, "I don't have my Water Blaster, so I'll use my bow and rubber suction cup arrows."

"Your aim with that," said Michael, "would be worse than the water pistol. We'd end up with rubber arrows stuck all over me and the ceiling."

"Then I'll just wear a disguise so if something is stealing your socks I can scare it off. My robot helmet looks pretty scary. See, if something sneaks in here, it'll expect to see kids in our beds. Not a robot. You should wear a disguise, too. Then it will get really scared."

Michael thought Norman's idea was dumb but wouldn't hurt. He dug around in his stacks and pulled out a rubber gorilla head.

"Where did you get that?" asked Norman, his eyes lighting up.

"I traded Jason Greensmith a lot of stuff for it. He terrified everybody in his neighborhood with it last Halloween."

"It doesn't look very scary," said Norman.

"It does when you have it on," replied Michael.

"Oh, good! Can I wear it? Please!"

Michael could see this would be the perfect thing to make a deal with the next time he wanted something big from Norman.

"No, maybe we can make a deal later," he said. "I'm going to wear it tonight. You get your robot helmet."

After they went to bed they whispered back and forth in
the dark until they heard their parents close their bedroom door.

Then they got their flashlights from under the blankets
where they had hidden them. Norman tied the string to Michael's
wrist. Michael tied the other end to the sock. Then they turned off
the flashlights, got back into bed, and put on their disguises.

"Ready?" asked Michael.

"Ready," said Norman.

They waited a long time.

Suddenly Norman whispered, "If your nose itches, remember, don't use the wrong hand."

"OK, OK."

They waited some more.

Norman whispered, "How will you scratch your nose with that mask on?"

"My nose is probably not going to itch. It hardly ever does."

"But what if it does?"

"The mask has big holes under the nose to breathe. I can scratch through there."

"Be sure not to use the wrong hand."

"Will you stop worrying about my nose!"

"I just want to be sure after what happened the last time."

"Norman, if we're going to find out what makes these socks disappear, we have to keep quiet. It only happens when we're asleep, so we have to pretend we are."

Norman was quiet for a long time. Nothing happened. Then he whispered, "I hope it's a raccoon."

"Why?"

"I like raccoons."

"Norman, stop it!"

"OK, OK."

Then Michael whispered, "Now don't get excited. I'm just going to scratch my nose."

"I knew this would happen," said Norman. "Are you using the wrong hand?"

"No!"

It was getting late. Lying there in the dark, pretending to be asleep, they could not stay awake.

Michael woke suddenly. Something was tugging on the string!

He whispered, "It's moving," to Norman and switched on his flashlight.

He saw something green curling around the white sock. A long vine from his plant was dragging it along the floor.

He yelled at Norman to wake up.

"Smurg," mumbled Norman, still completely konked out.

The vine lifted the sock up to one of the big curled leaves. The ice-cream cone shape slowly began sucking it in.

"Schlurrrrrp," said the plant as the sock disappeared.

"Wake up!" shouted Michael as he cut the string from his wrist.

Norman, who had fallen asleep holding his flashlight, turned it on.

Seeing a gorilla looming up in the dark, he gave a bloodcurdling "EEEEEEK," leaped from his bed, and zoomed out the door.

His parents, awakened by the horrible noises, were getting out of bed to come to the rescue. Suddenly they saw a ghostly robot hurtle into their room.

Dad, still half-asleep, grabbed Norman's Super Splasher Water Blaster from the bedside table. He let the robot have it right in the snoot.

At the first cold wet squirt, Norman ducked and disappeared.

Michael, running in right behind him, got the rest of the water.

Mom turned on the light. A short gorilla in wet pajamas stood at the end of the bed.

"You're not going to believe this," he said, "but my plant just ate my sock."

"You're right," said the gorilla's mother. "I don't believe any of this."

Dad looked around. "I saw something in the dark that looked like a robot. Where's Norman?"

"Down here," said a familiar voice from under the bed. "I thought a gorilla was after me."

Mom grabbed his feet and pulled him out.

"Remember," she asked, "when nights used to be normal around here? When everybody went to bed and just stayed there? What's next? Frankenstein and Wolfman?"

"My friend Bob's got a good Frankenstein mask I could borrow," Norman suggested helpfully.

"No way," said Dad. "Now Michael, what about this dream you had about your plant?"

"It wasn't a dream. I woke up and saw it suck up my sock!"

Dad said soothingly, "Everybody has amazing dreams once in a while that seem real."

Michael turned to Norman. "You woke up while it was happening. Tell Dad what you saw."

"All I saw was a gorilla coming at me in the dark. But I'm not going back in there. That plant might get me!" He clutched his throat and made a horrible noise.

"Nothing is going to get you," said Mom. "I think you've both been reading too many books like *The Glob That Ate Outer Space*. Let's find you some dry pajamas. Then we'll check out that plant. You'll see it was only a dream and there's nothing to be afraid of."

Michael explained, "It won't come after us. It only eats socks."

Dad led the way to the boys' room and turned on the light.

"See?" said Mom. "Your plant is just sitting there doing nothing as usual."

Michael walked up to it. "But I saw it eat the sock." He picked a black string off the floor. "This was tied to the sock. Here's the end I cut. The other end looks sort of chewed."

His parents looked closely.

"There must be some logical explanation for this," said Mom, "but I have no idea what it is."

Michael replied, "The logical explanation is that the plant ate my sock. Especially since I saw it."

"There is a Venus-flytrap plant that eats insects," said Dad, "but this is ridiculous."

"This must be a Sock Trap plant," said Norman.

"The way it's been growing," said Mom, "and with all the socks we're missing, I wouldn't be surprised."

"I'll prove it to you with an experiment," said Michael. He took a pair of socks from his dresser drawer and put one in front of his plant and the other in front of Norman's. He tied black string around them and fastened the other ends to the bedposts.

"Now Norman and I will sleep on the couch. We'll lock this door. In the morning you'll see what happened."

He turned out the lights, locked the door, and gave the key to Mom.

A moment after the door closed, Michael's plant rustled its leaves as if a little breeze were passing by. Then it made a funny noise that sounded like a contented burp after a good meal.

Michael woke up early and awakened everyone else. Mom handed over the key. Michael slowly opened the door.

They stared in amazement.

The sock in front of Michael's plant was still there. But the one in front of Norman's had vanished!

Michael was baffled.

Norman was upset. "Your plant reached over on my side of the room! It's not supposed to do that!"

"I don't think it did," said Michael. He pointed to the string still tied to Norman's bedpost. The other end was hanging from Norman's plant.

"My plant wouldn't eat your yukky old dirty socks," Norman protested.

"That's it!" exclaimed Michael. "Those socks weren't dirty. I got them out of the drawer. The ones that disappeared before were dirty. That's the only kind I leave on the floor. So my plant only likes dirty socks. It didn't want a clean one."

Would you rather be Michael's or Norman's friend? Explain your choice.

What do Michael and Norman do to solve the missing-sock mystery?

How is each boy's plant like its owner?

WRITE   Imagine that Norman is your brother. Would it bother you to share a room with him? Write a few journal entries that show what it is like to be Norman's roommate.

257

CARNIVOROUS PLANTS

A Lerner Natural Science Book

AWARD-WINNING
BOOK

by Cynthia Overbeck
Photographs by
Kiyoshi Shimizu

Exotic Plants

A black fly hovers in the air over a strange-looking plant. Attracted by a sweet smell, the fly lands on the flat, reddish surface of one of the plant's leaves. It begins to crawl across. Suddenly, the leaf moves! Before the fly can get away, the two halves of the leaf close around it. Two rows of "teeth" clamp together. All escape is cut off. The fly struggles to free itself, but the trap only closes more tightly. Soon, the fly is dead. In a few days, there is nothing left but the hard parts of its body.

This unlucky insect has become food for one of the world's most exotic plants—the Venus flytrap. The flytrap is one of about 450 species, or kinds, of carnivorous plants. **Carnivorous** (kar-NIH-vor-us) means "meat-eating." A plant that is carnivorous actually traps and eats insects, spiders, and, in some cases, tiny animals like frogs and mice. Carnivorous plants have developed this special way of feeding themselves in order to live and grow in a particular kind of environment.

In order to survive, most plants must take in water and minerals from the soil. These elements are combined with carbon dioxide and energy from sunlight to make the food that plants need to grow. Nitrogen is one of the most important minerals needed for plant growth. For this reason, most plants grow best in places where the soil is rich in nitrogen.

But carnivorous plants grow in wet, low-lying swamps and marshes. Here the damp soil is nitrogen-poor. Plants that take in nitrogen through their roots cannot live in such soil. Carnivorous plants stay alive by getting nitrogen and other minerals from another source. These plants get minerals from the bodies of the creatures that they trap and kill. The special leaves of carnivorous plants allow them to catch and use this handy source of food.

How do these unusual plants work? First, they must lure, or attract, animals. Unlike a frog or a bird, a carnivorous plant cannot reach out and grab an insect. It must wait until the insect comes to it. For this reason, carnivorous plants have special ways of attracting insects and other animals.

Some carnivorous plants give off a sweet smell like that of nectar, which attracts insects such as flies, bees, and ants. Others give off a smell of decay, to which flies and some other insects are equally attracted. Many carnivorous plants have bright colors and patterns that serve as lures. And a whole group has leaves covered with sparkling droplets that attract insects with bright color and light, as well as with a sweet smell.

Once an animal has been lured to the plant, it must be trapped. Generally, carnivorous plants have two main kinds of traps: **active,** or moving, traps and **passive,** or still, traps. Plants with active traps, like those of the Venus flytrap and the waterwheel, have parts that move quickly to trap any insect that lands on them. The moving parts may clamp together like jaws. Or they may swing shut like a trapdoor.

Passive traps do not depend on movement of their parts to trap animals. Some passive traps, like those of

A waterwheel plant

the sundews, are sticky traps. Although some of them may move after they have caught an insect, the actual trapping is done by a sticky substance on their leaves. This substance catches and holds insects without the need for movement.

Other passive traps are the "pitfall" type. They are found in the pitcher plants. Inside the leaves of these plants are cleverly made one-way tunnels into which insects are lured by sweet nectar. Once they are inside, the insects cannot get back out.

One type of pitcher plant

All of these traps help to feed the plants on which they grow. Usually, many traps grow on one plant. They all work together to catch, digest, and absorb the nutrition that the plant needs to survive.

ctive Traps

Perhaps the most familiar of the carnivorous plants is the Venus flytrap. This plant is found only in the United States, in the swamps of North Carolina. The entire plant grows about a foot (30 centimeters) tall. In spring it has pretty white flowers blooming on top of tall stalks. But the most interesting parts of this plant are its leaves.

The Venus flytrap

The flytrap's narrow green leaves grow in a circle around the plant's base. Each leaf blade opens into two halves, almost like a clamshell. The two halves, or **lobes,** are attached to a center rib. Each lobe averages about an inch (2.5 centimeters) in length. The inside surfaces of the lobes are usually a reddish color. Around the curved outer edge of each lobe is a row of stiff, pointed bristles, called **cilia** (SIL-ee-uh). On the inside surface of each lobe are three "trigger" hairs.

These strange leaves are the plant's traps. When the lobes are in an open position, the traps are set, ready for a meal. In the pictures, a spider has been attracted by a leaf's red color and by the sweet smell of a nectar-like substance produced on its edges. As the spider crawls onto the leaf's surface, it disturbs the trigger hairs. This is the signal for the lobes to move. But the trap must receive two signals in order to close. It will react only if one hair is touched twice or if two hairs are touched. This is the plant's way of making sure that it has caught a live, moving creature and not a piece of grass or a leaf.

Once the double signal has been given, the lobes close quickly around the spider. The cilia lock together to prevent escape. At this point, a very small spider or insect could still crawl out from between the cilia. The plant rejects such tiny animals because it would use more of its energy to digest them than it would gain from their bodies in food value.

As the trap closes, a fluid begins to ooze out of the inner surfaces of the lobes, and the spider is drowned. The fluid contains **digestive enzymes** (EN-zimes), substances that change the spider's body material into a form that the plant can absorb as nourishment. As more and more enzymes flow into the trap, the spider's soft body parts gradually dissolve.

In 8 to 10 days, the body parts of the animal have become a nitrogen-rich liquid that is absorbed into the plant. The trap opens, and out fall the hard body parts that the plant could not digest. The trap is now set again. One trap will usually catch and digest an average of three meals before it withers and dies.

Left: **The pictures show the leaf of a Venus flytrap capturing a spider.**

Right: **Another Venus flytrap catches an insect.**

A waterwheel plant with its leaves open

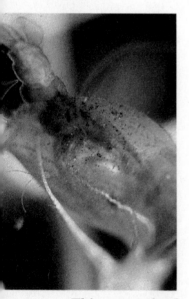

This waterwheel leaf has caught an insect larva.

Another carnivorous plant that uses an active trap much like that of the Venus flytrap is known as the waterwheel plant. It is found in Europe, Australia, India, Japan, and Africa. This small, rootless plant floats just under the surface of quiet ponds and swamps. The whole plant is only about 4 to 12 inches (10 to 30 centimeters) long. Its little white flowers, which bloom in the spring, show above the water's surface. The traps are underwater.

Each plant has a slender stem with leaves that are almost transparent. Groups of eight leaves are arranged around the stem like the spokes of a wheel. This is why the plant is called the waterwheel.

The waterwheel's leaves are its traps. Each leaf is very tiny—less than $\frac{1}{4}$ inch (6 millimeters) long. Such tiny traps can catch only very small creatures. The waterwheel feeds on water fleas, on **plankton,** or microscopic water animals, and on tiny **larvae** (LAR-vee)—insects in an early stage of development.

The waterwheel's leaves act just like underwater Venus flytraps. They have two lobes, rows of bristles, and trigger hairs inside their lobes. When an insect enters a trap, the halves snap shut in a fraction of a second. The waterwheel then digests its meal and reopens to catch the next one.

Both the Venus flytrap and the waterwheel plant use a clamping movement to trap animals. But another type of carnivorous plant with an active trap—the bladderwort—moves in a different way. The bladderwort has a kind of trapdoor for catching its meals.

Bladderworts are found in many parts of the world. Although some bladderworts grow on land, most grow in quiet ponds and swamps. Like the waterwheel plants, they do not have roots. They float in strands or clumps just below the water's surface. In summer, their tiny yellow or purple flowers bloom above the water.

Growing all along the bladderwort's thin stems are its leaves. Each leaf is actually a little air bag, or **bladder.** The bladders are very small; the biggest is only about $\frac{1}{5}$ inch (5 millimeters) long. These tiny, balloon-like leaves are the traps the bladderwort uses to catch water fleas, insect larvae, and sometimes small tadpoles.

At one end of each bladder are feathery hairs that serve as triggers. These hairs are arranged around an opening, across which is a tiny "trapdoor." This door swings open only one way—inward.

To trap insects, the bladder uses suction. When the door is closed and the bladder is empty, its walls are limp and collapsed. Then an insect swims by and brushes against the trigger hairs. Suddenly the bladder walls expand. This forces the trapdoor open and creates a sucking action. As the walls expand, water rushes in, pulling the insect with it. Then the trapdoor slams shut, and the insect is caught inside the bladder.

Immediately the digestive enzymes inside the bladder go to work. If the insect is tiny, the bladder takes only 15 to 30 minutes to absorb the nitrogen and other minerals from its body. If the insect is larger, digestion may take up to 2 hours. Sometimes, a bladder gets hold of an insect or larva that is too large to fit inside it. Then it digests the meal bit by bit. A single bladder can catch and digest about 15 small creatures before it dies.

This photograph, taken through a microscope, shows the many tiny bladders that grow on a single plant.

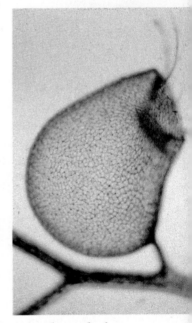

An enlarged picture of a single bladder

265

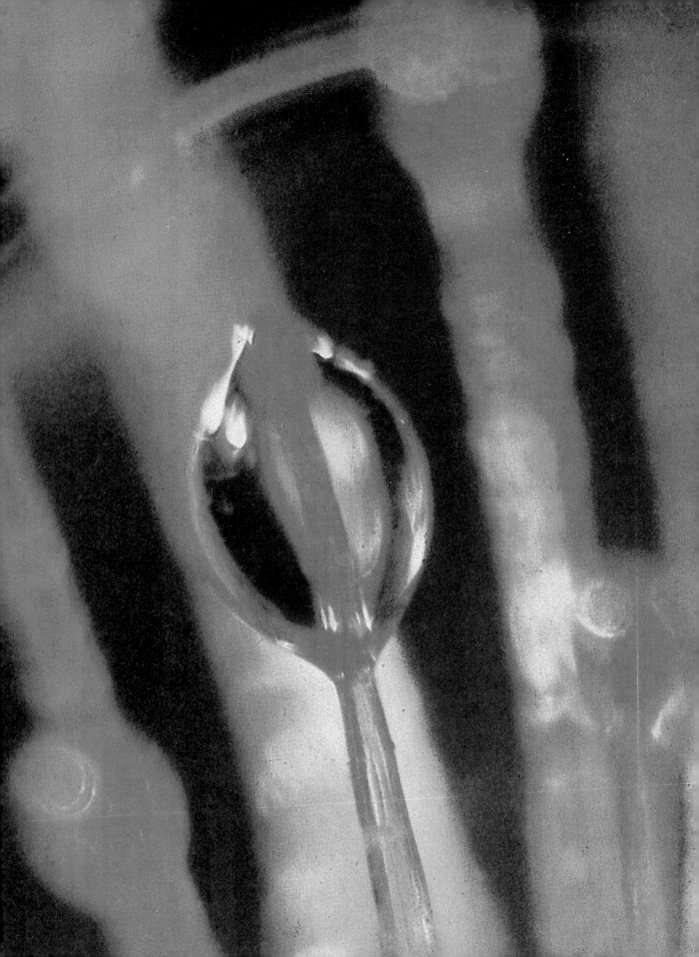

Above: Sundews growing among other marsh plants

Passive Traps

Flytraps, waterwheels, and bladderworts all use active traps to catch their food. But other carnivorous plants use passive traps—traps that do not depend on movement to capture insects. One group of plants, the sundews, uses a sticky trap.

Left: A closeup view of the surface of a sundew leaf

The small roundleaf sundew provides a good example of the way a sticky trap works. This plant grows in many swampy areas of the world, including parts of the United States. The plant is small—about $3\frac{1}{2}$ inches (8 centimeters) across. It is often partly hidden among taller weeds and plants that grow around it.

In summer the roundleaf's tall center stems carry white flowers. The leaves of the sundew look bright red. They seem to be covered with sparkling drops of dew. But what looks like a pretty red, dewdrop-covered leaf is really a deadly trap for flies and other insects.

The sundew's leaves are covered with many little stalks of different heights. At the top of each stalk is a tiny **gland,** or organ, that produces a clear, sticky liquid. This liquid forms a droplet on the tip of the stalk. Usually the gland is a reddish color, so the liquid on it appears to be red, too.

Flies and other insects are drawn to the sundew by the color and sparkling light, as well as by an attractive scent that the plant gives off. But when a fly lands on a sundew leaf, it is in trouble.

Immediately its feet are caught in the sticky liquid on top of the taller stalks. As the fly struggles to escape, more sticky liquid flows out of the glands. Now the fly is trapped for good. The stalks around the fly bend toward its body, giving off more liquid. The whole leaf curls slightly to cup the body. Digestive enzymes work until the soft parts of the fly have dissolved and become absorbed into the leaf. After four or five days, the leaf and stalks uncurl.

The pictures on these two pages show a fly being trapped and digested by a sundew leaf.

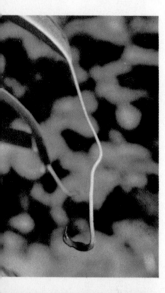

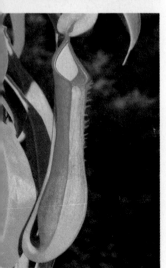

Of all the carnivorous plants with passive traps, perhaps none are more exotic-looking than the pitcher plants. These plants have special leaves that are hollow and can hold water, almost like a real jug or pitcher. The leaves are the plant's traps. Their structure and appearance are so unusual that people have given them many fanciful nicknames, such as huntsman's cup and Indian dipper.

There are about 80 kinds of pitcher plants growing in the wetlands of the world. Many, like the North American pitcher plant, grow close to the ground in a circle around a center base. All of the leaves of these plants are traps for catching insects.

Other pitcher plants are found in the tropical wetlands of Malaysia, Madagascar, and Sri Lanka. These plants have many brightly colored pitcher leaves growing on vines.

These tropical pitcher plants have ordinary green leaves as well as brightly colored pitcher leaves. The pictures show how their pitchers grow from a **tendril,** or threadlike stem. As the leaf grows, it swells to form a colorful "jug." The top opens to form a leafy hood. In some pitcher plants this hood is just a kind of frill around the pitcher's edges. In others it forms a flat "roof" above the whole opening.

The leaves of various kinds of pitcher plants may differ in size as well as in color, pattern, and shape. They can be from 2 inches (5 centimeters) to more than 2 feet (60 centimeters) tall. Small pitcher plants trap insects such as flies, beetles, and ants. The largest pitchers can also

Three stages in the development of a pitcher leaf

trap small frogs or mice. But whatever their size or outer appearance, all pitchers trap animals in basically the same way.

A pitcher trap is passive; it does not need to move in order to trap an insect. Instead, its clever design becomes a prison for almost any insect that crawls into it.

The leaf forms a kind of tube. At the top is an opening, usually brightly colored. The bottom part of the tube is shaped like a cup. Rainwater collects in this cup. (In the pitchers that grow close to the ground, water is also drawn up from the soil to fill the cup.) In most types of plants, the hood above the opening helps to keep too much rainwater from coming in. This hood always stays open. It never snaps shut to trap an insect, as some people believe.

A sweet nectar is produced around the lip of the pitcher opening. Attracted by the nectar and the bright colors of the pitcher, an insect flies or crawls onto the convenient lip. It begins to sip the nectar and soon crawls further into the opening, searching for more.

When the insect moves into the tube of the pitcher plant, it is in trouble. The inside walls of the tube are slick and slippery as ice. The insect slips further down. There it finds its footing along hairs that line the lower part of the tube. But the hairs all face downward, toward the pool of water below. Once the insect has crawled past them, it is impossible for it to get back up. The insect struggles but finally becomes exhausted and falls into the water below. There it drowns.

This x-ray picture shows a pitcher partly filled with water.

Now digestive enzymes flow into the pool. As in other carnivorous plants, the soft parts of the insect's body are digested and absorbed into the plant. The hard parts of the body collect in the bottom of the pitcher.

A cross-section view of a pitcher plant leaf. The fly is about to become a prisoner inside the pitcher tube.

Pitcher plants, like all the carnivorous plants in this article, have found ways to thrive in places where most plants could not live. With the help of their strange and often beautiful leaves, they feed on the creatures that share their marsh environment.

Plant Preservation

But as hardy as carnivorous plants are, today the lives of many of them may be in danger. As people drain more and more marshland to make way for buildings and roads, the plants have fewer places to grow. They are becoming increasingly rare.

Today people are trying to grow some carnivorous plants in indoor greenhouses. In this way, they hope to preserve these fascinating and unusual plants and to make sure that they do not disappear from our world.

What did you learn about carnivorous plants that you think is interesting?

Describe the important characteristics that all carnivorous plants share.

Briefly summarize the main difference between a passive trap and an active trap.

WRITE   What information about carnivorous plants was most surprising to you? Share these interesting facts in a short letter to a friend.

Some plants have very unusual eating habits. In what ways are the plants in the two selections you have read alike? How are they different?

WRITER'S WORKSHOP

Look through a book on caring for plants to find other plants with unusual names or interesting characteristics. Choose one plant, and gather information about it. Then write a how-to paragraph telling how to care for the plant you chose.

Writer's Choice
You have read about some unusual plants. Choose a topic, and write about it. You might want to write about characteristics that make these plants different from ordinary plants.

THEME

Picture yourself exploring a jungle or wandering through a beautiful garden as you read the following selections and poems.

CONTENTS

275

TEACHERS' CHOICE

THE GREAT KAPOK TREE

A TALE OF THE AMAZON RAIN FOREST

by Lynne Cherry

In the Amazon rain forest it is always hot, and in that heat everything grows, and grows, and grows. The tops of the trees in the rain forest are called the canopy. The canopy is a sunny place that touches the sky. The animals that live there like lots of light. Colorful parrots fly from tree to tree. Monkeys leap from branch to branch. The bottom of the rain forest is called the understory. The animals that live in the understory like darkness. There, silent snakes curl around hanging vines. Graceful jaguars watch and wait.

And in this steamy environment the great Kapok tree shoots up through the forest and emerges above the canopy.

This is the story of a community of animals that live in one such tree in the rain forest.

emerald tree boa

scarlet macaw

toucan

Brazilian tree frog

coati

scamander

red-necked tanager

tree frog

three-toed sloth

urania butterfly

cock-of-the-rock

tree porcupine

mother & baby tapir

mother & baby giant anteater

Vindula arsinoë butterfly

baby hoatzin

Amazonian katydid

poison arrow frog

ARCTIC OCEAN

GREENLAND

NORTH AMERICA

EUROPE

AFRICA

ATLANTIC OCEAN

Central America

CARIBBEAN SEA

THE AMAZON RAIN FOREST

Rio Negro

Manaus

AMAZON RIVER

Equator

Brazil

SOUTH AMERICA

Madag...

PACIFIC OCEAN

N
W   E
S

☐ today's rain forests
☐ original extent of rain forests

Tropical Rain Forests

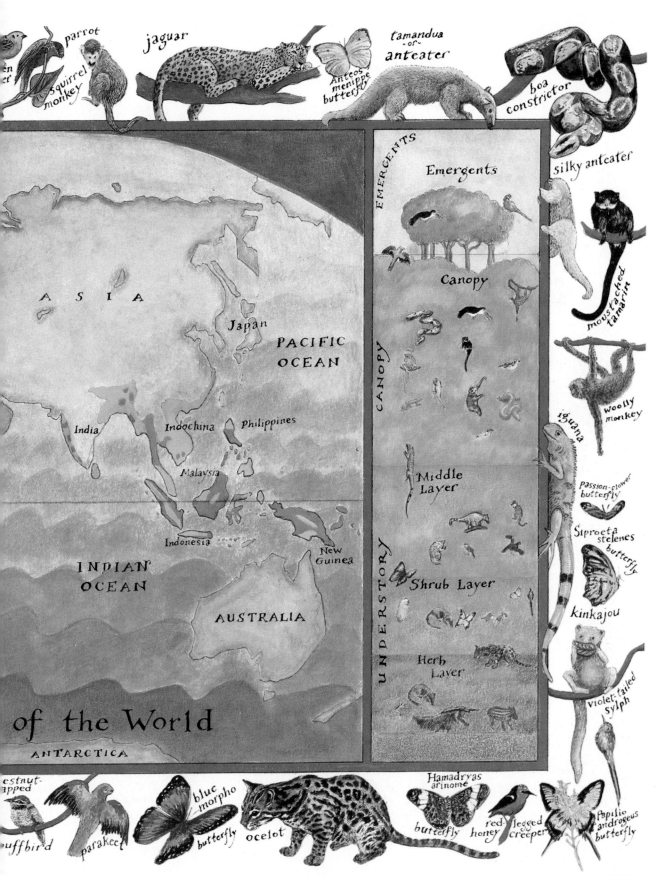

parrot

jaguar

tamandua
-or-
anteater

boa
constrictor

squirrel
monkey

Anteos
menippe
butterfly

silky anteater

EMERGENTS

Emergents

moustached
tamarin

CANOPY

Canopy

woolly
monkey

ASIA

Japan

PACIFIC
OCEAN

iguana

India

Indochina

Philippines

Passion-flower
butterfly

Malaysia

Middle
Layer

Siproeta
stelenes
butterfly

UNDERSTORY

Indonesia

New
Guinea

INDIAN
OCEAN

Shrub Layer

kinkajou

AUSTRALIA

Herb
Layer

of the World

violet-tailed
sylph

ANTARCTICA

chestnut-
capped

blue
morpho

Hamadryas
arinome

Papilio
androgeus
butterfly

buffbird

parakeet

butterfly

ocelot

butterfly

red-
legged
honey creeper

Two men walked into the rain forest. Moments before, the forest had been alive with the sounds of squawking birds and howling monkeys. Now all was quiet as the creatures watched the two men and wondered why they had come.

The larger man stopped and pointed to a great Kapok tree. Then he left.

The smaller man took the ax he carried and struck the trunk of the tree. Whack! Whack! Whack! The sounds of the blows rang through the forest. The wood of the tree was very hard. Chop! Chop! Chop! The man wiped off the sweat that ran down his face and neck. Whack! Chop! Whack! Chop!

Soon the man grew tired. He sat down to rest at the foot of the great Kapok tree. Before he knew it, the heat and hum of the forest had lulled him to sleep.

A boa constrictor lived in the Kapok tree. He slithered down its trunk to where the man was sleeping. He looked at the gash the ax had made in the tree. Then the huge snake slid very close to the man and hissed in his ear: "Senhor, this tree is a tree of miracles. It is my home, where generations of my ancestors have lived. Do not chop it down."

A bee buzzed in the sleeping man's ear: "Senhor, my hive is in this Kapok tree, and I fly from tree to tree and flower to flower collecting pollen. In this way I pollinate the trees and flowers throughout the rain forest. You see, all living things depend on one another."

A troupe of monkeys scampered down from the canopy of the Kapok tree. They chattered to the sleeping man: "Senhor, we have seen the ways of man. You chop down one tree, then come back for another and another. The roots of these great trees will wither and die, and there will be nothing left to hold the earth in place. When the heavy rains come, the soil will be washed away and the forest will become a desert."

A toucan, a macaw, and a cock-of-the-rock flew down from the canopy. "Senhor!" squawked the toucan, "you must not cut down this tree. We have flown over the rain forest and seen what happens once you begin to chop down the trees. Many people settle on the land. They set fires to clear the underbrush, and soon the forest disappears. Where once there was life and beauty only black and smoldering ruins remain."

A bright and small tree frog crawled along the edge of a leaf. In a squeaky voice he piped in the man's ear: "Senhor, a ruined rain forest means ruined lives . . . many ruined lives. You will leave many of us homeless if you chop down this great Kapok tree."

A jaguar had been sleeping along a branch in the middle of the tree. Because his spotted coat blended into the dappled light and shadows of the understory, no one had noticed him. Now he leapt down and padded silently over to the sleeping man. He growled in his ear: "Senhor, the Kapok tree is home to many birds and animals. If you cut it down, where will I find my dinner?"

Four tree porcupines swung down from branch to branch and whispered to the man: "Senhor, do you know what we animals and humans need in order to live? Oxygen. And, Senhor, do you know what trees produce? Oxygen! If you cut down the forests you will destroy that which gives us all life."

Several anteaters climbed down the Kapok tree with their young clinging to their backs. The unstriped anteater said to the sleeping man: "Senhor, you are chopping down this tree with no thought for the future. And surely you know that what happens tomorrow depends upon what you do today. The big man tells you to chop down a beautiful tree. He does not think of his own children, who tomorrow must live in a world without trees."

A three-toed sloth had begun climbing down from the canopy when the men first appeared. Only now did she reach the ground. Plodding ever so slowly over to the sleeping man, she spoke in her deep and lazy voice: "Senhor, how much is beauty worth? Can you live without it? If you destroy the beauty of the rain forest, on what would you feast your eyes?"

A child from the Yanomamo tribe who lived in the rain forest knelt over the sleeping man. He murmured in his ear: "Senhor, when you awake, please look upon us all with new eyes."

The man awoke with a start. Before him stood the rain forest child, and all around him, staring, were the creatures who depended upon the great Kapok tree. What wondrous and rare animals they were!

The man looked about and saw the sun streaming through the canopy. Spots of bright light glowed like jewels amidst the dark green forest. Strange and beautiful plants seemed to dangle in the air, suspended from the great Kapok tree.

The man smelled the fragrant perfume of their flowers. He felt the steamy mist rising from the forest floor. But he heard no sound, for the creatures were strangely silent.

The man stood and picked up his ax. He swung back his arm as though to strike the tree. Suddenly he stopped. He turned and looked at the animals and the child.

He hesitated. Then he dropped the ax and walked out of the rain forest.

How would you make the ending of this story different?

What do you think Lynne Cherry wants you to learn about rain forests? How do you know?

Why does the man drop his ax and walk out of the rain forest?

Do you think it is always wrong to cut down trees? Explain your answer.

WRITE   Write a descriptive paragraph that tells what you think the world would be like if there were no trees.

Wildflower

from Flower Moon Snow
by Kazue Mizumura
illustrated by Malcolm Farley

Is it waiting just for me,
This one wildflower
In the empty lot?

The Yellow Tulip

by George Swede

For weeks
it struggled
through the hard crust
of the spring earth
and a foot
of air

Just to be
scorched
by the sun
jolted
by raindrops
blasted
by the wind

But on this gentle
May morning
as it opens
yellow petals
to the sky

Nothing else matters

An underwater coral table

AWARD-WINNING
AUTHOR

DOWN UNDER
DOWN UNDER

BY ANN McGOVERN

Scuba diving on the Great Barrier Reef is an exciting adventure for a young girl. She is joined on the dive by her marine biologist mom, an expert diver named Sharon, the captain of the dive boat, and some eager underwater photographers.

When I told my friends I was going to the Great Barrier Reef, they wanted to know why it was so special.

First of all, it's huge! Picture a coral reef that stretches underwater from New York to Florida! The Great Barrier Reef is 1,250 miles long, extending from northeastern Australia to the shores of Papua New Guinea.

It's not one long reef, though. It's made up of 2,000 scattered reefs plus small, tree-covered islands and low, sandy islands called *cays*, separated by winding channels.

Just think! The Great Barrier Reef is the world's largest living thing. Yet it was built by individual pea-sized animals called *polyps*. The polyps' limestone skeletons piled on top of each other over the centuries, building huge reefs, each different than the others.

At low tide, I see the top of the reef breaking the surface of the water. Captain Chris says that there are about 1,500 species of fish living on the Great Barrier Reef and 400 different kinds of coral.

I was going to keep a list of the fish and coral I see, but with so many varieties it would turn out to be an encyclopedia!

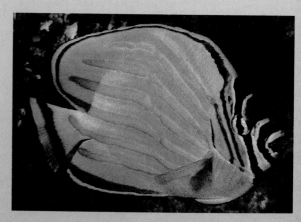

So many butterfly fish!

Long-snouted butterfly fish

The Great Barrier Reef must look the same today as it did in 1770, when British explorer Captain James Cook ran his ship aground on a coral reef. Captain Cook then spent four months charting what he called "submerged rock piles." Chris says it was a pity there were no face masks or snorkels or fins in those days. If Captain Cook had seen the unbelievable corals that he called "rock piles," he would have been just as amazed as I was.

The corals are absolutely awesome. And the colorful fish are out of a dream, too. I think about one family of fish—the butterfly fish. The masked butterfly, the long-snouted butterfly, the beaked butterfly, the banner butterfly—Chris says he can fill half a page with all the different names of this one family of fish.

Chris says that the Great Barrier Reef can be seen from the moon! Maybe one day I'll be able to walk on the moon, look down, and see the Great Barrier Reef. But right now, I'm thrilled to be on a boat on the Great Barrier Reef, looking up at the moon.

A clown fish in its anemone home

Every dive is like a wild dream come true. In my journal I write about some of the weird creatures I saw on *one* dive alone—

- funny-faced clown fish that live in a very strange home
- a school of one-horned unicorn fish
- a lumpy, frilly wobbegong shark
- five different, beautifully colored snails without shells, and a big one that I named ET.

After the dive and showers and a big lunch, Mom and I go into the lounge and begin tackling the books. I learn lots of fascinating facts about what I've seen on the morning dive.

A family of clown fish lives in each large anemone. They seldom swim more than a few feet away from their home. The clown fish are the only creatures that are safe from the stinging cells of the anemone's tentacles.

The anemone clearly protects the little clown fish. But what does the anemone get from the clown fish? Mom says that the colorful clown fish attract other fish to the anemone. These fish are stung by the anemone's writhing mass of tentacles and become the anemone's dinner.

Whenever I get too close to the clown fish, they quickly dive down into the anemone's tentacles. I could watch the darling clown fish for hours.

I love unicorns, even though I know they're not real. But unicorn fish are real. Today I saw a school of them—about twenty unicorn fish. Each one had a large spike that stuck out of its head, like the single horn of a unicorn.

Another weird creature is the wobbegong, or carpet shark. The one we saw was bigger than Mom. It's a harmless shark if it's left alone by divers. Sharon spotted it. If I hadn't been looking carefully, I wouldn't have known it was there. Colored brown and gray, it's hard to see on the brownish gray reef it lives on. The weedy growth around its mouth looks like whiskers and helps to hide its mouth. Sharon says the wobbegong is found only in Australia.

The underwater photographers are delighted with the beautiful snails without shells, molluscs called *nudibranchs*. Nudibranch means "naked gill," and I could see their gills on their backs, looking like delicate plumes. There are dozens of species of nudibranchs on the

The strange unicorn fish

The wobbegong, or carpet shark

A flatworm floats by my mask.

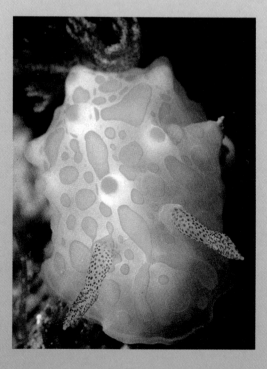

Colorful nudibranchs

Great Barrier Reef, most of them no bigger than two inches. But the one I found and named ET was the biggest nudibranch the crew had ever seen. Even Sharon, who knows all these creatures so well, had never seen anything like it before.

I measured ET—nearly a foot long!—and then we put it into a bucket to study. We'll return it to its watery home this afternoon.

I feel like a scientist making an important discovery.

ET—the big nudibranch!

You read that the Great Barrier Reef is 1,250 miles long. What other interesting or surprising information did you learn about the reef?

Describe the relationship between an anemone and a clown fish.

Why do you think Ann McGovern wrote about the Great Barrier Reef?

WRITE Write an advertisement that would persuade someone to go on a dive to the Great Barrier Reef.

Amazing Ecosystems

How are people's lives richer because of nature and its wonders? Use examples from the selections to support your ideas.

WRITER'S WORKSHOP

Choose the selection from this theme that has helped you learn the most about nature. Write a persuasive essay telling a student from another class why he or she should read the selection.

Writer's Choice

You have read about many natural wonders. You might want to choose one of these wonders and write about it. You might also want to illustrate your writing.

THEME

Harvest Humor

Have you ever heard an amazing story about a plant? Did you believe the story? The following riddles, story, and words from the author test your knowledge about the plant world in ways that will make you smile.

CONTENTS

303

Fruit and Vegetable Stew

AND

from *Alexander the Grape*

compiled by
Charles Keller

illustrated by Tuko Fujisaki

AWARD-WINNING
AUTHOR

Why aren't bananas ever lonely?
Because they come in bunches.

What vegetable do you
get when you drop a tomato?
Squash.

Why do watermelons
contain so much water?
They are planted in the spring.

How do you make gold stew?
Add fourteen carrots.

What's the most dangerous
vegetable to have on a boat?
A leek.

Why did the cornstalk get
mad at the farmer?
He kept pulling its ears.

When are vegetables like music?
When there are two beets to the measure.

What do you call a twisted path
through an Indian cornfield?
A maize.

Why did the tomato
go out with the prune?
Because he couldn't find a date.

MCBROOM

Tells The

TRUTH

BY SID FLEISCHMAN

ILLUSTRATIONS
DOUG PANTON

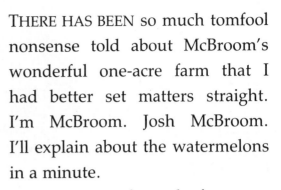

THERE HAS BEEN so much tomfool nonsense told about McBroom's wonderful one-acre farm that I had better set matters straight. I'm McBroom. Josh McBroom. I'll explain about the watermelons in a minute.

I aim to put down the facts, one after the other, the way things happened—exactly.

It began, you might say, the day we left the farm in Connecticut. We piled our youngsters and everything we owned in our old air-cooled Franklin automobile. We headed West.

To count noses, in addition to my own, there was my dear wife Melissa and our eleven red-headed, freckle-faced youngsters. Their names were Will*jill*hester-*chester*peter*polly*tim*tom*mary-*larry*andlittle*clarinda*.

It was summer, and the trees along the way were full of bird-song. We had got as far as Iowa when my dear wife Melissa made a startling discovery. We had *twelve* children along—one too many! She had just counted them again.

I slammed on the brakes and raised a cloud of dust.

307

"Will*jill*hester*chester*peter*polly* tim*tom*mary*larry*and-little*clarinda*!" I shouted. "Line up!"

The youngsters tumbled out of the car. I counted noses and there were twelve. I counted again. Twelve. It was a baffler as all the faces were familiar. Once more I made the count—but this time I caught Larry slipping around behind. He was having his nose counted twice, and the mystery was solved. The scamp! Didn't we laugh, though, and stretch our legs in the bargain.

Just then a thin, long-legged man came ambling down the road. He was so scrawny I do believe he could have hidden behind a flagpole, ears and all. He wore a tall stiff collar, a diamond stickpin in his tie, and a black hat.

"Lost, neighbor?" he asked, spitting out the pips of a green apple he was eating.

"Not a bit," said I. "We're heading West, sir. We gave up our farm—it was half rocks and the other half tree stumps. Folks tell us there's land out West and the sun shines in the winter."

The stranger pursed his lips. "You can't beat Iowa for farmland," he said.

"Maybe so," I nodded. "But I'm short of funds. Unless they're giving farms away in Iowa we'll keep a-going."

The man scratched his chin. "See here, I've got more land than I can plow. You look like nice folks. I'd like to have you for neighbors. I'll let you have eighty acres cheap. Not a stone or a tree stump anywhere on the place. Make me an offer."

"Thank you kindly, sir," I smiled. "But I'm afraid you would laugh at me if I offered you everything in my leather purse."

"How much is that?"

"Ten dollars exactly."

"Sold!" he said.

Well, I almost choked with surprise. I thought he must be joking, but quick as a flea he was scratching out a deed on the back of an old envelope.

"Hector Jones is my name, neighbor," he said. "You can call me Heck—everyone does."

Was there ever a more kindly and generous man? He signed the deed with a flourish, and I gladly opened the clasp of my purse.

Three milky white moths flew out. They had been gnawing on the ten dollar bill all the way from Connecticut, but enough remained to buy the farm. And not a stone or tree stump on it!

Mr. Heck Jones jumped on the running board and guided us a mile up the road. My youngsters tried to amuse him along the way. Will wiggled his ears, and Jill crossed her eyes, and Chester twitched his nose like a rabbit, but I reckoned Mr. Jones wasn't used to youngsters. Hester flapped her arms like a bird, Peter whistled through his front teeth, which were missing, and Tom tried to stand on his head in the back of the car. Mr. Heck Jones ignored them all.

Finally he raised his long arm and pointed.

"There's your property, neighbor," he said.

Didn't we tumble out of the car in a hurry? We gazed with delight at our new farm. It was broad and sunny, with an oak tree on a gentle hill. There was one defect, to be sure. A boggy looking pond spread across an acre beside the road. You could lose a cow in a place like that, but we had got a bargain—no doubt about it.

"Mama," I said to my dear Melissa. "See that fine old oak on the hill? That's where we'll build our farmhouse."

"No you won't," said Mr. Heck Jones. "That oak ain't on your property."

"But, sir—"

"All that's yours is what you see under water. Not a rock or a tree stump in it, like I said."

I thought he must be having his little joke, except that there wasn't a smile to be found on his face. "But *sir*!" I said. "You clearly stated that the farm was eighty acres."

"That's right."

"That marshy pond hardly covers an acre."

"That's wrong," he said. "There are a full eighty acres—one piled on the other, like griddle cakes. I didn't say your farm was all on the surface. It's eighty acres deep, McBroom. Read the deed."

I read the deed. It was true.

"*Hee-haw*! *Hee-haw*!" he snorted. "I got the best of you, McBroom! Good day, neighbor."

He scurried away, laughing up his sleeve all the way home. I soon learned that Mr. Heck was always laughing up his sleeve. Folks told me that when he'd hang up his coat and go to bed, all that stored-up laughter would pour out his sleeve and keep him awake nights. But there's no truth to that.

I'll tell you about the watermelons in a minute.

WELL, there we stood gazing at our one-acre farm that wasn't good for anything but jumping into on a hot day. And the day was the hottest I could remember. The hottest on record, as it turned out. That was the day, three minutes before noon, when the cornfields all over Iowa exploded into popcorn. That's history. You must have read about that. There are pictures to prove it.

I turned to my children. "Will*jill*hester*chester*peter*polly*tim*tom*mary*larry*andlittle*clarinda*," I said. "There's always a bright side to things. That pond we bought is a mite muddy, but it's wet. Let's jump in and cool off."

That idea met with favor and we were soon in our swimming togs. I gave the signal, and we took a running jump. At that moment such a dry spell struck that we landed in an acre of dry earth. The pond had evaporated. It was very surprising.

My boys had jumped in head first and there was nothing to be seen of them but their legs kicking in the air. I had to pluck them out of the earth like carrots. Some of my girls were still holding their noses. Of course, they were sorely disappointed to have that swimming hole pulled out from under them.

But the moment I ran the topsoil through my fingers, my farmer's heart skipped a beat. That pond bottom felt as soft and rich as black silk. "My dear Melissa!" I called. "Come look! This topsoil is so rich it ought to be kept in a bank."

I was in a sudden fever of excitement. That glorious topsoil seemed to cry out for seed. My dear Melissa had a sack of dried beans along, and I sent Will and Chester to fetch it. I saw no need to bother plowing the field. I directed Polly to draw a straight furrow with a stick and Tim to follow her, poking holes in the ground. Then I came along. I dropped a bean in each hole and stamped on it with my heel.

Well, I had hardly gone a couple of yards when something green and leafy tangled my foot. I looked behind me. There was a beanstalk traveling along in a hurry and looking for a pole to climb on.

"Glory be!" I exclaimed. That soil was *rich!* The stalks were spreading out all over. I had to rush along to keep ahead of them.

By the time I got to the end of the furrow the first stalks had blossomed, and the pods had formed, and they were ready for picking.

You can imagine our excitement. Will's ears wiggled. Jill's eyes crossed. Chester's nose twitched. Hester's arms flapped. Peter's missing front teeth whistled. And Tom stood on his head.

"Will*jill*hester*chester*peter*polly*tim*tom*mary*larry*and-little*clarinda,*" I shouted. "Harvest them beans!"

Within an hour we had planted and harvested that entire crop of beans. But was it hot working in the sun! I sent Larry to find a good acorn along the road. We planted it, but it didn't grow near as fast as I had expected. We had to wait an entire three hours for a shade tree.

WE MADE CAMP under our oak tree, and the next day we drove to Barnsville with our crop of beans. I traded it for various seeds—carrot and beet and cabbage and other items. The storekeeper found a few kernels of corn that hadn't popped, at the very bottom of the bin.

BEANS

BEANS

314

But we found out that corn was positively dangerous to plant. The stalk shot up so fast it would skin your nose.

Of course, there was a secret to that topsoil. A government man came out and made a study of the matter. He said there had once been a huge lake in that part of Iowa. It had taken thousands of years to shrink up to our pond, as you can imagine. The lake fish must have got packed in worse than sardines. There's nothing like fish to put nitrogen in the soil. That's a scientific fact. Nitrogen makes things grow to beat all. And we did occasionally turn up a fish bone.

It wasn't long before Mr. Heck Jones came around to pay us a neighborly call. He was eating a raw turnip. When he saw the way we were planting and harvesting cabbage his eyes popped out of his head. It almost cost him his eyesight.

He scurried away, muttering to himself.

"My dear Melissa," I said. "That man is up to mischief."

Folks in town had told me that Mr. Heck Jones had the worst farmland in Iowa. He couldn't give it away. Tornado winds had carried off his topsoil and left the hardpan right on top. He had to plow it with wedges and a sledge hammer. One day we heard a lot of booming on the other side of the hill, and my youngsters went up to see what was happening. It turned out he was planting seeds with a shotgun.

Meanwhile, we went about our business on the farm. I don't mind saying that before long we were showing a handsome profit. Back in Connecticut we had been lucky to harvest one crop a year. Now we were planting and harvesting three, four crops a *day*.

But there were things we had to be careful about. Weeds, for one thing. My youngsters took turns standing weed guard. The instant a weed popped out of the ground, they'd race to it and hoe it to death. You can imagine what would happen if weeds ever got going in rich soil like ours.

We also had to be careful about planting time. Once we planted lettuce just before my dear Melissa rang the noon bell for dinner. While we ate, the lettuce headed up and went to seed. We lost the whole crop.

One day back came Mr. Heck Jones with a grin on his face. He had figured out a loophole in the deed that made the farm ours.

"*Hee-haw!*" he laughed. He was munching a radish. "I got the best of you now, Neighbor McBroom. The deed says you were to pay me *everything* in your purse, and you *didn't.*"

"On the contrary, sir," I answered. "Ten dollars. There wasn't another cent in my purse."

"There were *moths* in the purse. I seen 'em flutter out. Three milky white moths, McBroom. I want three moths by three o'clock this afternoon, or I aim to take back the farm. *Hee-haw!*"

And off he went, laughing up his sleeve.

Mama was just ringing the noon bell so we didn't have much time. Confound that man! But he did have his legal point.

"Willjillhesterchesterpeterpollytimtommarylarryand-littleclarinda," I said. "We've got to catch three milky white moths! Hurry!"

We hurried in all directions. But moths are next to impossible to locate in the daytime. Try it yourself. Each of us came back empty-handed.

My dear Melissa began to cry, for we were sure to lose our farm. I don't mind telling you that things looked dark. Dark! That was it! I sent the youngsters running down the road to a lonely old pine tree and told them to rush back with a bushel of pine cones.

Didn't we get busy though! We planted a pine cone every three feet. They began to grow. We stood around anxiously, and I kept looking at my pocket watch. I'll tell you about the watermelons in a moment.

Sure enough, by ten minutes to three, those cones had grown into a thick pine forest.

It was dark inside, too! Not a ray of sunlight slipped through the green pine boughs. Deep in the forest I lit a lantern. Hardly a minute passed before I was surrounded by milky white moths—they thought it was night. I caught three on the wing and rushed out of the forest.

There stood Mr. Heck Jones waiting with the sheriff to foreclose.

"*Hee-haw! Hee-haw!*" old Heck laughed. He was eating a quince apple. "It's nigh onto three o'clock, and you can't catch moths in the day-time. The farm is mine!"

"Not so fast, Neighbor Jones," said I, with my hands cupped together. "Here are the three moths. Now, skedaddle, sir, before your feet take root and poison ivy grows out of your ears!"

He scurried away, muttering to himself.

"My dear Melissa," I said. "That man is up to mischief. He'll be back."

IT TOOK A GOOD BIT of work to clear the timber, I'll tell you. We had some of the pine milled and built ourselves a house on the corner of the farm. What was left we gave away to our neighbors. We were weeks blasting the roots out of the ground.

But I don't want you to think there was nothing but work on our farm. Some crops we grew just for the fun of it. Take pumpkins. The vines grew so fast we could hardly catch the pumpkins. It was something to see. The youngsters used to wear themselves out running after those pumpkins. Sometimes they'd have pumpkin races.

Sunday afternoons, just for the sport of it, the older boys would plant a pumpkin seed and try to catch a ride. It wasn't easy. You had to grab hold the instant the blossom dropped off and the pumpkin began to swell. Whoosh! It would yank you off your feet and take you whizzing over the farm until it wore itself out. Sometimes they'd use banana squash, which was faster.

And the girls learned to ride cornstalks like pogo sticks. It was just a matter of standing over the kernel as the stalk came busting up through the ground. It was good for quite a bounce.

We'd see Mr. Heck Jones standing on the hill in the distance, watching. He wasn't going to rest until he had pried us off our land.

Then, late one night, I was awakened by a hee-hawing outside the house. I went to the window and saw old Heck in the moonlight. He was cackling and chuckling and heeing and hawing and sprinkling seed every which way.

I pulled off my sleeping cap and rushed outside.

"What mischief are you up to, Neighbor Jones!" I shouted.

"*Hee-haw!*" he answered, and scurried away, laughing up his sleeve.

I had a sleepless night, as you can imagine. The next morning, as soon as the sun came up, that farm of ours broke out in weeds. You never saw such weeds! They heaved out of the ground and tumbled madly over each other—chickweed and milkweed, thistles and wild morning glory. In no time at all the weeds were in a tangle several feet thick and still rising.

We had a fight on our hands, I tell you! "Willjill-hesterchesterpeterpollytimtommarylarryandlittleclarinda!" I shouted. "There's work to do!"

We started hoeing and hacking away. For every weed we uprooted, another reseeded itself. We were a solid month battling those weeds. If our neighbors hadn't pitched in to help, we'd still be there burning weeds.

The day finally came when the farm was cleared and up popped old Heck Jones. He was eating a big slice of watermelon. That's what I was going to tell you about.

"Howdy, Neighbor McBroom," he said. "I came to say goodbye."

"Are you leaving, sir?" I asked.

"No, but *you* are."

I looked him squarely in the eye. "And if I don't, sir?"

"Why, *hee-haw*, McBroom! There's heaps more of weed seed where that came from!"

My dander was up. I rolled back my sleeves, meaning to give him a whipping he wouldn't forget. But what happened next saved me the bother.

As my youngsters gathered around, Mr. Heck Jones made the mistake of spitting out a mouthful of watermelon seeds.

Things did happen fast!

Before I had quite realized what he had done, a watermelon vine whipped up around old Heck's scrawny legs and jerked him off his feet. He went whizzing every which way over the farm. Watermelon seeds were flying. Soon he came zipping back and collided with a pumpkin left over from Sunday. In no time watermelons and pumpkins went galloping all over the place, and they were knocking him about something wild. He streaked here and there. Melons crashed and exploded. Old Heck was so covered with melon pulp he looked like he had been shot out of a ketchup bottle.

It was something to see. Will stood there wiggling his ears. Jill crossed her eyes. Chester twitched his nose. Hester flapped her arms like a bird. Peter whistled through his front teeth, which had grown in. Tom stood on his head. And little Clarinda took her first step.

By then the watermelons and pumpkins began to play themselves out. I figured Mr. Heck Jones would like to get home as fast as possible. So I asked Larry to fetch me the seed of a large banana squash.

"*Hee-haw!* Neighbor Jones," I said, and pitched the seed at his feet. I hardly had time to say goodbye before the vine had him. A long banana squash gave him a fast ride all the way home. I wish you could have been there to see it. He never came back.

That's the entire truth of the matter. Anything else you hear about McBroom's wonderful one-acre farm is an outright fib.

Why might it not be a good idea to buy something without examining it first?

What things happen in this story that would not happen in real life?

Does Hector Jones fool McBroom? Explain your answer.

WRITE If you had a farm like McBroom's, what would you plant on it? Write a list of plants you would grow, and give a reason for choosing each one.

WORDS FROM THE AUTHOR:

Sid Fleischman

AWARD-WINNING
AUTHOR

The idea for the *McBroom* books came to me while writing another book, *Chancy & the Grand Rascal*. In this book, there was a short scene about a liars' contest. That gave me the idea to do a tall tale, so I stopped writing the first book and started the new one.

Now that I had this new character, I needed a name for him. For years I have kept a name notebook, because using the right names is very important to an author. I checked my book, and there was the name McBroom. I have no idea where I got it originally, but it seemed perfect to me. Names also play a part in *McBroom* with those run-on names of the eleven McBroom children. How do you characterize eleven children? You can't, so I just strung all their names together, the way mothers do when they're calling their children. Those run-on names have become a popular part of the *McBroom* stories. Some classes have had contests to see how fast the students can say the names. The names have even been set to music!

With tall tales, my starting point has always been a concept—like the animals I used in *McBROOM's Zoo*. I think about that, and then I start writing. All kinds of interesting and exciting things happen as I go along.

To read more about McBroom and his family's adventures, check out these books by Sid Fleischman:

McBROOM and the Big Wind

McBROOM's Ear

McBROOM the Rainmaker

From the fruits and vegetables in the riddles, choose one that McBroom does not grow on his land. Describe how that crop might grow in McBroom's rich soil.

WRITER'S WORKSHOP

How would your friends and neighbors react if enormous fruits and vegetables grew in your garden? Write a story about this strange happening. You can make your story seem more believable if you include facts about the plants.

Writer's Choice   You have read some funny riddles and stories about plants. Plan a funny response of your own. Share your humor with your classmates.

CONNECTIONS

Multicultural Connection

Iroquois Harvest Celebrations

Native Americans have made huge contributions to the world's food supply by being the first to cultivate many important crops, including corn. Newcomers to America were saved from starving by corn provided by Native Americans.

As they did long ago, people of the Iroquois nations still hold ceremonies to give thanks for nature's gifts. The Green Corn Festival is held at harvesttime. In midwinter, a great thanksgiving feast begins the new year.

Look in copies of National Geographic World *magazine and other sources to find out what other ethnic groups or countries celebrate harvest festivals. Make a poster report about a group or a country, illustrating the foods, costumes, dances, and other activities of its festival.*

Iroquois men, dressed in bearskins and dried corn husks, go from house to house announcing the New Year's festival.

Social Studies/Art Connection

Please Don't Pick the Flowers

Every plant deserves its own celebration. Choose a national park, and make a map of it. In the border of the map, draw some wild plants that are protected there. Give facts that tell why each plant is valuable and why it needs protection. Display your map on a class bulletin board.

Science Connection

A Season for Everything

Why didn't the Iroquois plant corn year-round? They knew that plants grow well only if certain needs are met. Research four plants known to early American settlers. Find out how much heat or cold, water, and time each requires to grow. Report your findings to your classmates.

UNIT FOUR 4

DISCOVERIES

People in all cultures make discoveries. In this unit, you will read an African folktale that was discovered and written down by an African American. You'll follow a hometown detective as he sets out to solve a mystery. You'll share in the discovery of ancient treasures in Mexico. As you journey through this unit, you will feel the thrill of discovery shared by people all over the world.

THEMES

BOOKSHELF

BEAT THE STORY-DRUM, PUM-PUM

by Ashley Bryan

This collection of African folktales will make readers think and smile.

Coretta Scott King Award, ALA Notable Book, Parents' Choice

Harcourt Brace Library Book

JACE THE ACE

by Joanne Rocklin

Ten-year-old Jason Caputo, who prefers to be called "Jace the Ace, junior photojournalist," learns some valuable lessons as he solves the case of a "spy" named Sky.

Harcourt Brace Library Book

KNEE•KNOCK RISE

by Natalie Babbitt

Egan visits his relatives in the town of Instep and makes a discovery that the townspeople do not want to accept.

Newbery Honor, ALA Notable Book

FINDERS KEEPERS

by Emily Rodda

Patrick receives an invitation to participate in a television game show called "Finders Keepers." As a result, he finds himself in the midst of a very mysterious situation.

ANGRY RIVER

by Ruskin Bond

Sita and her grandparents live on an island in the middle of a river. As monsoon rains begin to fall, Grandmother becomes ill and has to be taken to the hospital. Alone on the island as the river rises, Sita faces the greatest challenge of her life.

T H E M E

Fun and Games

Do you remember a time when you were bored or just needed some company? The characters in the next three selections experience the same feeling. Then they discover new adventures and make new friends.

C O N T E N T S

"Now remember," Mother said, "your father and I are bringing some guests by after the opera, so please keep the house neat."

"Quite so," added Father, tucking his scarf inside his coat.

Mother peered into the hall mirror and carefully pinned her hat in place, then knelt and kissed both children good-bye.

When the front door closed, Judy and Peter giggled with delight. They took all the toys out of their toy chest and made a terrible mess. But their laughter slowly turned to silence till finally Peter slouched into a chair.

"You know what?" he said. "I'm really bored."

Written and Illustrated by
CHRIS VAN ALLSBURG

"Me too," sighed Judy. "Why don't we go outside and play?"

Peter agreed, so they set off across the street to the park. It was cold for November. The children could see their breath like steam. They rolled in the leaves and when Judy tried to stuff some leaves down Peter's sweater he jumped up and ran behind a tree. When his sister caught up with him, he was kneeling at the foot of the tree, looking at a long thin box.

"What's that?" Judy asked.

"It's a game," said Peter, handing her the box.

"'JUMANJI,'" Judy read from the box, "'A JUNGLE ADVENTURE GAME.'"

"Look," said Peter, pointing to a note taped to the bottom of the box. In a childlike handwriting were the words "Free game, fun for some but not for all. P.S. Read instructions carefully."

"Want to take it home?" Judy asked.

"Not really," said Peter. "I'm sure somebody left it here because it's so boring."

"Oh, come on," protested Judy. "Let's give it a try. Race you home!" And off she ran with Peter at her heels.

At home, the children spread the game out on a card table. It looked very much like the games they already had. There was a board that unfolded, revealing a path of colored squares. The squares had messages written on them. The path started in the deepest jungle and ended up in Jumanji, a city of golden buildings and towers. Peter began to shake the dice and play with the other pieces that were in the box.

"Put those down and listen," said Judy. "I'm going to read the instructions: 'Jumanji, a young people's jungle adventure especially designed for the bored and restless.

"'A. Player selects piece and places it in deepest jungle. B. Player rolls dice and moves piece along path through the dangers of the jungle. C. First player to reach Jumanji and yell the city's name aloud is the winner.'"

"Is that all?" asked Peter, sounding disappointed.

"No," said Judy, "there's one more thing, and this is in capital letters: 'D. VERY IMPORTANT: ONCE A GAME OF JUMANJI IS STARTED IT WILL NOT BE OVER UNTIL ONE PLAYER REACHES THE GOLDEN CITY.'"

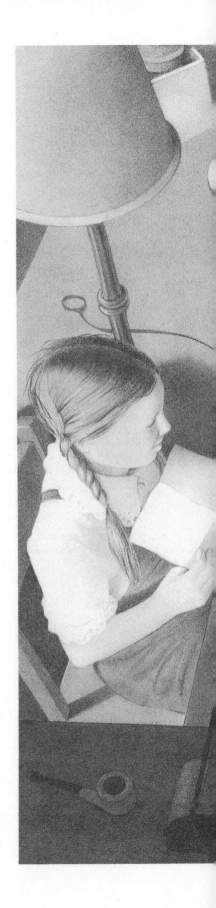

"Oh, big deal," said Peter, who gave a bored yawn.

"Here," said Judy, handing her brother the dice, "you go first."

Peter casually dropped the dice from his hand.

"Seven," said Judy.

Peter moved his piece to the seventh square.

"'Lion attacks, move back two spaces,'" read Judy.

"Gosh, how exciting," said Peter, in a very unexcited voice. As he reached for his piece he looked up at his sister. She had a look of absolute horror on her face.

"Peter," she whispered, "turn around very, very slowly."

The boy turned in his chair. He couldn't believe his eyes. Lying on the piano was a lion, staring at Peter and licking his lips.

The lion roared so loud it knocked Peter right off his chair. The big cat jumped to the floor. Peter was up on his feet, running through the house with the lion a whisker's length behind. He ran upstairs and dove under a bed. The lion tried to squeeze under, but got his head stuck. Peter scrambled out, ran from the bedroom, and slammed the door behind him. He stood in the hall with Judy, gasping for breath.

"I don't think," said Peter in between gasps of air, "that I want . . . to play . . . this game . . . anymore."

"But we have to," said Judy as she helped Peter back downstairs. "I'm sure that's what the instructions mean. That lion won't go away until one of us wins the game."

Peter stood next to the card table. "Can't we just call the zoo and have him taken away?" From upstairs came the sounds of growling and clawing at the bedroom door. "Or maybe we could wait till Father comes home."

"No one would come from the zoo because they wouldn't believe us," said Judy. "And you know how upset Mother would be if there was a lion in the bedroom. We started this game, and now we have to finish it."

Peter looked down at the game board. What if Judy rolled a seven? Then there'd be two lions. For an instant Peter thought he was going to cry. Then he sat firmly in his chair and said, "Let's play."

Judy picked up the dice, rolled an eight, and moved her piece. "'Monkeys steal food, miss one turn,'" she read. From the kitchen came the sounds of banging pots and falling jars. The children ran in to see a dozen monkeys tearing the room apart.

"Oh boy," said Peter, "this would upset Mother even more than the lion."

"Quick," said Judy, "back to the game."

Peter took his turn. Thank heavens, he landed on a blank space. He rolled again. "'Monsoon season begins, lose one turn.'" Little raindrops began to fall in the living room. Then a roll of thunder shook the walls and scared the monkeys out of the kitchen. The rain began to fall in buckets as Judy took the dice.

"'Guide gets lost, lose one turn.'" The rain suddenly stopped. The children turned to see a man hunched over a map.

"Oh dear, I say, spot of bad luck now," he mumbled. "Perhaps a left turn here then . . . No, no . . . a right turn here . . . Yes, absolutely, I think, a right turn . . . or maybe . . ."

"Excuse me," said Judy, but the guide just ignored her.

". . . around here, then over . . . No, no . . . over here and around this . . . Yes, good . . . but then . . . Hm . . ."

Judy shrugged her shoulders and handed the dice to Peter.

". . . four, five, six," he counted. "'Bitten by tsetse fly, contract sleeping sickness, lose one turn.'"

Judy heard a faint buzzing noise and watched a small insect land on Peter's nose. Peter lifted his hand to brush the bug away, but then stopped, gave a tremendous yawn, and fell sound asleep, his head on the table.

"Peter, Peter, wake up!" cried Judy. But it was no use. She grabbed the dice and moved to a blank. She rolled again and waited in amazement. "'Rhinoceros stampede, go back two spaces.'"

As fast as he had fallen asleep, Peter awoke. Together they listened to a rumble in the hallway. It grew louder and louder. Suddenly a herd of rhinos charged through the living room and into the dining room, crushing all the furniture in their path. Peter and Judy covered their ears as sounds of splintering wood and breaking china filled the house.

Peter gave the dice a quick tumble. "'Python sneaks into camp, go back one space.'"

Judy shrieked and jumped up on her chair.

"Over the fireplace," said Peter. Judy sat down again, nervously eyeing the eight-foot snake that was wrapping itself around the mantel clock. The guide looked up from his map, took one look at the snake, and moved to the far corner of the room, joining the monkeys on the couch.

Judy took her turn and landed on a blank space. Her brother took the dice and rolled a three.

"Oh, no," he moaned. "'Volcano erupts, go back three spaces.'" The room became warm and started to shake a little. Molten lava poured from the fireplace opening. It hit the water on the floor and the room filled with steam. Judy rolled the dice and moved ahead.

"'Discover shortcut, roll again.' Oh dear!" she cried. Judy saw the snake unwrapping itself from the clock.

"If you roll a twelve you can get out of the jungle," said Peter.

"Please, please," Judy begged as she shook the dice. The snake was wriggling its way to the floor. She dropped the dice from her hand. One six, then another. Judy grabbed her piece and slammed it to the board. "JUMANJI," she yelled, as loud as she could.

The steam in the room became thicker and thicker. Judy could not even see Peter across the table. Then, as if all the doors and windows had been opened, a cool breeze cleared the steam from the room. Everything was just as it had been before the game. No monkeys, no guide, no water, no broken furniture, no snake, no lion roaring upstairs, no rhinos. Without saying a word to each other, Peter and Judy threw the game into its box. They bolted out the door, ran across the street to the park, and dropped the game under a tree. Back home, they quickly put all their toys away. But both children were too excited to sit quietly, so Peter took out a picture puzzle. As they fit the pieces together, their excitement slowly turned to relief, and then exhaustion. With the puzzle half done Peter and Judy fell sound asleep on the sofa.

"Wake up, dears," Mother's voice called.

Judy opened her eyes. Mother and Father had returned and their guests were arriving. Judy gave Peter a nudge to wake him. Yawning and stretching, they got to their feet.

Mother introduced them to some of the guests, then asked, "Did you have an exciting afternoon?"

"Oh yes," said Peter. "We had a flood, a stampede, a volcano, I got sleeping sickness, and—" Peter was interrupted by the adults' laughter.

"Well," said Mother, "I think you both got sleeping sickness. Why don't you go upstairs and put your pajamas on? Then you can finish your puzzle and have some dinner."

When Peter and Judy came back downstairs they found that Father had moved the puzzle into the den. While the children were working on it, one of the guests, Mrs. Budwing, brought them a tray of food.

"Such a hard puzzle," she said to the children. "Daniel and Walter are always starting puzzles and never finishing them." Daniel and Walter were Mrs. Budwing's sons. "They never read instructions either. Oh well," said Mrs. Budwing, turning to rejoin the guests, "I guess they'll learn."

Both children answered, "I hope so," but they weren't looking at Mrs. Budwing. They were looking out the window. Two boys were running through the park. It was Danny and Walter Budwing, and Danny had a long thin box under his arm.

Peter didn't want to take the Jumanji game home from the park. What would you have done? Why?

Why was winning Jumanji so important?

Peter and Judy had different feelings at different points in the story. What were some of the feelings they had?

WRITE The message on the Jumanji game box read, "Fun for some but not for all." Write a message for the next person who finds the game, telling what you think of it.

AN INTERVIEW WITH THE AUTHOR AND ILLUSTRATOR:

Chris Van Allsburg

Chris Van Allsburg is both an author and an illustrator. He has written and illustrated many books about strange happenings. Read what he told writer Ilene Cooper about how his mind works when he writes and draws.

MS. COOPER: Where did you get the idea for *Jumanji*?

MR. VAN ALLSBURG: I see images in my mind's eye. Usually they're images of things that are unexplainable. With *Jumanji*, it wasn't a jungle scene, but more the idea of something not being where it's supposed to be.

MS. COOPER: Like a lion on top of the piano?

MR. VAN ALLSBURG: Yes, but first I saw the idea of a house, which we like to think of as a safe place, being overrun by beasts of some sort.

MS. COOPER: What about the board game?

MR. VAN ALLSBURG:
One thing about board games is that they require your imagination to make them fun. When you play some board games, even when you win, you're not rich, so the excitement of the game really comes from inside your head. So with *Jumanji*, I thought of this game that wouldn't require an imagination. Those animals really are there. In the game, the object is to get to the Golden City, but what the kids understand at the end is that the real payoff is to get your world back to where it was.

MS. COOPER: Did you think about being a writer when you were young?

MR. VAN ALLSBURG: No, I never thought about writing for anyone, adults or children. Even now, when I know the challenges and the opportunities of being a writer, I still am a writer who is motivated by the images that I see in my mind.

Why Frog and Snake Never Play Together

written and illustrated by
Ashley Bryan

Beat the
Story-Drum,
Pum-Pum

by ASHLEY BRYAN

ALA NOTABLE
BOOK
CORETTA SCOTT
KING AWARD

MAMA FROG had a son. Mama Snake also had a son. One morning both children went out to play.

Mama Snake called after her child:

"Watch out for big things with sharp claws and teeth that gnaw. Don't lose your way in the bush, baby, and be back to the burrow before dark."

"Clawsangnaws," sang Snake as he went looping through the grass. "Beware of the Clawsangnaws."

Mama Frog called after her son:

"Watch out for things that peck or bite. Don't go into the bush alone, dear. Don't fight, and get home before night."

"Peckorbite," sang Frog as he went hopping from stone to stone. "Beware of the Peckorbite!"

Snake was singing his Clawsangnaws song, and Frog was singing of Peckorbites when they met along the way. They had never met before.

"Who are you?" asked Frog. "Are you a Peckorbite?" and he prepared to spring out of reach.

"Oh no! I'm Snake, called by my Mama 'Snakeson': I'm slick, lithe and slithery. Who are you? Are you a Clawsangnaws?" and he got ready to move, just in case.

"No no! I'm Frog, called by my Mama 'Frogchild.' I'm hip, quick and hoppy."

They stood and stared at each other, and then they said together:

"You don't look anything like me."

Their eyes brightened. They did not look alike, that's true, but some of their customs were alike. Both knew what to do when two say the same thing at the same time.

They clasped each other, closed their eyes and sang:

"You wish a wish
I'll wish a wish, too;
May your wish and my wish
Both come true."

Each made a wish then let go.

Just then a fly flew by, right past Frog's eyes. Flip! out went his tongue as he flicked in the fly.

A bug whizzed past Snake's nose. Flash! Snake flicked out his tongue and caught the bug.

They looked in admiration at each other and smiled. The two new friends now knew something of what each other could do. They felt at ease with each other, like old friends.

"Let's play!" said Frog.

"Hey!" said Snake, "that was my wish. Let's play in the bush."

"The bush! In the bush!" cried Frog. "That was my wish. If you go with me, it's all right 'cause Mama said I shouldn't go alone."

Frog and Snake raced to the bush and started playing games.

"Watch this," said Frog. He crouched down and counted. "One a fly, two a fly, three a fly, four!"

He popped way up into the air, somersaulted and came down, whop!

"Can you do that, Snake?"

Snake bounded for a nearby mound to try the Frog-Hop. He got to the top of the slope, stood on the tip of his tail and tossed himself into the air. Down he came, flop! a tangle of coils. He laughed and tried again.

Sometimes Snake and Frog jumped together and bumped in midair. No matter how hard they hit, it didn't hurt. They had fun.

Then Snake said, "Watch this!" He stretched out at the top of the mound and counted, "One a bug, two a bug, three a bug, four!" Then swoosh! he slithered down the slope on his stomach.

"Try that, Frog. It's called the Snake-Slither."

Frog lay on his stomach and slipped down the hill. His arms and legs flailed about as he slithered. He turned over at the bottom of the slope, *blump!* and rolled up in a lump.

Frog and Snake slithered down together, entangling as they went. Their calls and laughter could be heard all over the bush. One game led to another. They were having such a good time that the day passed swiftly. By late afternoon there were not two better friends in all the bush.

The sun was going down when Snake remembered his promise to his mother.

"I promised to be home before dark," he said.

"Me too," said Frog. "Good-bye!"

They hugged. Snake was so happy that he'd found a real friend that he forgot himself and squeezed Frog very tightly. It felt good, very, very good.

"Ow! easy!" said Frog. "Not too tight."

"Oh, sorry," said Snake loosening his hug-hold. " My! but you sure feel good, good enough to eat."

At that they burst out laughing and hugged again, lightly this time.

"I like you," said Frog. "Bye, Snake."

"Bye, Frog. You're my best friend."

"Let's play again tomorrow," they said together.

Aha! they clasped and sang once again:

"You wish a wish
I'll wish a wish, too;
May your wish and my wish
Both come true."

Off they went, Snake hopping and Frog slithering all the way home.

When Frog reached home, he knocked his knock, and Mama Frog unlocked the rock door. She was startled to see her child come slithering in across the floor.

"Now what is this, eh?" she said. "Look at you, all covered with grass and dirt."

"It doesn't hurt," said Frog. "I had fun."

"Fun? Now what is this, eh? I can tell you haven't been playing in ponds or bogs with the good frogs. Where have you been all day? You look as if you've just come out of the bush."

"But I didn't go alone, Ma. I went with a good boy. He's my best friend."

"Best friend? Now what is this, eh?" said Mama Frog. "What good boy could that be, playing in the bush?"

"Look at this trick that he taught me, Ma," said Frogchild. He flopped on his stomach and wriggled across the floor, bungling up Mama Frog's neatly stitched lily-pad rug.

"That's no trick for a frog! Get up from there, child!" cried Mama Frog. "Now what is this, eh? Look how you've balled up my rug. Just you tell me, who was this playmate?"

"His name is Snakeson, Mama."

"Snake, son! Did you say Snake, son?"

"Yes. What's the matter, Mama?"

Mama Frog trembled and turned a pale green. She sat down to keep from fainting. When she had recovered herself, she said:

"Listen, Frogchild, listen carefully to what I have to say." She pulled her son close. "Snake comes from the Snake family. They are bad people. Keep away from them. You hear me, child?"

"Bad people?" asked Frog.

"Bad, too bad!" said Mama Frog. "Snakes are sneaks. They hide poison in their tongues, and they crush you in their coils."

Frogchild gulped.

"You be sure to hop out of Snake's reach if ever you meet again. And stop this slithering foolishness. Slithering's not for frogs."

Mama Frog set the table muttering to herself: "Playing with Snake! Now what is this, eh?" She rolled a steaming ball of gleaming cornmeal onto Frogchild's plate.

"Sit down and eat your funji, child," said Mama Frog.

"And remember, I'm not fattening frogs for snakes, eh?"

Snake too reached home. He rustled the braided twig hatch-cover to his home. His mother knew his rustle and undid the vine latch. Snake toppled in.

"I'm hungry, Ma," he said, hopping all about.

"Eh, eh! Do good bless you! What a sight you are!" said Mama Snake. "Just look at you. And listen to your panting and wheezing. Where have you been all day?"

"In the bush, Mama, with my new friend. We played games. See what he taught me."

Snakeson jumped up on top of the table and leaped into the air. He came down on a stool, knocking it over and entangling himself in its legs.

"Eh, eh! Do good bless you. What a dangerous game that is," said Mama Snake. "Keep it up and see if you don't break every bone in your back. What new friend taught you that?"

She bent over and untangled her son from the stool.

"My frog friend taught me that. His name's Frogchild. It's the Frog-Hop, Mama. Try it. It's fun."

"Frog, child?" Mama Snake's jaws hung open showing her fangs. "Did you say Frog, child?"

"Yes," said Snakeson. "He's my best friend."

"You mean you played all day with a frog and you come home hungry?"

"He was hungry too, Mama, after playing the Snake-Slither game that I taught him."

"Eh, eh! Well do good bless you! Come, curl up here, son, and listen carefully to what I have to tell you."

Snakeson curled up on the stool.

"Don't you know, son, that it is the custom of our house to eat frogs? Frogs are delicious people!"

Snakeson's small eyes widened.

"Ah, for true!" said Mama Snake. "Eating frogs is the custom of our house, a tradition in our family. Hopping isn't, so cut it out, you hear me?"

"Oh, Mama," cried Snakeson. "I can't eat frogs. Frog's a friend."

"Frog a friend! Do good bless you!" said Mama Snake.

"That's not natural. Now you listen to me, baby. The next time you play with Frog, jump, roll and romp all you like. But when you get hungry, his game is up. Catch him and eat him!"

The next morning Snakeson was up early. He pushed off his dry-leaf cover and stretched himself. He remembered his mother's words, and the delicious feel of his frog friend when they had hugged. He was ready to go.

Mama Snake fixed her son a light breakfast of spiced insects and goldfinch eggs. Snakeson was soon on his way.

"Now don't you forget my instructions about frogs, do good bless you," Mama Snake called out after him. "And don't let me have to tell you again to watch out for big things with sharp claws and teeth that gnaw."

"Clawsangnaw," sang Snakeson. "Clawsangnaw."

He reached the bush and waited for his friend. He looked forward to fun with Frog, and he looked forward to finishing the fun with a feast of his fine frog friend. He lolled about in the sun, laughing and singing:

"You wish a wish
I'll wish a wish, too;
Can your wish and my wish
Both come true?"

The sun rose higher and higher, but Frog did not come.

"What's taking Frogchild so long?" said Snakeson. "Perhaps too much slithering has given him the bellyache. I'll go and look for him."

Snake found Frog's rock home by the pond. He rolled up a stone in his tail and knocked on the rock door.

"Anybody home?"

"Just me," answered Frogchild.

"May I come in?"

"Ah, it's you Snakeson. Sorry, my Mama's out, and she said not to open the door to anyone."

"Come on out then and let's play," said Snakeson. "I waited all morning for you in the bush."

"I can't," said Frog, "Not now, anyway."

"Oh, that's too bad," said Snake. "My mother taught me a new game. I'd love to teach it to you."

"I'll bet you would," said Frog.

"You don't know what you're missing," said Snake.

"But I do know what you're missing," said Frog, and he burst out laughing.

"Aha!" said Snake. "I see that your mother has given you instructions. My mother has given me instructions too."

Snake sighed. There was nothing more to say or do, so he slithered away.

Frog and Snake never forgot that day when they played together as friends. Neither ever again had that much fun with anybody.

Today you will see them, quiet and alone in the sun, still as stone. They are deep in thought remembering that day of games in the bush, and both of them wonder:

"What if we had just kept on playing together, and no one had ever said anything?"

But from that day to this, Frog and Snake have never played together again.

You wish a wish
I'll wish a wish, too;
May your wish and my wish
Both come true.

What do you think the author's message is about friendship? Do you agree with the message? Why or why not?

What might have happened if Frog and Snake had tried to keep their friendship a secret?

WRITE　Frog and Snake admired each other's insect-catching ability. Think of one of your friends. Write sentences that tell about some talents and abilities you admire in that friend.

Words About the Author and Illustrator:

Ashley Bryan

Ashley Bryan grew up in a tough neighborhood, but he didn't want to spend time fighting. Instead, he spent time drawing. Ashley Bryan knew since he was in kindergarten what he wanted to be. When a teacher showed his class how a book gets made, Ashley wrote, illustrated, edited, published, and bound his own alphabet book. Throughout his life, Ashley's family supported his desire to be an artist.

When Ashley Bryan was an adult, he discovered that the stories he most liked to write and illustrate were stories from Africa and the West Indies, the lands of his ancestors. Ashley Bryan hears the stories in his head before he writes, and he likes to play with the sounds. He is famous for his story-telling and poetry readings, which he enjoys performing in front of audiences.

AWARD-WINNING AUTHOR AND ILLUSTRATOR

CLOSE ENCOUNTER
OF A WEIRD KIND

by A. F. Bauman • illustrated by David Groff
from *Space and Science Fiction Plays for Young People*

Characters:
MR. WILSON
MRS. WILSON
THERESA WILSON }
TOM WILSON } twins, 12
JIM WILSON, 9
THREE LETONIANS,
creatures from the planet Leto

TIME: *Evening, the present.*
SETTING: *Living room of the Wilson home. Exit to bedrooms is left; door to outside is center back, with windows on either side; exit to kitchen is right. A coffee table is in middle of room, with couch and chairs arranged around it. A Monopoly game is set up on coffee table. Magazines and an evening bag are on couch.*
AT RISE: TOM, THERESA, *and* **JIM** *are sitting around coffee table, playing Monopoly.*

JIM (*Moving his piece on Monopoly board*): One, two, three! Hooray! I landed on Boardwalk. I'll buy it.

TOM: Sorry, Jim, you can't. You spent most of your money the last time around buying your third railroad.

THERESA: Yes, Jim. You've got to be careful how you use your money in Monopoly.

JIM: Stop telling me how to spend my money, Theresa! (MR. *and* MRS. WILSON *enter right.*)

MRS. WILSON (*To* JIM *and* THERESA): Did I hear you two fighting again? I thought you all said you'd be good tonight.

TOM: We will, Mom. Don't worry.

MRS. WILSON: All right. I guess I'm a little uneasy about leaving you children here alone.

TOM (*Reassuringly*): Sure, Mom. We understand. But we really are old enough to take care of ourselves.

MR. WILSON (*To* MRS. WILSON): Yes, dear. Tom and Theresa can handle things much better than that last babysitter we had.

JIM: All she did was yell at me. She wouldn't let me play games or watch TV or anything. We just had to be quiet all evening while she talked to her boyfriend on the phone.

MR. WILSON (*Sternly, to* JIM): That's enough, Jim.

THERESA: We'll keep all the lights on, Mom, and all the doors and windows locked. Don't worry.

TOM: And we've got the fire department and police phone numbers right here. (*TOM holds up a small piece of paper.*) And the number of the place where you'll be.

THERESA: Besides, you'll only be gone two or three hours.

MRS. WILSON (*To* THERESA): All right. But, Theresa, just one more thing—don't you tell Jim any ghost stories. You know what an imagination he has. Those stories of yours give him bad dreams for a week.

THERESA: O.K., Mom, I promise. Go ahead and have a good time.

TOM: Everything's cool. Enjoy yourselves.

MR. WILSON (*To* MRS. WILSON): Come on, dear, we'll be late. (*He picks up evening bag from couch and hands it to her.*)

MRS. WILSON (*To* MR. WILSON): I wouldn't be so worried if we lived in town. Out here the nearest house is two miles away.

MR. WILSON: Everything will be fine, honey. Come on, it's late. Let's go. (*They exit center.* TOM, THERESA, *and* JIM *go to window left, wave, then return to the Monopoly game.*)

TOM: I think it was my turn. (*They ad lib playing game.*)

THERESA: Jim, isn't it about time you put your cat outside?

JIM: I almost forgot. Reginald's in the kitchen. I'll go let him out the back door. (JIM *exits.*)

TOM: Whose turn is it now?

THERESA: Jim's. We'll have to wait for him. (JIM *returns and sits.*)

TOM: It's your turn, Jim. Throw the dice. (*Suddenly, sound of a loud "boom" is heard, followed by a bright flash of light, seen through windows. Then a blinking light is seen through right window.* TOM, JIM, *and* THERESA *jump up, startled.*) What could that be?

JIM: Maybe it's a thunderstorm!

THERESA: No, Jim, the moon is bright, and the stars are out.

TOM: It's not a fire. That light keeps going on and off.

JIM (*Excitedly*): I don't smell any smoke.

TOM (*Trying to be calm*): It can't be burglars. They would sneak in quietly.

THERESA: It's O.K. We're safe. All the doors are locked.

JIM (*Sheepishly*): They *were* locked. But remember when I put out the cat?

THERESA: You left the back door unlocked! Oh, no!

TOM: But nobody is coming in, yet. (*Bravely*) I'm going over to the window to see what's making that light. (TOM *walks to window right and peers out.*) Look at that! A huge round thing as big as a fifty-foot-wide saucer.

THERESA: What? Let me see. (*She walks to window.* JIM *follows close behind.*) It does look like a saucer. And it's got a big flashing light on top!

JIM (*Looking out window*): Look—something's opening up on the bottom—it's a set of stairs unfolding down to the ground!

THERESA (*Watching*): And three weird creatures are climbing down!

TOM (*Trying to remain calm*): Well, gang, I guess we've got a UFO right in our own back yard.

THERESA: Those creatures are walking over to our back door! (TOM, JIM, *and* THERESA *run left, huddling close to one another. Sound of footsteps is heard from offstage.*)

JIM: They must be inside the house! What are we going to do?

TOM: There's nothing we can do. Just try to stop shaking and be cool. (THREE LETONIANS *enter right, walking stiffly, wearing silvery costumes and green leotards. They lift their visors, revealing green faces.* TOM, JIM, *and* THERESA *jump back, frightened.* LETONIANS *speak in robot-like monotones.*)

1ST LETONIAN: Do not be afraid.

2ND LETONIAN: We will not harm you.

TOM (*Trying to be calm*): Who are you?

3RD LETONIAN: We are from the planet Leto.

THERESA (*Scared*): What do you want?

1ST LETONIAN: We are on a special mission. We have been sent to bring something back from the earth to our planet.

2ND LETONIAN: You earthlings have what we need.

1ST LETONIAN: On earth, you have something that will keep cold things cold for a long time. The same device will keep hot things hot for a long time.

2ND LETONIAN: This is a strange but useful item. We do not know how it can tell whether to keep things cold or hot.

3RD LETONIAN: This is our assignment: To bring this invention back to Leto.

1ST LETONIAN: Can you help us?

JIM (*Helpfully*): I know what you need! I'll go get it! (JIM *runs, exits right.*)

THERESA: I wonder what he's going after?

TOM: I sure don't know. With his imagination, he can think up just about anything. (JIM *returns, carrying a bowl of ice. He hands it to* 2ND LETONIAN.)

JIM: Here's what you need!

2ND LETONIAN (*Looking in bowl*): We have ice on Leto. Thank you, but this is not what we need.

THERESA: Besides, Jim, ice certainly won't keep hot things hot.

JIM: Oh, now I know! Wait a second; I know just where it is! (JIM *exits right and quickly returns with an immersion heater.*) Mom uses this to heat up her coffee. (*Excited,* 1ST LETONIAN *takes off gloves, revealing green hands. He tries to stuff gloves into pocket, but one falls to floor and remains there, unnoticed.* 1ST LETONIAN *takes immersion heater from* JIM *and examines it.*)

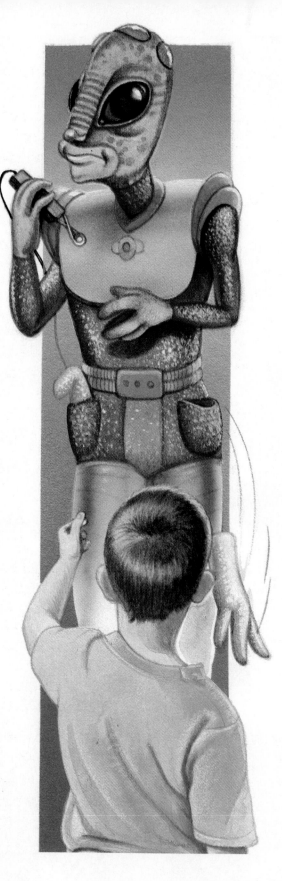

2ND LETONIAN (*To* JIM): Will it keep hot things hot?

JIM: Sure. Mom can keep the coffee in her mug hot all day with that thing.

3RD LETONIAN (*To* JIM): And will it keep things cold?

JIM: No, it won't.

1ST LETONIAN: This is not what we want.

2ND LETONIAN: Our commander will be disappointed if we return from our trip without this invention.

3RD LETONIAN: We are told that it does not cost a lot of—of—of—what is it called?

THERESA: Money?

3RD LETONIAN: Yes, it does not cost a lot of money.

2ND LETONIAN: Our commander told us that almost every household in America has one.

TOM (*Wondering*): What could it be?

THERESA (*Thinking*): Beats me. Let's see—it keeps cold things cold for a long time.

1ST LETONIAN: And hot things hot for a long time.

TOM: And it doesn't cost a lot and most Americans have it in their homes.

JIM: At lunchtime, I always have a cold drink.

THERESA: And I always have a hot drink with my lunch.

TOM (*Triumphantly*): Hey, we've got what you need, Letonians! Wait right here. (TOM *runs offstage to kitchen carrying immersion heater, and comes back quickly with a thermos bottle.*) Here it is!

375

THERESA (*Excited*): Of course! A thermos! Nice going, Tom! Why didn't we think of that before?

JIM (*Also excited*): Yes, the same thing keeps hot things hot and cold things cold!

1ST LETONIAN (*Puzzled*): What is this great invention?

TOM: We call it a thermos bottle. (*Shows thermos to* THREE LETONIANS) Here, let me show you how it works. You take the lid off, like this, see? Then you put in whatever you want to stay hot or cold.

THERESA: Then you make sure the lid is on tight. (*She takes thermos and lid from* TOM *and screws lid on thermos.*)

1ST LETONIAN: Will it keep cold things cold for a long time?

JIM (*Proudly*): Sure it will! My mom puts ice cubes in it in the morning when she fixes my cold drink. By lunchtime at school, the ice isn't even melted and my drink is icy cold.

2ND LETONIAN: Does this same invention keep hot things hot for a long time?

THERESA: Easily! Every morning Mom makes hot chocolate and puts it in my thermos. When I open it hours later for lunch, the hot chocolate is steaming.

3RD LETONIAN: How does it know which is which, to keep hot or cold?

TOM: Gosh, I sure don't know. But it works.

THERESA: And it's really easy to use!

JIM (*Proudly*): That thermos bottle is the one from *my* lunchbox. You can have it if you like. (THERESA *gives thermos to* 1ST LETONIAN.)

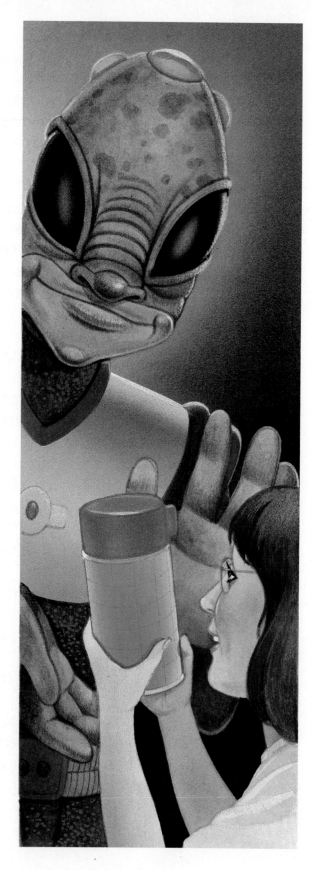

1ST LETONIAN (*Taking thermos carefully*):
Thank you. Our special mission is
completed. Now we can return to Leto.

2ND LETONIAN (*Slowly*): A thermos bottle.
A thermos bottle. A thermos bottle. (3RD
LETONIAN *hits him gently on the back.*)

3RD LETONIAN: Thank you, earthlings, for
sharing this great invention with us.

2ND LETONIAN: Our commander will be
satisfied with this thermos bottle, thermos
bottle, thermos bottle. (1ST LETONIAN *hits*
2ND LETONIAN *on the back.*)

1ST LETONIAN: We do not need to write
down the name of this invention. My co-
captain (*Pointing to* 2ND LETONIAN)
knows the name well.

3RD LETONIAN: We are very grateful for
your help.

1ST LETONIAN: We must return to our
planet now. Let us get back to our space
vehicle.

JIM: O.K. I'll lock the door after you.
(LETONIANS *and* JIM *walk offstage right.*
THERESA *and* TOM *walk to window right,
look out.*)

TOM: Look, Theresa. They're walking over
to their spacecraft.

THERESA: And there they go up the
steps. I can't see them any more.

TOM: The steps are folding back up into
the spacecraft. (*There is another loud
boom and flash of bright light. Flicker of
light is seen, then fades and goes off.*)

JIM (*Walking quickly onstage from right*):
Wow! What weird visitors!

THERESA: Boy, was I ever scared when
they walked into the house.

TOM: Me, too. Maybe they were just as scared of us. But you could never tell by the way they talked.

JIM (*Imitating* LETONIANS): Yes, we are scared of you, too, but we have a special mission.

THERESA: Wasn't that something? All they wanted was a thermos bottle.

JIM: Some special mission! I really liked the way they looked.

TOM: Just like space creatures in the movies. (MR. *and* MRS. WILSON *open center door and enter.*)

MR. WILSON (*Taking* MRS. WILSON's *coat*): How did it go, kids? Everything O.K.?

JIM (*Running up to* MR. *and* MRS. WILSON): Mom! Dad! A flying saucer landed in our back yard!

MRS. WILSON (*Humoring* JIM): Really, Jim?

JIM: Yes, Mom. Three space people from the planet Leto came inside our house!

MRS. WILSON (*Still humoring* JIM): My, what an adventure! Jimmy, you've got a big imagination. (TOM *sits and shakes his head.*)

THERESA: But he's right, Mother. They're called Letonians and they came here on a special mission. They talked funny and had green skin and silver suits and gloves and helmets!

MRS. WILSON: Now, Theresa, were you telling Jimmy scary stories again?

THERESA (*Exasperated*): No, Mother. It really happened.

MRS. WILSON: Theresa, you should write books. You're so good at thinking up stories that now even you are beginning to believe them. Anyway, I'm glad you had a nice evening.

MR. WILSON (*Looking around room*): It looks as if playing Monopoly is about all you did while we were gone. Everything's all right. The doors and windows are still locked. (*To* MRS. WILSON) See, honey, I told you nothing would happen.

JIM (*Exasperated*): But it did! It really happened! Honest! The Letonians were here, right in our own living room.

MRS. WILSON: Yes, dear. Now you three put away your game and get ready for bed. (*To* MR. WILSON) Let's go and get some coffee, dear. (MR. *and* MRS. WILSON *exit*.)

JIM (*Exasperated*): But, Theresa, why won't they believe us? (TOM *and* THERESA *start putting the Monopoly game away*.)

THERESA: It's hard to convince them it really happened. The whole thing sounds so unbelievable I almost think I imagined it myself.

TOM: Mom and Dad would never in a million years believe our story about those Letonians. Let's just keep it a secret for ourselves.

JIM: Just wait till Mom tries to find my thermos!

THERESA: Come on, let's go to bed. (*They exit left.* MR. *and* MRS. WILSON *enter right, holding coffee mugs*.)

MR. WILSON: That story about the spaceship is ridiculous!

MRS. WILSON: Flying saucer, indeed! Theresa always did have a vivid imagination. (*Pause*) I wonder what my immersion heater was doing out on the counter? (MRS. WILSON *sets down her mug and begins straightening pillows on the couch*.)

MR. WILSON (*Sitting left*): You probably forgot to put it away in your rush getting ready to go out.

MRS. WILSON (*Straightening magazines on coffee table*): But I wasn't in any rush. I had everything put away when we left.

MR. WILSON: O.K., dear, O.K. (*He drinks coffee.* MRS. WILSON *walks toward the chair on right where* 1ST LETONIAN *dropped his glove. With a quizzical look, she goes over and picks it up, holding it up for* MR. WILSON *to see.*)

MRS. WILSON: But where did this silver glove come from? I've never seen anything like it before! (*Musing*) I wonder if the children were telling the truth, after all? (*Quick curtain*)

THE END

How would you feel about meeting some creatures like the Letonians? Tell why you feel as you do.

What does the title of this play mean?

Do you think Mr. and Mrs. Wilson believe that the Letonians really visited their home? Explain your answer.

WRITE Suppose you were going to travel to another planet. Write a list of useful items you would take along, and tell why you would take each thing.

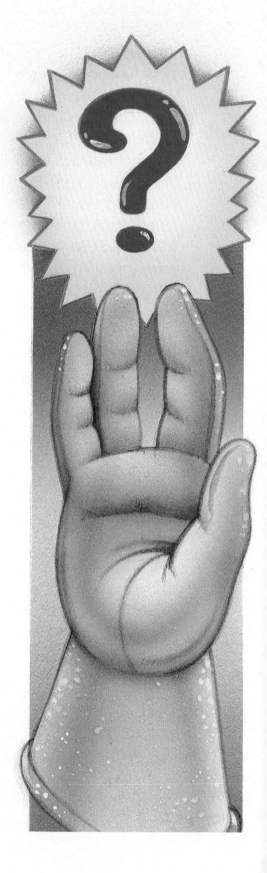

Fun and Games

Which adventure in this theme would you most like to share? Explain why you feel as you do.

WRITER'S WORKSHOP

What board games do you like to play? List some of your favorite board games, and then list some words and phrases that tell why you enjoy them. Use the lists to write a poem about the games you enjoy. Share your poem with some classmates.

Writer's Choice Which of the stories in this theme did you enjoy the most? Choose a way to share your feelings. Then plan how to share your work with some classmates.

THEME

Solve It!

Donald J. Sobol writes about brilliant detectives who are challenged by mysterious crimes. Read the following cases and the author interview to see how the characters solve the puzzling crimes that Mr. Sobol creates.

CONTENTS

Words About the Author:
Donald J. Sobol

"I didn't become a serious reader until I went to college and decided I wanted to be a writer and I had better develop a pleasure in reading all kinds, not just for information, which is the kind of reading I'd mainly been doing."

Donald J. Sobol

Since he began writing, Donald Sobol has won many awards for his mysteries. He began by writing a newspaper column called "Two-Minute Mysteries." But Mr. Sobol is perhaps best known for his Encyclopedia Brown detective stories. It has been thirty years since the first story about the crime-solving boy detective was published. The next two selections were written by Donald Sobol. See if you can match wits with Dr. Haledjian and Encyclopedia Brown to solve the cases.

THE CASE OF THE LOCKED ROOM

from *Two-Minute Mysteries*

by Donald J. Sobol

"I think I've been taken for ten thousand dollars, but I can't figure out how it was done," said Archer Skeat, the blind violinist, to Dr. Haledjian, as the two friends sat in the musician's library.

"Last night Marty Scopes dropped by," continued Skeat. "Marty had a ginger ale—and we got to chatting about the locked room mysteries till I made this crazy ten-thousand-dollar bet.

"Marty then went to the bar over there, filled a glass with six cubes of ice and gave it to me. He took a bottle of ginger ale and left the room.

"I locked the door and the windows from the inside, felt to make sure that Marty's glass held only ice, and put it into the wall safe behind you. Then I turned off the lights and sat down to wait.

"The bet was that within an hour Marty could enter the dark, locked room, open the locked safe, take out the glass, remove the ice, pour in half a glass of ginger ale, lock the safe, and leave the room, locking it behind him—all without my hearing him!

---

illustrated by Steven Meyers

"When the alarm rang after an hour, I had heard nothing. Confidently, I unlocked the door. I kept Marty whistling in the hall when I crossed the room to the opposite wall and opened the safe. The glass was inside. By heavens, it was half filled with ginger ale and only ginger ale. I tasted it! How did he do it?"

"Undoubtedly by means of an insulated bag," replied Haledjian after a moment's thought. "There is nothing wrong with your hearing. But no man could have heard—"

Heard what?

Ice melting. Marty had brought with him frozen cubes of ginger ale. After setting up the bet, he had slipped the ginger ale cubes into the glass. While they melted in the glass inside the safe, Marty waited in the hall!

Do you think the bet is a fair one? Tell why you think as you do.

Describe the mystery that Archer Skeat is trying to solve.

WRITE Write a clue that would have helped Archer Skeat solve the mystery.

THE CASE OF THE MILLION PESOS

from *Encyclopedia Brown Gets His Man*

by Donald J. Sobol

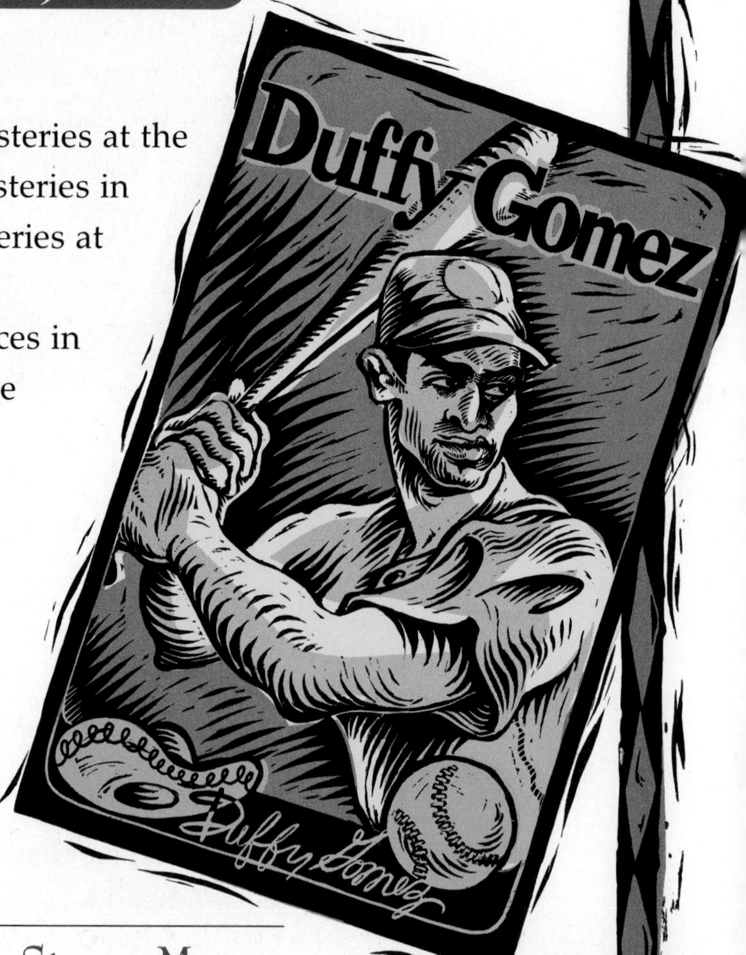

Encyclopedia solved mysteries at the dinner table. He solved mysteries in the garage. He solved mysteries at the scene of the crime.

There were no other places in Idaville, he thought, to solve mysteries.

He was wrong.

There was second base.

While sitting on second base, he solved a robbery that had taken place in a country a thousand miles away.

Duffy Gomez

illustrated by Steven Meyers

Encyclopedia got his start as an international detective during an evening baseball game. His grounder slipped through Benny Breslin at short-stop. Encyclopedia wound up with a double.

Tim Gomez, the next batter, ended the inning by striking out. The game was immediately called on account of darkness. The score was 12 to 3.

Encyclopedia sat down on second base, discouraged. Benny Breslin flopped upon the grass beside him.

"We were going good," said Encyclopedia. "All we needed were nine runs to tie."

"I'm glad they stopped it," said Benny, a home-run hitter. "I've raced around the bases five times. My legs are falling off."

Sally walked over from first base. She looked troubled.

"What's bothering Tim Gomez?" she asked Encyclopedia. "He struck out six times in a row. Something is on his mind."

"Baseballs," said Benny. "He fielded every fly with the top of his head. He didn't catch one all game."

"Be quiet," whispered Encyclopedia, for Tim was passing near them.

"Sorry," Tim apologized. "I played like a cow on crutches."

"Forget it," said Encyclopedia.

"Aren't you feeling well?" asked Sally.

"I'm worried about my uncle, Duffy Gomez," said Tim. "He's in jail in Mexico City."

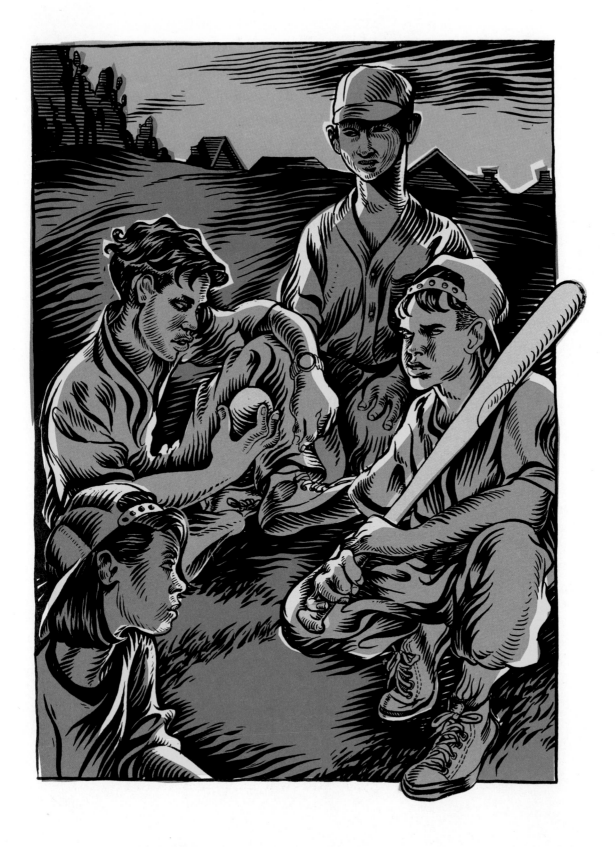

Duffy Gomez, Mexico's greatest baseball player, in jail! Encyclopedia, Sally, and Benny were stunned by the news.

"What did he do?" asked Benny.

"The police say he robbed a bank," answered Tim. "But I don't believe it!"

"What does your uncle say?" asked Encyclopedia.

"He says he's innocent," replied Tim. "The police threw him in jail just the same. He's being framed!"

"By whom?" asked Sally.

"By a man named Pedro Morales. He's hated my uncle for years," said Tim. "Pedro was in love with my Aunt Molly. She turned him down to marry Uncle Duffy."

"So Pedro accused your uncle of robbing a bank," said Sally. "What a low way to get back!"

"Doesn't your uncle have an alibi?" asked Encyclopedia. "Can't he prove he was somewhere else when the bank was robbed?"

"He was at a movie. Nobody saw him, though," said Tim. "Uncle Duffy wears a fake beard when he goes out in public. If he didn't disguise himself, baseball fans would mob him."

"Being at a movie is a pretty weak alibi," said Encyclopedia regretfully. "Your uncle will have a hard time making a judge and jury believe him."

"The real robber is bound to be caught," said Sally. "Don't you worry, Tim."

"There isn't much time left," said Tim. "Uncle Duffy goes on trial next week. Pedro will testify against him."

Sally glanced at Encyclopedia for help.

"Don't ask me," mumbled Encyclopedia.

"You *can't* say no," urged Sally. "Give it a try, Encyclopedia!"

"I can tell you everything about the case," said Tim eagerly. "I've read the newspaper stories my uncle sent from Mexico."

Encyclopedia considered the problem; namely, trying to solve a bank robbery in Mexico while sitting on second base in Idaville.

"You can't do Tim's uncle any harm," said Sally.

Encyclopedia couldn't argue with that. "You win," he said. "Tell me what you know, Tim."

"The National Bank of Mexico City was robbed last month by two masked men. They got away with a million pesos in one-peso bills," said Tim.

"That's about eighty thousand dollars," exclaimed Encyclopedia.

"Two weeks later," continued Tim, "Pedro Morales says he passed my uncle's house. It was late at night. There was a light in the living room. Pedro says he saw my uncle arguing with another man."

"Did Pedro overhear what was said?" asked Encyclopedia.

"Yes, the window was open," replied Tim. "Pedro claims my uncle said that he had counted the money again that afternoon. His share wasn't half the million pesos—it was a thousand pesos short."

"What happened next?" said Sally.

"According to Pedro," said Tim, "the other man got excited. He threw some money into my uncle's face and shouted, 'There's a thousand pesos. I never want to see your ugly face again!'"

"How did Pedro know they were talking about the stolen money?" asked Encyclopedia.

"Pedro says he didn't know—then," replied Tim. "Some of the one-peso bills the man threw at my uncle flew out the open window. Pedro picked them up. On a hunch, he brought them to the police. The numbers on the bills proved they were stolen from the bank."

"If Pedro had some of the stolen money," said Sally, "he must have had something to do with the robbery himself!"

"I agree," said Encyclopedia. "Pedro lied. His story just doesn't add up!"

WHAT WAS PEDRO'S LIE?

Solution

Pedro's mistake was in claiming that Tim's uncle said that he had "counted the money again that afternoon," and that "his share wasn't half the million pesos."

Remember, the stolen money was in the form of one million one-peso bills.

Tim's uncle could not have counted half a million bills, his share, in one afternoon.

It would have taken him five days—counting day and night!

Were you surprised by the solution to this mystery? Explain your answer.

Why was Uncle Duffy's alibi weak?

How did Encyclopedia know that Duffy Gomez was innocent?

WRITE Write a letter to Encyclopedia Brown telling him why you think he is or is not a good detective.

Solve It!

How are Dr. Haledjian and Encyclopedia Brown alike? What characteristics do they share that make them good detectives?

WRITER'S WORKSHOP

Imagine that you are a mystery writer like Donald Sobol. Write a letter to Mr. Sobol, explaining an idea for a two-minute mystery that he might like to write about in one of his books. Remember to include a possible solution in the body of your letter.

Writer's Choice

In this theme, you have read about mysteries. You might want to write a new ending for one of these mysteries. You might want to respond in some other way. Decide how to share your response with some classmates.

T H E M E

Hidden Riches

Sometimes when you are searching for something, you find a more valuable treasure along the way. The following selection and poem tell about some hidden riches that change the people who discover them.

C O N T E N T S

397

THE GOLD COIN

by Alma Flor Ada

illustrated by Neil Waldman

Juan had been a thief for many years. Because he did his stealing by night, his skin had become pale and sickly. Because he spent his time either hiding or sneaking about, his body had become shriveled and bent. And because he had neither friend nor relative to make him smile, his face was always twisted into an angry frown.

One night, drawn by a light shining through the trees, Juan came upon a hut. He crept up to the door and through a crack saw an old woman sitting at a plain, wooden table.

What was that shining in her hand? Juan wondered. He could not believe his eyes: It was a gold coin. Then he heard the woman say to herself, "I must be the richest person in the world."

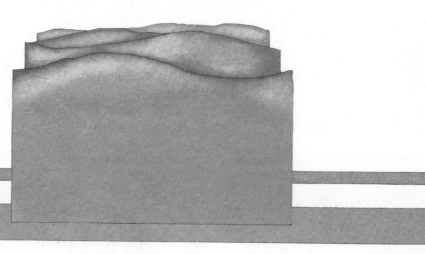

Juan decided instantly that all the woman's gold must be his. He thought that the easiest thing to do was to watch until the woman left. Juan hid in the bushes and huddled under his poncho, waiting for the right moment to enter the hut.

Juan was half asleep when he heard knocking at the door and the sound of insistent voices. A few minutes later, he saw the woman, wrapped in a black cloak, leave the hut with two men at her side.

Here's my chance! Juan thought. And, forcing open a window, he climbed into the empty hut.

He looked about eagerly for the gold. He looked under the bed. It wasn't there. He looked in the cupboard. It wasn't there, either. Where could it be? Close to despair, Juan tore away some beams supporting the thatch roof.

Finally, he gave up. There was simply no gold in the hut.

All I can do, he thought, is to find the old woman and make her tell me where she's hidden it.

So he set out along the path that she and her two companions had taken.

It was daylight by the time Juan reached the river. The countryside had been deserted, but here, along the riverbank, were two huts. Nearby, a man and his son were hard at work, hoeing potatoes.

It had been a long, long time since Juan had spoken to another human being. Yet his desire to find the woman was so strong that he went up to the farmers and asked, in a hoarse, raspy voice, "Have you seen a short, gray-haired woman, wearing a black cloak?"

"Oh, you must be looking for Doña Josefa," the young boy said. "Yes, we've seen her. We went to fetch her this morning, because my grandfather had another attack of—"

"Where is she now?" Juan broke in.

"She is long gone," said the father with a smile. "Some people from across the river came looking for her, because someone in their family is sick."

"How can I get across the river?" Juan asked anxiously.

"Only by boat," the boy answered. "We'll row you across later, if you'd like." Then turning back to his work, he added, "But first we must finish digging up the potatoes."

The thief muttered, "Thanks." But he quickly grew impatient. He grabbed a hoe and began to help the pair of farmers. The sooner we finish, the sooner we'll get across the river, he thought. And the sooner I'll get to my gold!

It was dusk when they finally laid down their hoes. The soil had been turned, and the wicker baskets were brimming with potatoes.

"Now can you row me across?" Juan asked the father anxiously.

"Certainly," the man said. "But let's eat supper first."

Juan had forgotten the taste of a home-cooked meal and the pleasure that comes from sharing it with others. As he sopped up the last of the stew with a chunk of dark bread, memories of other meals came back to him from far away and long ago.

By the light of the moon, father and son guided their boat across the river.

"What a wonderful healer Doña Josefa is!" the boy told Juan. "All she had to do to make Abuelo better was give him a cup of her special tea."

"Yes, and not only that," his father added, "she brought him a gold coin."

Juan was stunned. It was one thing for Doña Josefa to go around helping people. But how could she go around handing out gold coins—*his gold coins*?

When the threesome finally reached the other side of the river, they saw a young man sitting outside his hut.

"This fellow is looking for Doña Josefa," the father said, pointing to Juan.

"Oh, she left some time ago," the young man said.

"Where to?" Juan asked tensely.

"Over to the other side of the mountain," the young man replied, pointing to the vague outline of mountains in the night sky.

"How did she get there?" Juan asked, trying to hide his impatience.

"By horse," the young man answered. "They came on horseback to get her because someone had broken his leg."

"Well, then, I need a horse, too," Juan said urgently.

"Tomorrow," the young man replied softly. "Perhaps I can take you tomorrow, maybe the next day. First I must finish harvesting the corn."

So Juan spent the next day in the fields, bathed in sweat from sunup to sundown.

Yet each ear of corn that he picked seemed to bring him closer to his treasure. And later that evening, when he helped the young man husk several ears so they could boil them for supper, the yellow kernels glittered like gold coins.

While they were eating, Juan thought about Doña Josefa. Why, he wondered, would someone who said she was the world's richest woman spend her time taking care of every sick person for miles around?

The following day, the two set off at dawn. Juan could not recall when he last had noticed the beauty of the sunrise. He felt strangely moved by the sight of the mountains, barely lit by the faint rays of the morning sun.

As they neared the foothills, the young man said, "I'm not surprised you're looking for Doña Josefa. The whole countryside needs her. I went for her because my wife had been running a high fever. In no time at all, Doña Josefa had her on the road to recovery. And what's more, my friend, she brought her a gold coin!"

Juan groaned inwardly. To think that someone could hand out gold so freely! What a strange woman Doña Josefa is, Juan thought. Not only is she willing to help one person after another, but she doesn't mind traveling all over the countryside to do it!

"Well, my friend," said the young man finally, "this is where I must leave you. But you don't have far to walk. See that house over there? It belongs to the man who broke his leg."

The young man stretched out his hand to say good-bye. Juan stared at it for a moment. It had been a long, long time since the thief had shaken hands with anyone. Slowly, he pulled out a hand from under his poncho. When his companion grasped it firmly in his own, Juan felt suddenly warmed, as if by the rays of the sun.

But after he thanked the young man, Juan ran down the road. He was still eager to catch up with Doña Josefa. When he reached the house, a woman and a child were stepping down from a wagon.

"Have you seen Doña Josefa?" Juan asked.

"We've just taken her to Don Teodosio's," the woman said. "His wife is sick, you know—"

"How do I get there?" Juan broke in. "I've got to see her."

"It's too far to walk," the woman said amiably. "If you'd like, I'll take you there tomorrow. But first I must gather my squash and beans."

So Juan spent yet another long day in the fields. Working beneath the summer sun, Juan noticed that his skin had begun to tan. And although he had to stoop down to pick the squash, he found that he could now stretch his body. His back had begun to straighten, too.

Later, when the little girl took him by the hand to show him a family of rabbits burrowed under a fallen tree, Juan's face broke into a smile. It had been a long, long time since Juan had smiled.

Yet his thoughts kept coming back to the gold.

The following day, the wagon carrying Juan and the woman lumbered along a road lined with coffee fields.

The woman said, "I don't know what we would have done without Doña Josefa. I sent my daughter to our neighbor's house, who then brought Doña Josefa on horseback. She set my husband's leg and then showed me how to brew a special tea to lessen the pain."

Getting no reply, she went on. "And, as if that weren't enough, she brought him a gold coin. Can you imagine such a thing?"

Juan could only sigh. No doubt about it, he thought, Doña Josefa is someone special. But Juan didn't know whether to be happy that Doña Josefa had so much gold she could freely hand it out, or angry for her having already given so much of it away.

When they finally reached Don Teodosio's house, Doña Josefa was already gone. But here, too, there was work that needed to be done. . . .

Juan stayed to help with the coffee harvest. As he picked the red berries, he gazed up from time to time at the trees that grew, row upon row, along the hillsides. What a calm, peaceful place this is! he thought.

The next morning, Juan was up at daybreak. Bathed in the soft, dawn light, the mountains seemed to smile at him. When Don Teodosio offered him a lift on horseback, Juan found it difficult to have to say good-bye.

"What a good woman Doña Josefa is!" Don Teodosio said, as they rode down the hill toward the sugarcane fields. "The minute she heard about my wife being sick, she came with her special herbs. And as if that weren't enough, she brought my wife a gold coin!"

In the stifling heat, the kind that often signals the approach of a storm, Juan simply sighed and mopped his brow. The pair continued riding for several hours in silence.

Juan then realized he was back in familiar territory, for they were now on the stretch of road he had traveled only a week ago—though how much longer it now seemed to him. He jumped off Don Teodosio's horse and broke into a run.

This time the gold would not escape him! But he had to move quickly, so he could find shelter before the storm broke.

Out of breath, Juan finally reached Doña Josefa's

hut. She was standing by the door, shaking her head slowly as she surveyed the ransacked house.

"So I've caught up with you at last!" Juan shouted, startling the old woman. "Where's the gold?"

"The gold coin?" Doña Josefa said, surprised and looking at Juan intently. "Have you come for the gold coin? I've been trying hard to give it to someone who might need it," Doña Josefa said. "First to an old man who had just gotten over a bad attack. Then to a young woman who had been running a fever. Then to a man with a broken leg. And finally to Don Teodosio's wife. But none of them would take it. They all said, 'Keep it. There must be someone who needs it more.'"

Juan did not say a word.

"You must be the one who needs it," Doña Josefa said.

She took the coin out of her pocket and handed it to him. Juan stared at the coin, speechless.

At that moment a young girl appeared, her long braid bouncing as she ran. "Hurry, Doña Josefa, please!" she said breathlessly. "My mother is all alone, and the baby is due any minute."

"Of course, dear," Doña Josefa replied. But as she glanced up at the sky, she saw nothing but black clouds. The storm was nearly upon them. Doña Josefa sighed deeply.

"But how can I leave now? Look at my house! I don't know what has happened to the roof. The storm will wash the whole place away!"

And there was a deep sadness in her voice.

Juan took in the child's frightened eyes, Doña Josefa's sad, distressed face, and the ransacked hut.

"Go ahead, Doña Josefa," he said. "Don't worry about your house. I'll see that the roof is back in shape, good as new."

The woman nodded gratefully, drew her cloak about her shoulders, and took the child by the hand. As she turned to leave, Juan held out his hand.

"Here, take this," he said, giving her the gold coin. "I'm sure the newborn will need it more than I."

Did Juan do the right thing? Explain why you think as you do.

In what way was Doña Josefa rich? Explain your answer.

WRITE Do you know someone who is like Doña Josefa? Write a poem telling how that person is special and how you feel about him or her.

Pearls

from *Hey World, Here I Am!*
by Jean Little
illustrated by Denise Hilton Putnam

Dad gave me a string of pearls for my birthday.
They aren't real pearls but they look real.
They came nested in deep, deep blue velvet
    in a hinged box with a silvery lid.
His sister had some like them when she was my age.
She was thrilled.
He thought I'd really like them.
I said I did.

I love the box.

Hidden Riches

Think about the treasures that Juan and the girl in the poem discover. Which kind of treasure would you rather have? Why?

WRITER'S WORKSHOP

Think about something you own and treasure. What makes it special to you? Write a description of your treasure. Tell why it is valuable to you.

Writer's Choice
A treasure can be something you own, or it can be something like a special memory. You might want to choose some other kind of treasure to write about. Plan how you will share your writing.

CONNECTIONS

Mexican Masks

Dr. Eduardo Matos Moctezuma of Mexico has directed many archaeological projects in order to learn more about the ancient people of his country. Dr. Moctezuma and other archaeologists around the world often are puzzled by what they find.

Many ancient Mexican masks have been discovered, but we can't be sure why these masks were made and worn. We know more about the Mexican masks of recent centuries. Generations of carvers handed down the art of mask-making. Their striking masks were worn by dancers acting out folktales.

Mexican girl with festive mask

Mexican masks have made their way north. Today you might see the masks on the actors of a Mexican American theater group. Or you might see them displayed in a museum as the work of modern artists.

With your classmates, choose a Mexican folktale or a folktale from another culture. Then create masks for all the characters.

416

Mexican Indian cat mask

Social Studies Connection

Mysteries of the Maya

Who were the mysterious people who created the early masks of Mexico? Read about one of the Mexican native groups, such as the Maya, the Aztecs, or the Toltecs. Use what you learn to create a bulletin board display. List some questions that archaeologists have answered and some they have not answered.

Art Connection

What Is It?

Archaeologists are often puzzled by the things they find. Puzzle your classmates in the same way by drawing a useful object that doesn't exist. Design the object so that its use makes sense once someone knows what it is. Challenge your classmates to tell what the object is for and to name it.

An archaeologist examines Mayan artifacts in a cave.

417

UNIT FIVE

ACROSS AMERICA

From the wetlands of the Southeast to the northern reaches of Alaska, America is a diverse land of diverse people. In this unit you will travel across America, visiting the unique regions Americans call home. You will read about pioneers on the plains and Native Americans in the Northwest. You will discover a steel-making town in the East and a canyon town in the Southwest. Think about how these places are like your home and how your home is different from any other place in America.

THEMES

BOOKSHELF

THE BEST TOWN IN THE WORLD

by Byrd Baylor

This poetic story describes a small town where the best of everything could be found—the best neighbors, the best swimming spots, the best dogs, and the best chocolate cakes.

ALA Notable Book

Harcourt Brace Library Book

PUEBLO STORYTELLER

by Diane Hoyt-Goldsmith

April, a ten-year-old Native American girl, learns many crafts and Pueblo traditions from her storyteller grandparents.

Award-Winning Author

Harcourt Brace Library Book

ON THE BANKS OF PLUM CREEK

by Laura Ingalls Wilder

In the fourth book of Ms. Wilder's *Little House* series, Laura and her family move to Walnut Grove, Minnesota, and settle on the banks of Plum Creek.

Newbery Honor

A PARADISE CALLED TEXAS

by Janice Jordan Shefelman

Looking for a better life, Mina Jordan and her parents leave their home in Germany and set sail for the Republic of Texas.

ELLIS ISLAND: NEW HOPE IN A NEW LAND

by William Jay Jacobs

As hopeful immigrants look over the rail of a ship at the looming Statue of Liberty, tears come to their eyes. Will they be welcomed in America?

Notable Children's Trade Book in the Field of Social Studies

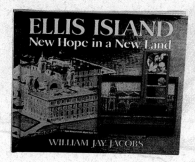

THEME

The Changing Land

Imagine what it would have been like to live in America long ago, when most of its land was still wilderness. These selections will help you see how America has grown and changed.

CONTENTS

A River

Ran Wild

written and illustrated by
Lynne Cherry

NOTABLE
TRADE BOOK IN
SOCIAL STUDIES
TEACHERS' CHOICE
OUTSTANDING
SCIENCE TRADE
BOOK

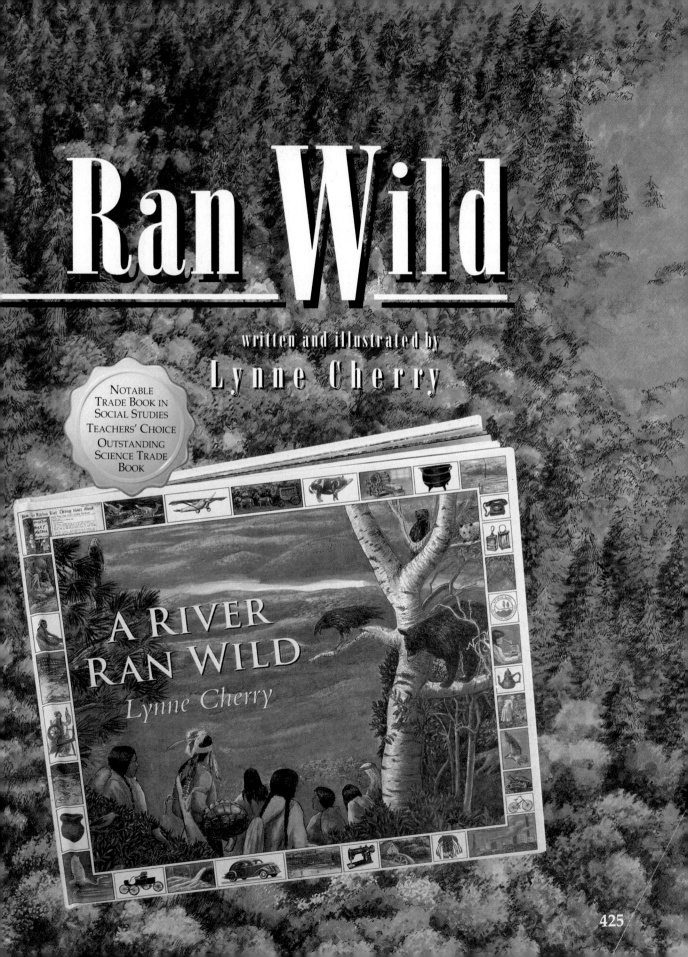

A RIVER
RAN WILD

Lynne Cherry

7000 years ago: Indian peoples come through the Nashua River Valley.

1400: Nashua Indian people of the Pennacook Confederacy settle along the Nashua River.

1600s: First colonial settlements in New England

1616–17: Indian settlements devastated by smallpox epidemic

1628: Massachusetts Bay Colony founded

1675–76: King Philip's (Metacomet) War

1776: Declaration of Independence

1830: Indian Removal Act

1848–60: Wave of immigrants come from Europe, many work in factories.

1850: Paper manufacture, textiles, and shoe products become the prevalent industries on the river.

1899: Largest dam on the Nashua River—the Wachusett Dam in Clinton—built to provide Boston with water.

1910: Manufacture of Bakelite begins plastic age.

1962: Marion Stoddart organizes the Nashua River Cleanup Committee, and the city of Leominster gets permission from the Massachusetts Department of Public Health to dump 150 million gallons of raw sewage per day into the Nashua.

1965: U.S. Congress passes Clean Water Act. Paper companies along the Nashua join together to build a treatment plant, and 400–500 youths work for five months to clear trash from Nashua's riverbed and banks.

1970: U.S. Environmental Protection Agency (EPA) formed, and Federal Clean Water Act states that all U.S. waters be fishable and swimmable by 1983.

1979: Bass, pickerel, perch, trout, bald eagles, osprey, and great blue heron return to the Nashua.

bald eagle

moose

opossum

trout

wolf

black-capped chickadee

kingfisher

porcupine

owl

red-headed woodpecker

turkey

red-tailed hawk

black bear

wolverine

bass

passenger pigeon

gray squirrel

muskrat

otter

flying squirrel

wren

pine grosbeak

red squirrel

mountain lion

painted bunting

red fox

Canada goose

beaver

Long ago a river ran wild through a land of towering forests. Bears, moose, and herds of deer, hawks and owls all made their homes in the peaceful river valley. Geese paused on their long migration and rested on its banks. Beavers, turtles, and schools of fish swam in its clear waters.

One day a group of native people, searching for a place to settle, came upon the river valley. From atop the highest mountain, known today as Mt. Wachusett, they saw the river nestled in its valley, a silver sliver in the sun.

They came down from the mountain, and at the river's edge they knelt to quench their thirst with its clear water. Pebbles shone up from the bottom.

428

wampum belt

wampum

spoon

squash

purse

woven baskets

zucchini

woven baskets

clay pipes

pestle

comb

clay pipes

clay pots

"Let us settle by this river," said the chief of the native people. He named the river Nash-a-way—River with the Pebbled Bottom.

By the Nash-a-way, Chief Weeawa's people built a village. They gathered cattails from the riverbanks to thatch their dwellings. In the forest they set fires to clear brush from the forest floor. In these clearings they planted corn and squash for eating. They made arrows for hunting and canoes for river travel.

When the Indians hunted in the forest or caught salmon in the river, they killed only what they needed for themselves for food and clothing. They asked all the forest creatures that they killed to please forgive them.

The Nashua people saw a rhythm in their lives and in the seasons. The river, land, and forest provided all they needed.

mortar

arrowheads

quiver and bow

arrow

antler flaking tools

wooden bowl

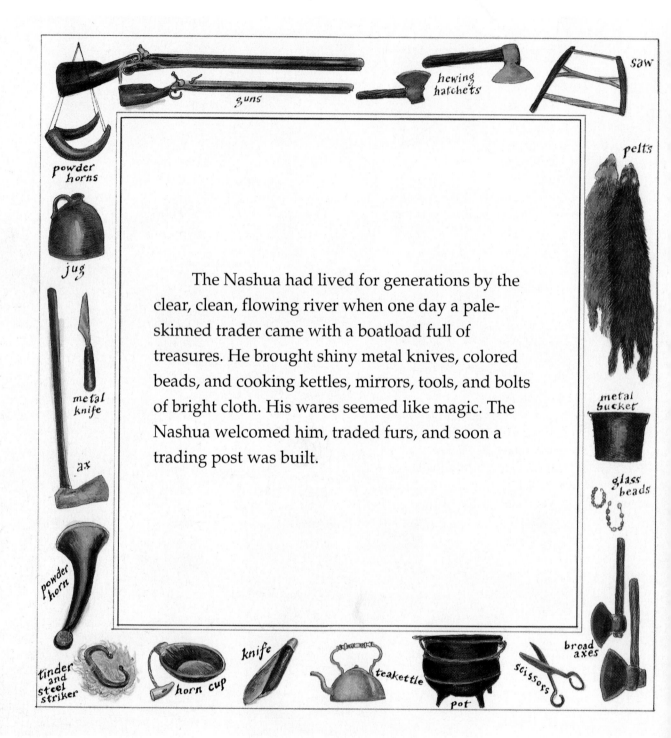

The Nashua had lived for generations by the clear, clean, flowing river when one day a pale-skinned trader came with a boatload full of treasures. He brought shiny metal knives, colored beads, and cooking kettles, mirrors, tools, and bolts of bright cloth. His wares seemed like magic. The Nashua welcomed him, traded furs, and soon a trading post was built.

In the many years that followed, the settlers' village and others like it grew and the Nash-a-way became the Nashua. The settlers worked together to clear land by cutting down the forests, which they thought were full of danger—wilderness that they would conquer. They hunted wolves and beaver, killing much more than they needed. Extra pelts were sent to England in return for goods and money.

The settlers built sawmills along the river, which the Nashua's current powered. They built dams to make the millponds that were used to store the water. They cut down the towering forest and floated tree trunks down the river. The logs were cut up into lumber, which was used for building houses.

435

The settlers built fences for their pastures, plowed the fields, and planted crops. They called the land their own and told the Indians not to trespass. Hunting land disappeared as the settlers cleared the forest. Indian fishing rights vanished as the settlers claimed the river.

The Indians' ways were disrupted and they began to fight the settlers. The wars raged for many years but the Indians' bows and arrows were no match against gunpowder, and so the settlers' rifles drove the Indians from the land.

Through a hundred years of fighting, the Nashua was a healthy river, sometimes dammed for grist and sawmills, but still flowing wild and free. Muskrats, fish, and turtles still swam from bank to bank. Deer still came to drink from the river, and owls, raccoons, and beaver fed there.

first sewing machine

Civil War

loom

Shortest and Most Direct Route From Points in New England "FIVE EXPRESS TRAINS LEAVE ALBANY DAILY"

mill

first telephone

Edison electric light invented

camera invented 1839

clock

typewriter invented

bicycle invented

young factory workers

Crompton Loom 1876

Edison phonograph

At the start of the new century, an industrial revolution came to the Nashua's banks and waters. Many new machines were invented. Some spun thread from wool and cotton. Others wove the thread into cloth. Some machines turned wood to pulp, and others made the pulp into paper. Leftover pulp and dye and fiber was dumped into the Nashua River, whose swiftly flowing current washed away the waste.

canal at West Boylston

old bridge in Boylston

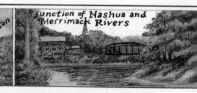
junction of Nashua and Merrimack Rivers

1882 first Bell telephone

mill at South Lancaster

These were times of much excitement, times of "progress" and "invention." Factories along the Nashua River made new things of new materials. Telephones and radios and other things were made of plastics. Chemicals and plastic waste were also dumped into the river. Soon the Nashua's fish and wildlife grew sick from this pollution.

Wright biplane first airplane

1902 Oldsmobile

radio invented

Model-T Ford

plastic hoola hoops

plastic eyeglass frames

camera

I WANT YOU
U.S. ARMY
World War II poster

T.V.

1st nuclear explosion

plastic telephone

adding machine

rubber band

plastic paintbrush

camera

The paper mills continued to pollute the Nashua's waters. Every day for many decades pulp was dumped into the Nashua, and as the pulp clogged up the river, it began to run more slowly.

As the pulp decomposed, bad smells welled up from the river. People who lived near the river smelled its stench and stayed far from it. Each day as the mills dyed paper red, green, blue, and yellow, the Nashua ran whatever color the paper was dyed.

Soon no fish lived in the river. No birds stopped on their migration. No one could see pebbles shining up through murky water. The Nashua was dark and dirty. The Nashua was slowly dying.

Sewing machine

airplane

typewriter

1955 Cadillac

movie projector

One night Oweana, a descendant of Weeawa who still lived by the Nashua, had a dream so vivid that he awoke in wide-eyed wonder. In his dream Chief Weeawa's spirit returned to the river and saw it as it was now—still and deadly.

Chief Weeawa mourned for the Nash-a-way, but where his tears fell upon the dirty waters, the waters were cleansed until the river once again flowed freely.

The next morning Oweana went to speak to his friend Marion. When he told her of his dream, she said, "I had this dream also! River with the Pebbled Bottom is the name Weeawa gave it, but today no pebbles shine up through the Nashua River's waters." Together they decided something must be done.

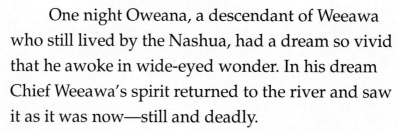

Marion traveled to each town along the
Nashua. She spoke of the river's history and of her
vision to restore it. "No longer do we have a river—
it's a stinking, smelly sewer. But it wasn't always
this way."

People listened and imagined a sparkling
river, full of fish. They imagined pebbles shining up
through clear waters. They signed petitions and
sent letters. They protested to politicians and
showed them jars of dirty water. They convinced
the paper mills to build a plant to process the waste.
They persuaded the factories to stop dumping.
Finally, new laws were passed and the factories
stopped polluting.

Slowly, slowly, the Nashua's current began to clean its water. Year by year the river carried away the dyes and fiber to the ocean. Marion and Oweana thanked the people who had helped to clean the Nashua.

Through the meadows, towns, and cities, the Nashua once again flows freely. Paper pulp no longer clogs it. Chemicals no longer foul it.

Now we walk along its banks and row upon its fragrant waters. We can set our boats upon it and with its current, drift downstream.

Once again the river runs wild through a towering forest greenway. Red-tailed hawks and barred owls live here. Geese pause from their long migration and rest on the riverbanks. Deer come to drink from the river's waters. We, too, have settled by this river. Pebbles shine up through clear water. Nashua is what we call it—River with the Pebbled Bottom.

What do you admire most about the Nashua people? Tell why you feel as you do.

Summarize what happened when people settled the land around the Nashua River and built homes and factories.

What did you learn from Lynne Cherry's words and pictures that helped you better understand life in early America?

WRITE   Think of a naturally beautiful place in your town or state. List words that describe the sights, the sounds, and the smells of that place. Then use your list to write a brief description.

Lynne Cherry

Lynne Cherry grew up in a wooded area of
Pennsylvania, and she loved the peace she
found there. Lynne liked to write and
to draw, and she found the woods an
excellent place to sketch animals and
to become closer to nature.

A River Ran Wild is a very special book to
Lynne Cherry. It took her an entire year to do
the research. "I traveled to Massachusetts
to canoe the Nashua River, visited historical
societies to find old photographs, and went to
Indian pow-wows and met with other
Indians . . . I flew in a small airplane to
take aerial photographs of the river and
visited the Colonial Farm in Maryland,
and Plimoth Plantation and
Sturbridge Village in Massachusetts.
It was a lot of work, but it was fun
because I was learning as I went."

451

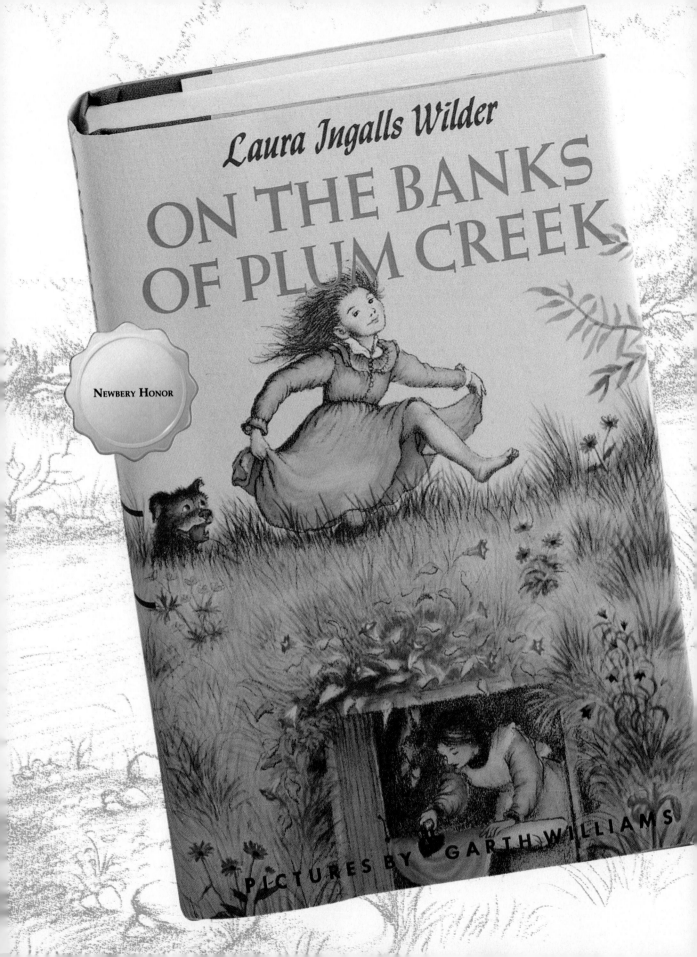

*W*hen Pa, Ma, and little Carrie went into town for the day, Laura and Mary were left alone with Jack, their dog, to take care of everything. After lunch, the three were faced with a big problem. The cattle were tearing into the hay-stacks and eating all the hay. Jack and Laura and Mary finally were able to chase the cattle into the high prairie grasses away from the banks of Plum Creek.

*A*ll that long, quiet afternoon they stayed in the dugout. The cattle did not come back to the hay-stacks. Slowly the sun went down the western sky. Soon it would be time to meet the cattle at the big grey rock, and Laura and Mary wished that Pa and Ma would come home.

Again and again they went up the path to look for the wagon. At last they sat waiting with Jack on the grassy top of their house. The lower the sun went, the more attentive Jack's ears were. Often he and Laura stood up to look at the edge of the sky where the wagon had gone, though they could see it just as well when they were sitting down.

Finally Jack turned one ear that way, then the other. Then he looked up at Laura and a waggle went from his neck to his stubby tail. The wagon was coming!

They all stood and watched till it came out of the
prairie. When Laura saw the oxen, and Ma and Carrie
on the wagon seat, she jumped up and down, swinging
her sunbonnet and shouting, "They're coming! They're
coming!"

"They're coming awful fast," Mary said.

Laura was still. She heard the wagon rattling loudly.
Pete and Bright were coming very fast. They were
running. They were running away.

The wagon came bumpity-banging and bouncing.
Laura saw Ma down in a corner of the wagon box,
hanging onto it and hugging Carrie. Pa came bounding
in long jumps beside Bright, shouting and hitting at
Bright with the goad.

He was trying to turn Bright back from the creek bank.

He could not do it. The big oxen galloped nearer and
nearer the steep edge. Bright was pushing Pa off it.
They were all going over. The wagon, Ma and Carrie,
were going to fall down the bank, all the way down to
the creek.

Pa shouted a terrible shout. He struck Bright's head with all his might, and Bright swerved. Laura ran screaming. Jack jumped at Bright's nose. Then the wagon, Ma, and Carrie flashed by. Bright crashed against the stable and suddenly everything was still.

Pa ran after the wagon and Laura ran behind him.

"Whoa, Bright! Whoa, Pete," Pa said. He held onto the wagon box and looked at Ma.

"We're all right, Charles," Ma said. Her face was grey and she was shaking all over.

Pete was trying to go on through the doorway into the stable, but he was yoked to Bright and Bright was headed against the stable wall. Pa lifted Ma and Carrie out of the wagon, and Ma said, "Don't cry, Carrie. See, we're all right."

Carrie's pink dress was torn down the front. She snuffled against Ma's neck and tried to stop crying as Ma told her.

"Oh, Caroline! I thought you were going over the bank," Pa said.

"I thought so, too, for a minute," Ma answered. "But I might have known you wouldn't let that happen."

"Pshaw!" said Pa. "It was good old Pete. He wasn't running away. Bright was, but Pete was only going along. He saw the stable and wanted his supper."

But Laura knew that Ma and Carrie would have fallen down into the creek with the wagon and oxen, if Pa had not run so fast and hit Bright so hard. She crowded against Ma's hoopskirt and hugged her tight and said, "Oh, Ma! Oh, Ma!" So did Mary.

"There, there," said Ma. "All's well that ends well. Now, girls, help bring in the packages while Pa puts up the oxen."

They carried all the little packages into the dugout. They met the cattle at the grey rock and put Spot into the stable, and Laura helped milk her while Mary helped Ma get supper.

At supper, they told how the cattle had got into the hay-stacks and how they had driven them away. Pa said they had done exactly the right thing. He said, "We knew we could depend on you to take care of everything. Didn't we, Caroline?"

They had completely forgotten that Pa always brought them presents from town, until after supper he pushed back his bench and looked as if he expected something. Then Laura jumped on his knee, and Mary sat on the other, and Laura bounced and asked, "What did you bring us, Pa? What? What?"

"Guess," Pa said.

They could not guess. But Laura felt something crackle in his jumper pocket and she pounced on it. She pulled out a paper bag, beautifully striped with tiny red and green stripes. And in the bag were two sticks of candy, one for Mary and one for Laura!

They were maple-sugar-coloured, and they were flat on one side.

Mary licked hers. But Laura bit her stick, and the outside of it came off, crumbly. The inside was hard and clear and dark brown. And it had a rich, brown, tangy taste. Pa said it was hoarhound candy.

After the dishes were done, Laura and Mary each took her stick of candy and they sat on Pa's knees, outside the door in the cool dusk. Ma sat just inside the dugout, humming to Carrie in her arms.

The creek was talking to itself under the yellow willows. One by one the great stars swung low and seemed to quiver and flicker in the little wind.

Laura was snug in Pa's arm. His beard softly tickled her cheek and the delicious candy-taste melted on her tongue.

After a while she said, "Pa."

"What, little half-pint?" Pa's voice asked against her hair.

"I think I like wolves better than cattle," she said.

"Cattle are more useful, Laura," Pa said.

She thought about that a while. Then she said, "Anyway, I like wolves better."

She was not contradicting; she was only saying what she thought.

"Well, Laura, we're going to have a good team of horses before long," Pa said. She knew when that would be. It would be when they had a wheat crop.

Would you have enjoyed living on a prairie farm in the 1870s? Tell why.

What is Pa like? How do you know?

Why do you think people like to read about Laura Ingalls Wilder's experiences?

WRITE Think of something you use today that wasn't available to Laura. Write her a letter about it.

WORDS
ABOUT THE
AUTHOR:
LAURA INGALLS WILDER

Laura was born in a little log cabin in the big woods of
Wisconsin in 1867. In *Little House in the Big Woods*, her first
book, she wrote about her experiences growing up.

In her next book, *Little House on the Prairie*,
Laura described the wagon-train trip that took
the Ingalls family from Wisconsin to the Kansas prairie.
The landscape of the prairie was very different from
that of the Wisconsin woods. On the
prairie, the sky seemed to go on forever.
There weren't many other settlers, but
there were Indians living on the land,
which had once been their
hunting ground.

When it appeared that the
government was going to return the
land to the Indians, the Ingalls family
went back to Wisconsin, but Pa soon
had an "itchy foot" and wanted
to try the West again. This
time, the family settled in
Walnut Grove, Minnesota,
which is the setting for
On the Banks of Plum Creek.

458

The Changing Land

These selections helped you understand what life was like in some parts of America long ago. Now that you have read the selections, would you rather live on the prairie in the 1850s or by the Nashua River during one of the times described in "A River Ran Wild"? Why?

WRITER'S WORKSHOP

Today we can travel across America or across an ocean in a matter of hours. Write paragraphs comparing and contrasting ways we travel today with ways Americans traveled long ago. Use an encyclopedia and other reference books for help.

Writer's Choice You may want to write on another topic about life in early America. List several possible topics, and then choose one to write about.

THEME

Hometown, U.S.A.

What do you like most about the place where you live? Is it a noisy and exciting city, or is it a quiet suburb where you know all of your neighbors? Wherever people grow up, they have special memories about their homes. In the following selections, you'll read about the memories of some people who grew up in American towns.

CONTENTS

461

The Best Town in the World

by Byrd Baylor
illustrated by Ronald Himler

All my life I've heard about
a little, dirt-road,
one-store,
country town
not far from a rocky canyon
way back
in the Texas hills.

The
Best Town in the World

By Byrd Baylor   Pictures by Ronald Himler

This town had lots of space
around it
with caves to find
and honey trees
and giant rocks to climb.

It had a creek
and there were panther tracks
to follow
and you could swing
on the wild grapevines.
My father said it was
the best town in the world
and he just happened
to be born there.
How's that for being
lucky?

We always liked
to hear about
that town
where everything was
perfect.

Of course it had a name
but people called the town
and all the ranches
and the farms around it
just *The Canyon*,
and they called each other
Canyon People.
The way my father said it,
you could tell
it was a special thing
to be
one of those people.

No Star Nights

by Anna Egan Smucker

paintings by Steve Johnson

When I was little, we couldn't see the stars in the nighttime sky because the furnaces of the mill turned the darkness into a red glow. But we would lie on the hill and look up at the sky anyway and wait for a bright orange light that seemed to breathe in and out to spread across it. And we would know that the golden spark-spitting steel was being poured out of giant buckets into molds to cool.

Then we would look down on a train pulling cars mounted with giant thimbles rocking back and forth. They were filled with fiery hot molten slag that in the night glowed orange. And when they were dumped, the sky lit up again.

ALA
NOTABLE BOOK
IRA CHILDREN'S
BOOK AWARD
NOTABLE CHILDREN'S
TRADE BOOK IN
SOCIAL
STUDIES

NO
STAR
NIGHTS

by Anna Egan Smucker · paintings by Steve Johnson

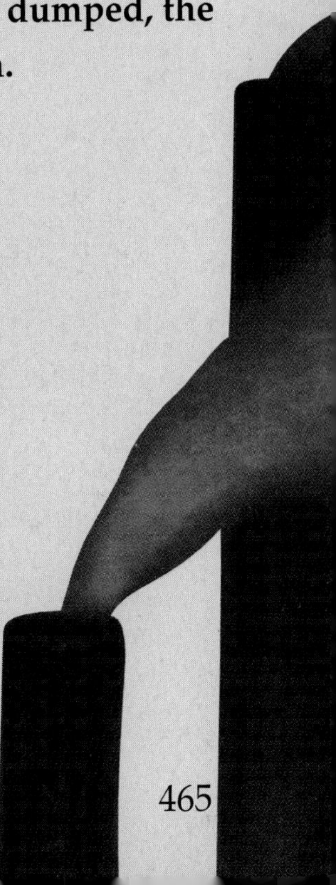

A loud steam whistle that echoed off the hills announced the change of shifts, and hundreds of men streamed out of the mill's gates. Everyone's dad worked in the mill, and carried a tin lunchbox and a big metal thermos bottle.

Work at the mill went on night and day. When Dad worked night shift, we children had to whisper and play quietly during the day so that we didn't wake him up. His job was too dangerous for him to go without sleep. He operated a crane that lifted heavy ingots of steel into a pit that was thousands of degrees hot.

When Dad worked the three-to-eleven shift, Mom made dinner early so we could all eat together. She made the best stuffed cabbage of anyone in the neighborhood. We sometimes tried to help fold the cabbage leaves around the meat and rice like she did, but our cabbage leaves always came unrolled.

During the school year days went by when we didn't see Dad at all because he was either at work or sleeping. When he changed shifts from daylight to night and back again it took him a while to get used to the different waking and sleeping times. We called these his grumpy times. We liked it best when he had daylight hours to spend with us. We played baseball until it was too dark to see the ball.

On a few very special summer afternoons he would load us all into the car for a hot, sweaty trip to Pittsburgh and a doubleheader Pirates game at Forbes Field. We sat in the bleachers way out in left field, eating popcorn and drinking lemonade that we brought from home, yelling our heads off for the Pirates. Our brother always wore his baseball glove, hoping to catch a foul ball that might come into the stands. Dad helped us mark our scorecards and bought us hot dogs during the seventh-inning stretch.

On our way home we passed the black silhouettes of Pittsburgh's steel mills, with their great heavy clouds of smoke billowing from endless rows of smokestacks. The road wound along as the river wound, and

between us and the river were the mills, and on the other side of the road were the hills—the river, the mills, and the hills. And we sang as we rode home, "She'll be comin' round the mountain when she comes . . ."

July was just about the best month of the year. Everyone who worked in the mill got their vacation pay then. We called it Christmas in July. All the stores had big sales. Even though it wasn't really Christmas, we each got a present.

And the Fourth of July parade was something everyone looked forward to. We were busy for weeks making flowers out of Kleenex to cover our Girl Scout float. Some of our friends took baton lessons and were part of a marching unit called the Steel Town Strutters. They wore shiny black-and-gold-spangled leotards and threw their batons high up into the air and caught them! Something we sure couldn't do. But our favorites were the baby strutters. Some of them were only two years old. They did a good job just carrying their batons.

With all the bands and fire engines and floats, the
parade went on and on. There were convertibles with
beauty queens sitting on the back. Members of the Kennel
Club marched their dogs in circles and figure eights.

Kids rode bikes decorated with colored crepe paper, flags,
and balloons. The mayor drove an old-fashioned car, and
his children threw bubblegum and candies into the crowds.

We went to school across from the mill. The smokestacks towered above us and the smoke billowed out in great puffy clouds of red, orange, and yellow, but mostly the color of rust. Everything—houses, hedges, old cars—was a rusty red color. Everything but the little bits of graphite, and they glinted like silver in the dust. At recess when the wind whirled these sharp, shiny metal pieces around, we girls would crouch so that our skirts touched the ground and kept our bare legs from being stung.

We would squint our eyes when the wind blew to keep the graphite out. Once a piece got caught in my eye, and no matter how much I blinked or how much my eye watered it wouldn't come out. When the eye doctor finally took it out and showed it to me, I was amazed that a speck that small could feel so big.

We played on the steep street that ran up the hill beside our school. Our favorite game was dodge ball. The kids on the bottom row knew they had to catch the ball. If they didn't, it would roll down onto the busy county road that ran in front of the school. Too often a truck carrying a heavy roll of steel would run over it and with a loud *bang* the ball would be flattened.

The windows in our school were kept closed to try to keep the graphite and smoke out. On really windy days we could hear the dry, dusty sound of grit hitting against the glass. Dusting the room was a daily job. The best duster got to dust the teacher's desk with a soft white cloth and a spray that made the whole room smell like lemons. It was always a mystery to us how the nuns who were our teachers could keep the white parts of their habits so clean.

Some days it seemed as though there was a giant lid covering the valley, keeping the smoke in. It was so thick you couldn't see anything clearly. On days like that I felt as if we were living in a whirling world of smoke.

The road we took home from school went right through part of the mill. Tall cement walls with strands of barbed wire at the top kept us on the sidewalk and out of the mill. But when we got to the bridge that spanned the railroad tracks, there was just a steel mesh fence. From there we could look straight down into the mill! There was always something wonderful to watch. Through a huge open doorway we could see the mammoth open-hearth furnace. A giant ladle would tilt to give the fiery furnace a "drink" of orange, molten iron. Sometimes we would see the golden, liquid steel pouring out the bottom of the open hearth into enormous bucketlike ladles. The workers were just small dark figures made even smaller by the great size of the ladles and the furnace. The hot glow of the liquid steel made the dark mill light up as if the sun itself was being poured out. And standing on the bridge we could feel its awful heat.

Warning sirens and the toots of steam whistles, the screeching sounds of train wheels and the wham-wham of cars being coupled and uncoupled—all these sounds surrounded us as we stood on the bridge. From the other side we could look into another part of the mill. Rows of lights hung from girders across the ceiling. White-hot steel bars glided smoothly over rollers on long tables. Men were using torches on the big slabs of steel. The torches gave off streaks of burning, white light and showers of sparks that looked like our Fourth of July sparklers.

Behind the mill rose huge piles of black shiny coal and rich red iron ore, and a hill of rusting scrap metal. A crane that to us looked like a dinosaur with huge jaws was constantly at work picking up twisted, jagged pieces of metal and dropping them into railroad cars to be taken into the mill. Sometimes we would imagine that the mill itself was a huge beast, glowing hot, breathing heavily, always hungry, always needing to be fed. And we would run home, not stopping once to look over our shoulders.

Not too far from our house was a hill made of boulders of slag from the mill. Our grandfather told us that long ago it had been a deep ravine. Over the years truckload after truckload of slag from the mill had been dumped into it until the hole had become a hill. Now it towered over the old houses that were near it.

For an adventure, my best friend and I once decided to climb the slag hill. We slipped and slid and sent the pitted rocks rolling down as we scrambled up. Our younger sisters spied us, by now near the top, and started climbing too. It was then that my friend and I saw the dump truck with a heavy load of slag from the mill slowly winding its way up the hill.

"Don't dump! Don't dump!" we screamed. But the deep
engine sounds of the truck straining under its great load
drowned out our cries. Chunks of slag fell onto the roadway.
The truck backed onto the flat place to dump its load.
Stumbling toward it, we waved our arms and screamed
again, "Don't dump! Please don't dump! Our sisters are
down there!" The driver finally heard us, and leaning out
the window of the cab he saw the little girls. He nodded and
waved his hand, then the truck lurched forward back onto
the road and disappeared around the curve.

We sank exhausted to the ground, our hearts pounding in our ears. The roar of the truck's engine became fainter and fainter. The sky around us was turning red and orange and gold. We looked down on the mill that seemed to go on forever into the valley. From its long straight row of stacks, clouds of orange smoke swirled into the colors of the sunset. In the distance a whistle blew.

Many years have passed since then, and now the slag hill is covered with grasses and blackberry bushes and sumac trees. The night sky is clear and star filled because the mill is shut down. The big buckets no longer pour the hot, yellow steel. The furnaces whose fires lit up everything are rusting and cold.

Not many children live in the town now. Most of the younger people have moved away to other places to find work. The valley's steelworking way of life is gone forever. But whenever the grandchildren come back to visit, they love more than anything else to listen to stories about the days when all night long the sky glowed red.

486

Do you think you and your friends are very different from or very much like the children in this story? Explain your answer.

What do you think was the best thing about living in the steel-mill town? Tell why you think as you do.

The author of this story grew up in a town like the one she describes in "No Star Nights." How do you think she feels about the place where she grew up? How do you know?

WRITE   Think about how the author describes the sights, sounds, and experiences of her hometown. Write five sentences about your hometown. Use one of these senses in each sentence: sight, hearing, smell, touch, or taste.

An Interview with the Author:
Anna Egan Smucker

Anna Egan Smucker, a former teacher, now works as a children's librarian in Clarksburg, West Virginia. In this interview, Ms. Smucker shares with writer Ilene Cooper some of her personal history and some tips for young writers.

COOPER: What made you want to write *No Star Nights*?

SMUCKER: The place where I grew up, Weirton, West Virginia, is a steel-mill town near Pittsburgh. I wrote the story during the time many mills were closing down around the Pittsburgh area. That whole way of life I knew, growing up in a steel-mill town, was disappearing all across the country. I wanted to capture it before it was gone.

COOPER: Was Steve Johnson, your illustrator, from a mill town, too?

SMUCKER: No. He had never been to one when he started the book. He did a lot of research at a library in Minneapolis, where he lived. He did pencil sketches, using the library's photo collection. He would send these to our editor, and she'd pass them on to me.

COOPER: What kind of advice do you have for kids who would like to write histories of themselves or their families?

SMUCKER: I would encourage kids to talk to older relatives and other adults in their lives. I think it's fascinating to find out what it was like to grow up in another era. If young people don't write down the stories, they'll be lost forever.

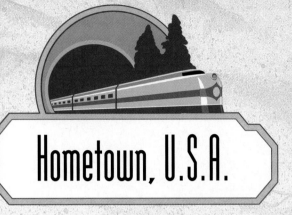

Hometown, U.S.A.

How do the narrators in the selections feel about life in the towns they describe? Explain your answer.

WRITER'S WORKSHOP

What makes a town or an area a great place to grow up? Make a list of reasons. Then use your list to write a persuasive paragraph. Explain why someone looking for a new home should move to an area like the one you described.

Writer's Choice

The poem "The Best Town in the World" and the story "No Star Nights" both tell about life in a small town. Share your feelings about the message in these selections through a poem, a song, or another way of your choice.

Traditions

Traditions are usually customs that began many years ago and have been passed down from one generation to another. Some customs celebrate a young person's steps toward adulthood. Other customs help people remember their heritage. As you read the selections that follow, think about why traditions are important.

CONTENTS

SUN DANCERS

by Patricia Irving
illustrated by Cary Henrie

Sun dancers
Whirling, twirling madly—
Feet churning Mother Earth
Until clouds weep.

Sun dancers
Bringing song to life
With forlorn drumbeat,
With feathers bright.

Sun dancers'
Feathers bowing to four winds,
Feathers dampened by the rain;
Corn feathering on the stalk.

Sun dancers
Throw humble gratitude to sky
In thundering beat
From whirling, churning feet.

TOTEM POLE

BY DIANE HOYT-GOLDSMITH • PHOTOGRAPHS BY LAWRENCE MIGDALE

My name is David. I live in a small town called Kingston in Washington State. In the summer, I like to hunt for salmonberries and blackberries in the fields near our house.

My brother and I like to look out over Puget Sound, watching for the ferry from Seattle. Sometimes, we spot a pair of eagles flying high overhead. This makes us feel lucky because our family belongs to the Eagle Clan, which is our family group within the Tsimshian *(TSIM-shee-an)* tribe.

Our father is an Indian. He was brought up by his grandparents in Metlakatla *(MET-lah-CAT-lah),* on Annette Island in Alaska. He was raised in the old ways and traditions. He learned how to hunt, to fish, and to carve.

In our tribe, a person belongs to the same clan as his mother does. Our mother is not Indian. Her ancestors emigrated to the United States from Europe many generations ago. When I was two years old, she was adopted in a special ceremony by two members of the Eagle Clan in Metlakatla. This makes my brother and me members of the Eagle Clan too.

My father is an artist, a wood-carver. Ever since I was little, I have watched him take a piece of wood and carve a creature from it. Sometimes it is a wolf, sometimes a bear, and sometimes an eagle, the symbol and totem of our clan.

 My father has a special cedar box. It is very important to him because it was made by my great-great-grandfather five generations ago. My father painted an eagle on the lid, and now he keeps his carving tools inside.

The box was first used to store food. When my father was a young boy, he was in charge of keeping the food box safe. When his family went out to hunt or fish, he carried the box from the boat up to the camp and stored it in a safe place. The foods his family had prepared for the journey were kept inside the box—the dried meat and fish, and the hardtack. These were the only foods the family would have to eat while they were camping.

My father says that even now, when he opens the box to take out a tool, he can smell the foods that were once stored inside. The faint scent brings him strong memories of the salt air, the hardtack, the fresh salmon, and even the smoke of the cooking fire where his family gathered. These memories are precious to him. The smells make the past come alive, he says.

When I open the box, all I can smell are the steel and leather tools inside. But the past comes alive for me when I hear the strike of the adze and hear my father tell his stories. He likes to tell me what it was like to grow up in Alaska.

One of my favorite stories is a Tsimshian tale called "The Legend of the Eagle and the Young Chief." Maybe I like it best because I belong to the Eagle Clan.

When my father first began to teach me about the Tsimshian songs, dances, and legends, he made some special clothes for me to wear. These clothes are called "regalia." They are worn for certain ceremonies, dances, and celebrations.

Sometimes in the afternoons, I go to my father's workshop. I look inside the trunk that holds all the regalia he has made. I dress in my special clothes to practice the dances my father taught me.

The first thing my father made for me is a headdress out of leather and decorated with ermine skins. On the front, there is a small eagle's face carved from a piece of cedar wood and painted blue and brown. This is called a frontlet. The eagle is shown on all our regalia because the eagle is our family crest. My Indian name is Lap'aigh laskeeg (lah-pah-AG-a-lah-SKEEK). It means "He Who Flies Like the Eagle" in the Tsimshian language.

My father made me an apron out of deerskin which is painted with an eagle design. I have leggings made of soft leather. They have a fringe with deer hooves hanging down. The hooves knock together as I dance and make a rattling sound as I move.

I also have a button blanket that I wear. On the back there is another large eagle design. It is outlined in hundreds of tiny white buttons. In the old days, the Tsimshian blankets were first woven from cedar bark and then decorated with rows of tiny white shells. But in the 1800s, when Europeans began to trade with the tribes along the coast, the Indians began to use bright red "trade cloth" for the blankets and machine-made buttons of mother-of-pearl for decoration.

CARVING THE POLE

My father is carving a totem pole for the Klallam (*KLAH-lum*) Indians who live on the Port Gamble Reservation near our home. Although my father belongs to a different tribe, the Tsimshian, he was asked to carve the pole because of his skill. It is common among the Northwest Coast Indians for one tribe to invite an artist from another tribe to carve a pole for them. The pole will be made from a single log, forty feet long. It will have animals and figures carved on it, important characters from Klallam myths and legends.

My father says that a totem pole is like a signboard. He tells me that it is a system for passing on legends and stories from one generation to another for people who have no written language. A totem pole is like a library for a tribe!

The first step in making a totem pole is to find a straight tree. It must be wide enough to make a strong pole. The best trees for a totem pole have few branches. Where a branch joins the trunk a knot forms, making the carving very difficult.

Nearly all totem poles are carved from cedar logs. Cedar trees grow very straight and are common in the evergreen forests along the coastline near our home. The wood of the cedar is soft and easy to carve. It does not rot and insects will not destroy it. A totem pole carved from a cedar log can last a hundred years or more.

After the right tree is found and cut down, all the branches are removed with an axe and the bark is stripped from the outside of the log. In the old days, the Indians had no saws or axes, so even cutting the tree down was a harder job than it is today. Back then, the carvers used a hammer and chisel to cut a wedge at the base of the tree. This weakened the tree, and in a strong wind storm, the tree would fall.

When the log is ready to be carved, my father makes a drawing of how the pole will look when it is finished. He draws the animals for the totem pole on a sheet of paper. He might begin by drawing each animal separately, but before he starts to carve he will draw a picture of how the completed pole will look.

Next he uses a stick of charcoal to make a drawing on the log itself. Then he stands up on the log to see how the figures and animals look. When he is satisfied with the drawing, he takes up his tools and begins to carve.

The totem pole for the Klallam tribe has six figures, one on top of the other. At the very top of the pole is the Thunderbird. He brings good luck to the Klallam village. The Klallam people believe the Thunderbird lives on the Olympic mountain range, across the water from their reservation, in the place where the mountains touch the sky. They say that when Thunderbird catches the great Killer Whale, you can hear thunder and see lightning in the sky.

Below Thunderbird is the figure who represents the Klallam people. The figure holds Killer Whale by the tail. Together, they tell the legend of a tribal member named Charlie who rode out to sea on the back of a Killer Whale.

The fourth animal on the pole is Bear, who provided the Indian people with many important things. His fur gave warmth and clothing. His meat gave food. His claws and teeth were used for trinkets and charms and to decorate clothing.

The next figure is Raven, who brought light to the Indian people by stealing the Sun from Darkness. Raven is the great trickster. Sometimes he does things that are good, but sometimes he does things that are bad.

The last figure on the pole is a Klallam Chief. The chief on the pole holds a "speaker stick," a symbol of his leadership and his important position in the tribe. In the Klallam culture, when a chief holds the speaker stick, all the people pay attention and listen to what he says.

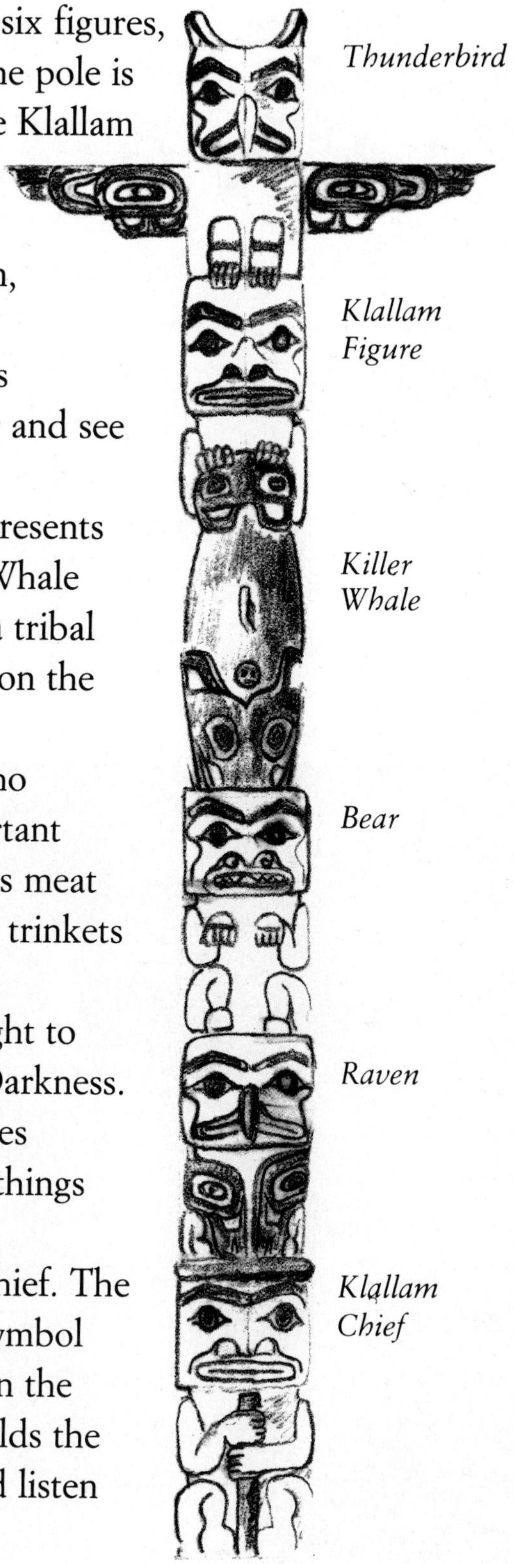

Thunderbird

Klallam Figure

Killer Whale

Bear

Raven

Klallam Chief

As my father carves the pole, he brings all of these characters to life. He works on the pole every day. He uses many tools: the adze, chisels, and handmade knives. He even uses a chain saw for the largest cuts!

This totem pole is special to me. I am finally old enough to help my father with the work. He lets me sweep away the wood shavings as he carves. I can also take care of the tools he uses—the adze, the saws, the handmade knives, and the chisels.

As I get older, I'll learn how to use my father's carving tools safely and to help him really carve a pole. But for now, I just practice on some bits of wood I find lying around. Like my father, I look for the animal shapes hidden inside the wood.

In the old days, it used to take a year to carve a totem pole. In those days, the blade of the adze was made of stone and wasn't nearly as sharp as the steel blades my father uses today. Knives, for the carving of fine details, were made from beaver teeth or from large shells.

My father says that it is the artist's skill with the adze that makes a totem pole great. Each artist has his own way of carving. The strokes of the adze create a pattern in the wood, like small ripples across the wide water.

My father makes the work look easy. He cuts into the wood quickly, as if it were as soft as soap. I know carving is much harder than he makes it look. I know because I've tried it.

After all the figures and animals are carved into the log, I help my father paint the pole. We make the eyes dark. We paint the mouths red. Whale's back and dorsal fin are black. Raven and Thunderbird have wings with patterns of red and black. The colors my father shows me are taken from the old traditions of the Tsimshian people. From a distance, the pole will look powerful and strong.

Finally, after two months of hard work, my father puts away his tools and packs up his paintbrushes. The totem pole is finished.

RAISING THE POLE

The Klallam tribe decides to hold a special ceremony to raise the totem pole. It will follow the ancient traditions of the Northwest Coast Indian people. After the ceremony, there will be a feast like the potlatch of the old days. There will be many guests. There will be traditional songs and dances, and food prepared by the villagers. If this were a traditional potlatch, the Klallam would give money or gifts to every guest.

On the day of the ceremony, we arrive on the Klallam Reservation early. I look at the pole, lying on its back in the early morning light. Each figure on the pole is strong and seems to have a spirit all its own. Looking at the totem pole, I can hardly believe my father made it.

Soon the guests begin to arrive. Many are from the Klallam village. Others are from Seattle and the surrounding towns. Some people have even come from other states.

My father and I dress in our regalia. Although my little brother is too young to dance, he wears his button blanket and headdress for the occasion. Most of my family have come to celebrate the raising of the pole. My mother is here with my grandmother and grandfather. I know my father wishes that *his* grandfather could be here too. Although my great-grandfather is in Alaska, we know he is thinking about us today.

When all the guests have arrived, my father invites
everyone to help carry the pole to the place where it
will be raised. It weighs over three thousand pounds
and it takes fifty strong men and women to carry it.
Long pieces of wood are placed underneath the back
of the pole. Standing two by two, the people lift the
pole when my father gives the command. They carry it
slowly down the road to the place where it will stand.

In the old days, every totem pole stood so it faced
the water. This was because the visitors to a village
would always arrive by canoe. But today, things are
different. Since people come to the reservation by car,
the pole is placed to face the road.

It used to be that a totem pole was raised in position by hand, with many people pulling it up with ropes. The modern way is to use a powerful truck with a crane attached. The crane slowly lifts the pole while a group of singers chant and dance.

As the pole is raised higher and higher, their voices grow louder and louder. It takes a number of tries to get the pole in the right position, but finally it is done. The pole stands straight, facing south toward the road that leads into the Klallam Reservation.

Now it is time for my father and me to dance. Holding ceremonial wooden adzes, we begin to perform the Carver's Dance at the base of the totem pole. This dance was created by my father to show that the work on the pole is finished. We dance to show how proud we are.

Tell about the part of David's life that you think is the most interesting.

How do the members of David's tribe feel about animals and nature? Tell how you know.

WRITE Write a brief description of what a totem pole about your family would look like. You might want to draw a picture to go with your description.

510

Traditions

Family traditions are important to many people. What feelings about traditions are expressed in "Sun Dancers" and "Totem Pole"? Do you share any of these feelings? Explain your answer.

WRITER'S WORKSHOP

Choose a tradition that you and your family share. How did the tradition begin? Gather information about the tradition, and present what you learn in a research report.

Writer's Choice You might want to share some information about a tradition celebrated by other families. Choose and plan your own way to tell about how traditions can be important.

CONNECTIONS

Multicultural Connection

Miami's Cuban Americans

Miami is the second largest city in Florida and one of the busiest cities in the United States. Much of the city's success is due to Miami's Cuban Americans.

In 1959, a new leader named Fidel Castro took power in Cuba. Many skilled and educated Cubans were afraid for their future and left their country. They came to Miami, Florida, about two hundred miles from Cuba. At that time, Miami's economy was not doing well. When Cuban teachers, doctors, engineers, lawyers, and accountants flowed into the city, they were just what Miami needed. The new citizens started businesses and helped to bring the city back to life. Today, Cuban Americans are still an important part of the exciting culture of Miami.

The United States is the home of immigrants from all over the world. Choose one immigrant group— Cuban, Mexican, Irish, Polish, Korean, or any other group—and find out how some of its members have contributed to American culture.

512

Immigrant businesses have had a positive effect on Miami's economy.

Miami Beach, Florida

Social Studies Connection

Family Heritage Scrapbook

Your family may have come from another country, whether long ago or recently. Or you may be a Native American, and your family may have been here long before other groups arrived. Find out about your own family heritage, and start a scrapbook about it. Collect information, sayings, stories, pictures, and whatever else you can find that reminds you of your family's past.

Music Connection

American Folk Songs

Music is a part of our country's heritage. Some songs have been around so long that no one knows who first made them up. With a group, look through a book of folk songs and choose one. Practice singing it together. You might use homemade instruments, too. Perform your song for other classmates.

513

6

Dreamers

. . . i'm gonna beat
out my own rhythm
—Nikki Giovanni

Everyone has a dream and a rhythm, a way of making that dream come true. Dr. Martin Luther King, Jr., had one of the most important dreams of our times. Do you dream of growing up to be like him or like another adult whom you admire? Or do you dream of having an exciting adventure or reaching a special goal? As you read the selections in this unit, think about your own dream. You may find someone who shares it.

T H E M E S

BOOKSHELF

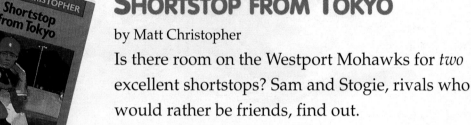

SHORTSTOP FROM TOKYO

by Matt Christopher

Is there room on the Westport Mohawks for *two* excellent shortstops? Sam and Stogie, rivals who would rather be friends, find out.

Harcourt Brace Library Book

CARVER

by Ruth Yaffe Radin

Jon, blind since he was two years old, wants to carve wood just as his father used to. With the help of an older sculptor, Jon finds that it is possible to achieve his dreams.

Award-Winning Author

Harcourt Brace Library Book

Go Fish

by Mary Stolz

Thomas is tired of resting his broken ankle. Then Grandfather suggests that the two of them go fishing. During their time together, Thomas learns to appreciate Grandfather's wisdom.

Notable Trade Book in the Field of Social Studies

Bonolo and the Peach Tree

by Njabulo S. Ndebele

Every day Bonolo sits under his peach tree, dreaming and telling stories. When the tree gets sick, suddenly Bonolo's dreaming cannot help him. How will he deal with this real-life crisis?

Award-Winning Author

Man from the Sky

by Avi

One day Jamie Peters sees a man falling from the sky. Will anyone believe Jamie when he tells what he has seen, or will people think he has been daydreaming again?

Children's Choice

THEME

Dream Journeys

Sometimes dreams can take you to places where your feet can't travel. These journeys can be exciting, and they can also help you learn what is important to you. As you read the following stories, think about what the characters learn through their dreams.

CONTENTS

519

JUST A DREAM

STORY AND PICTURES BY CHRIS VAN ALLSBURG

NOTABLE CHILDREN'S TRADE BOOK IN SOCIAL STUDIES

OUTSTANDING SCIENCE TRADE BOOK

As usual, Walter stopped at the bakery on his way home from school. He bought one large jelly-filled doughnut. He took the pastry from its bag, eating quickly as he walked along. He licked the red jelly from his fingers. Then he crumpled up the empty bag and threw it at a fire hydrant.

At home Walter saw Rose, the little girl next door, watering a tree that had just been planted. "It's my birthday present," she said proudly. Walter couldn't

understand why anyone would want a tree for a present.
His own birthday was just a few days away, "And I'm not
getting some dumb plant," he told Rose.

  After dinner Walter took out the trash. Three cans stood
next to the garage. One was for bottles, one for cans, and
one for everything else. As usual, Walter dumped
everything into one can. He was too busy to sort through
garbage, especially when there was something good on
television.

The show that Walter was so eager to watch was about a boy who lived in the future. The boy flew around in a tiny airplane that he parked on the roof of his house. He had a robot and a small machine that could make any kind of food with the push of a button.

Walter went to bed wishing he lived in the future. He couldn't wait to have his own tiny plane, a robot to take out the trash, and a machine that could make jelly doughnuts by the thousands. When he fell asleep, his wish came true. That night Walter's bed traveled to . . .

the future.

Walter woke up in the middle of a huge dump. A
bulldozer was pushing a heap of bulging trash bags
toward him. "Stop!" he yelled.

The man driving the bulldozer put his machine in
neutral. "Oh, sorry," he said. "Didn't see you."

Walter looked at the distant mountains of trash and
saw half-buried houses. "Do people live here?" he asked.

"Not anymore," answered the man.

A few feet from the bed was a rusty old street sign that
read FLORAL AVENUE. "Oh no," gasped Walter. He lived on
Floral Avenue.

The driver revved up his bulldozer. "Well," he
shouted, "back to work!"

Walter pulled the covers over his head. This can't be
the future, he thought. I'm sure it's just a dream. He went
back to sleep.

But not for long . . .

Walter peered over the edge of his bed, which was caught in the branches of a tall tree. Down below, he could see two men carrying a large saw. "Hello!" Walter yelled out.

"Hello to you!" they shouted back.

"You aren't going to cut down this tree, are you?" Walter asked.

But the woodcutters didn't answer. They took off their jackets, rolled up their sleeves, and got to work. Back and forth they pushed the saw, slicing through the trunk of Walter's tree. "You must need this tree for something important," Walter called down.

"Oh yes," they said, "very important." Then Walter noticed lettering on the woodcutters' jackets. He could just make out the words: QUALITY TOOTHPICK COMPANY. Walter sighed and slid back under the blankets.

Until . . .

Walter couldn't stop coughing. His bed was balanced on the rim of a giant smokestack. The air was filled with smoke that burned his throat and made his eyes itch. All around him, dozens of smokestacks belched thick clouds of hot, foul smoke. A workman climbed one of the stacks.

"What is this place?" Walter called out.

"This is the Maximum Strength Medicine Factory," the man answered.

"Gosh," said Walter, looking at all the smoke, "what kind of medicine do they make here?"

"Wonderful medicine," the workman replied, "for burning throats and itchy eyes."

Walter started coughing again.

"I can get you some," the man offered.

"No thanks," said Walter. He buried his head in his pillow and, when his coughing stopped, fell asleep.

But then . . .

Snowflakes fell on Walter. He was high in the mountains. A group of people wearing snowshoes and long fur coats hiked past his bed.

"Where are you going?" Walter asked.

"To the hotel," one of them replied.

Walter turned around and saw an enormous building. A sign on it read HOTEL EVEREST. "Is that hotel," asked Walter, "on the top of Mount Everest?"

"Yes," said one of the hikers. "Isn't it beautiful?"

"Well," Walter began. But the group didn't wait for his answer. They waved goodbye and marched away. Walter stared at the flashing yellow sign, then crawled back beneath his sheets.

But there was more to see . . .

Walter's hand was wet and cold. When he opened his eyes, he found himself floating on the open sea, drifting toward a fishing boat. The men on the boat were laughing and dancing.

"Ship ahoy!" Walter shouted.

The fishermen waved to him.

"What's the celebration for?" he asked.

"We've just caught a fish," one of them yelled back. "Our second one this week!" They held up their small fish for Walter to see.

"Aren't you supposed to throw the little ones back?" Walter asked.

But the fishermen didn't hear him. They were busy singing and dancing.

Walter turned away. Soon the rocking of the bed put him to sleep.

But only for a moment . . .

A loud, shrieking horn nearly lifted Walter off his mattress. He jumped up. There were cars and trucks all around him, horns honking loudly, creeping along inch by inch. Every driver had a car phone in one hand and a big cup of coffee in the other. When the traffic stopped completely, the honking grew even louder. Walter could not get back to sleep.

Hours passed, and he wondered if he'd be stuck on this highway forever. He pulled his pillow tightly around his head. This can't be the future, he thought. Where are the tiny airplanes, the robots? The honking continued into the night, until finally, one by one, the cars became quiet as their drivers, and Walter, went to sleep.

But his bed traveled on . . .

Walter looked up. A horse stood right over his bed, staring directly at him. In the saddle was a woman wearing cowboy clothes. "My horse likes you," she said.

"Good," replied Walter, who wondered where he'd ended up this time. All he could see was a dull yellow haze.

"Son," the woman told him, spreading her arms in front of her, "this is the mighty Grand Canyon."

Walter gazed into the foggy distance.

"Of course," she went on, "with all this smog, nobody's gotten a good look at it for years." The woman offered to sell Walter some postcards that showed the canyon in the old days. "They're real pretty," she said.

But he couldn't look. It's just a dream, he told himself. I know I'll wake up soon, back in my room.

But he didn't . . .

Walter looked out from under his sheets. His bed was flying through the night sky. A flock of ducks passed overhead. One of them landed on the bed, and to Walter's surprise, he began to speak. "I hope you don't mind," the bird said, "if I take a short rest here." The ducks had been flying for days, looking for the pond where they had always stopped to eat.

"I'm sure it's down there somewhere," Walter said, though he suspected something awful might have happened. After a while the duck waddled to the edge of the bed, took a deep breath, and flew off. "Good luck," Walter called to him. Then he pulled the blanket over his head. "It's just a dream," he whispered, and wondered if it would ever end.

Then finally . . .

Walter's bed returned to the present. He was safe in his
room again, but he felt terrible. The future he'd seen was
not what he'd expected. Robots and little airplanes didn't
seem very important now. He looked out his window at
the trees and lawns in the early morning light, then jumped
out of bed.

He ran outside and down the block, still in his pajamas. He found the empty jelly doughnut bag he'd thrown at the fire hydrant the day before. Then Walter went back home and, before the sun came up, sorted all the trash by the garage.

A few days later, on Walter's birthday, all his friends came over for cake and ice cream. They loved his new toys: the laser gun set, electric yo-yo, and inflatable dinosaurs. "My best present," Walter told them, "is outside." Then he showed them the gift that he'd picked out that morning—a tree.

After the party, Walter and his dad planted the birthday present. When he went to bed, Walter looked out his window. He could see his tree and the tree Rose had planted on her birthday. He liked the way they looked, side by side. Then he went to sleep, but not for long, because that night Walter's bed took him away again.

When Walter woke up, his bed was standing in the shade of two tall trees. The sky was blue. Laundry hanging from a clothesline flapped in the breeze. A man pushed an old motorless lawn mower. This isn't the future, Walter thought. It's the past.

"Good morning," the man said. "You've found a nice place to sleep."

"Yes, I have," Walter agreed. There was something very peaceful about the huge trees next to his bed.

The man looked up at the rustling leaves. "My great-grandmother planted one of these trees," he said, "when she was a little girl."

Walter looked up at the leaves too, and realized where his bed had taken him. This was the future, after all, a different kind of future. There were still no robots or tiny airplanes. There weren't even any clothes dryers or gas-powered lawn mowers. Walter lay back and smiled. "I like it here," he told the man, then drifted off to sleep in the shade of the two giant trees—the trees he and Rose had planted so many years ago.

Think about why the children in this story planted trees. What could you do to help the environment?

How would you describe this story to a friend?

What do you think Chris Van Allsburg wants you to learn from "Just a Dream"?

WRITE Write a brief description of what you hope the world will be like in the future.

A RIVER DREAM

ALLEN SAY

The week that Mark had a high fever, Uncle Scott sent him a small metal box for trout flies. Mark was thrilled to have his uncle's favorite fly box. And what's more, it brought back memories of his first fishing trip.

541

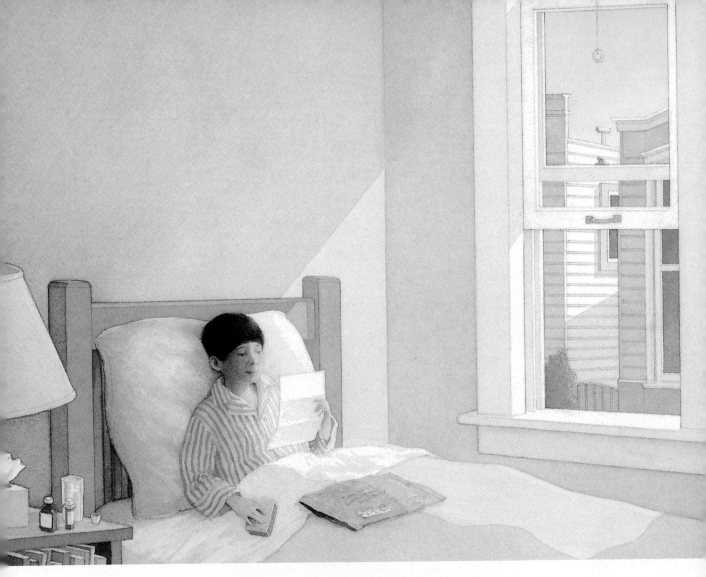

Last summer, Uncle Scott had taken him to a secret place on a sparkling river, and Mark had hooked a rainbow trout with a fly. How the little fish had jumped! More than anything else, Mark wanted to show his catch to his mother and father, but the fish got away and he never caught another.

"Better luck next time," Uncle Scott had said.

When Mark opened the box, he was startled by a cloud of mayflies that rose up from it. As the flies fluttered out the window, he looked outside and rubbed his eyes in wonder.

The whole neighborhood had disappeared! A river
flowed where the street had been, and a forest spread out
as far as he could see. Then he noticed the mayflies
hovering over the water, and shiny fish began to leap up
after them. Mark rushed outside.

He saw a rowboat bobbing in the shallow water.

"I wonder whose it is," he whispered. He looked all
around but saw no one. But the mayflies had moved
down the river, with the leaping fish after them.

"Well, I'm going to borrow this, just for a little while,"
he said and got into the boat.

As Mark drifted around the first bend in the river, he saw a lone fisherman below him.

Then, quite near Mark, a fish leapt out of the water, almost splashing him. It was the largest trout he had ever seen. It had a hook in its mouth.

"How about that, Mark!" shouted the fisherman.

"Uncle Scott!" Mark cried. "What are you doing here?"

"Funny you should ask," said Uncle, reeling in the fish. "I was about to ask what you were doing in my boat."

"This is your boat?" said Mark.

Uncle nodded. "Well, I'm glad to see you're feeling better. So, did you like the box I sent you?"

"Oh, yes, thank you very much. But you know what? All the flies flew away. I mean, they were real flies!"

"What magic!" Uncle laughed. "This fellow certainly thought my fly was real."

Uncle Scott netted the fish, removed the fly from its mouth, and let it swim away. Mark was amazed.

"Why did you do that?" asked Mark.

"Why didn't I kill the fish?" said Uncle. "I like to leave the river the way I found it. It's like cutting trees, Mark. You keep cutting trees and soon you're going to have bald mountains."

"Then why do you fish?"

"Just for the fun of it," Uncle replied. "Besides, maybe one day I will catch a mermaid. A wise old fisherman said that."

"But mermaids aren't real," said Mark.

"Aren't they?" Uncle smiled.

Mayflies began to flit all around them, and rising trout made rings on the water.

"The magic hour, my boy," said Uncle, climbing into the boat. "Do you remember your roll cast?"

"Yes, like this." Mark nodded, swinging his hand back and forth.

"Well, this may be your lucky night." Uncle handed Mark the rod.

Mark flushed with excitement. He raised the rod tip high, until the line hung behind his shoulder—just as his uncle had taught him. Then, with a quick, chopping stroke, he whipped the rod downward. The line shot out, and the cream-colored fly drifted down on the slick water like a snowflake. Mark took a deep breath.

"Fine cast!" Uncle exclaimed. "Now keep your eye on the fly. Remember, you're not going to feel the strike. You're going to see it. When you see a fish take your fly, raise your rod. Easy does it, my boy, you don't want to break your line."

Mark kept his eye on the fly, and suddenly the water swelled under it. Then a gaping mouth broke the surface and the fly was gone!

"Set the hook!" Uncle shouted.

Mark raised the rod, and the rod bent over from some heavy weight. The reel screeched as the line ran out. A large trout leapt in the air.

"It's bigger than the one you caught!" yelled Mark.

"Some rainbow!" Uncle agreed. "Let him run! Keep the rod up!"

The great trout put up a mighty fight, running again and again, leaping and twisting, but it could not break the line. When it could fight no more, Mark reeled it in. It barely fitted in Uncle's net.

"He's beautiful!" said Mark.

"Magnificent!" said Uncle. "And you're some fisherman!"

Mark sat down to admire his prize.

"Can I keep it?" he asked finally.

"Kill it, you mean?" said Uncle.

"Well . . . I want to show it to Mom and Dad. . . . It's my fish."

"That it is," said his uncle. "You must kill it quickly." He opened his knife and gave it to his nephew.

"I have to do it?" asked Mark.

"It's your fish," said Uncle, lighting his pipe.

"How?" The boy waved the knife.

"Give it a quick stab there." Uncle Scott pointed at the rainbow's head. "Mind your hand, it's very sharp."

Mark stared at the gasping fish, then at the gleaming blade.

The knife dropped from Mark's hand with a loud
clatter. Then he lifted his catch with both hands and
lowered it into the river. The limp fish did not move.

"Is it dead?" asked Mark.

"It'll be all right," said his uncle. "Rock it back and
forth and let water go through the gills."

So Mark rocked the fish, back and forth, back and
forth—until the fins began to wave. Then the sleek fish
stirred, as though waking from a long sleep. With a flick
of its tail the rainbow slipped out of the boy's hands, and
the boy watched his trout swim away.

"That was fun," he whispered.

"So what's the use in fishing if you don't keep any fish?" Uncle Scott asked.

"Oh, it's good to leave the river the way I found it," said Mark. "Besides, I might catch a mermaid some day."

"That's my man," Uncle said, laughing. "Just for that I'm going to build you a rod."

"A rod like yours?" shouted Mark.

"Exactly like mine, with your name on it," said Uncle.

Just then they heard someone talking quite nearby.

"Sounds like a woman," said Uncle Scott. "Maybe that *was* your mermaid."

They looked upstream and saw a house. All the windows were lit except for Mark's. It was still open, and his mother's voice drifted out of it.

"I've kept you out long enough," Uncle Scott said and took the oars.

Mark said good night to his uncle and climbed into his room through the window. A short while later, when his parents opened the door, Mark pretended to be fast asleep.

"Leave it to my brother," Mother whispered. "Sending fishing lures to a sick child. Why, they're all over the bed. He could have hurt himself!"

"Look," said his father. "His temperature seems almost normal."

"Thank goodness," said his mother.

And Mark fell asleep.

Mark decides to let the beautiful fish he catches go free. Would you have made the same choice in his place? Explain your answer.

Does Mark's uncle enjoy nature? What information from the story makes you think as you do?

In your opinion, what does Mark learn through his river dream?

WRITE Mark was able to make a difficult decision. Write a few sentences about a time when you had to make a difficult decision.

WORDS ABOUT THE AUTHOR AND ILLUSTRATOR:
ALLEN SAY

Allen Say didn't start out to be an artist. He wanted to be a cartoonist. The son of a Korean father and a Japanese mother, twelve-year-old Allen went to the studio of a great Japanese cartoonist and asked if the man would teach him. Noro Shinpei agreed, and he taught Allen everything he knew about Western and Japanese styles of drawing and art.

When Allen Say was sixteen, he went to California. He lived with his father, who had moved there after he and Allen's mother were divorced. Since Allen did not speak any English, he had a tough time growing up and going to school in America. In addition, World War II had been over for only eight years, and many people were still angry at Japan and at Japanese Americans. Although his family had encouraged him to be a businessman, Allen Say became a successful commercial photographer, even though painting was still what he wanted to do. His first real achievement as an author and illustrator came in 1982, when he wrote *The Bicycle Man*, about a group of Japanese children and two Americans in post–World War II Japan.

Say likes to write about both his memories of Japan and his life here in his adopted country. "I start out with a very vague idea. Then the story comes to me as I start painting, and when the scenes and the characters I'm trying to depict become real to me, then somehow the words happen. Because I came late to English, I have a fear of writing it, but I don't agonize too much. I let the pictures tell the story."

Dream Journeys

Do you think that you can learn through your dreams? Tell why you think as you do.

WRITER'S WORKSHOP

Walter and Mark both learn how to care for the environment. Think about something you have learned to do. How would you teach it to someone else? Write a how-to paragraph explaining how to do the activity, and include the necessary steps in the correct order.

Writer's Choice   If you wish, respond to the selections in another way. Plan your response and how you will share it with others.

T H E M E

Dream Makers

Do you ever daydream about what kind of person you will grow up to be? What qualities do you have now that you are proud of? The characters in the following selections will help you think about what kind of person you are—and will show you ways to become the person you want to be.

C O N T E N T S

Daydreamers

by Eloise Greenfield
illustrated by Tom Feelings

Daydreamers . . .
holding their bodies still
for a time
letting the world turn around them
while their dreams hopscotch,
doubledutch, dance,
thoughts rollerskate,
crisscross,
bump into hopes and wishes.

Dreamers
thinking up new ways,
looking toward new days,
planning new tries,
asking new whys.

Before long,
hands will start to move again,
eyes turn outward,
bodies shift for action,
but for this moment they are still,
they are
the daydreamers,
letting the world dizzy itself
without them.

Scenes passing through their minds
make no sound
glide from hiding places
promenade and return
silently
the children watch their memories
with spirit-eyes
seeing more than they saw before
feeling more
or maybe less
than they felt the time before
reaching with spirit-hands
to touch the dreams
drawn from their yesterdays.

They will not be the same
after this growing time,
this dreaming.

In their stillness they have moved
forward
toward womanhood
toward manhood.

This dreaming
has made them
new.

JOHN STEPTOE

Mufaro's Beautiful Daughters

AN AFRICAN TALE

A LONG TIME AGO, in a certain place in Africa, a small village lay across a river and half a day's journey from a city where a great king lived. A man named Mufaro lived in this village with his two daughters, who were called Manyara and Nyasha. Everyone agreed that Manyara and Nyasha were very beautiful.

Manyara was almost always in a bad temper. She teased her sister whenever their father's back was turned, and she had been heard to say, "Someday, Nyasha, I will be a queen, and you will be a servant in my household."

"If that should come to pass," Nyasha responded, "I will be pleased to serve you. But why do you say such things? You are clever and strong and beautiful. Why are you so unhappy?"

"Because everyone talks about how kind you are, and they praise everything you do," Manyara replied. "I'm certain that Father loves you best. But when I am a queen, everyone will know that your silly kindness is only weakness."

Nyasha was sad that Manyara felt this way, but she ignored her sister's words and went about her chores. Nyasha kept a small plot of land, on which she grew millet, sunflowers, yams, and vegetables. She always sang as she worked, and some said it was her singing that made her crops more bountiful than anyone else's.

One day, Nyasha noticed a small garden snake resting beneath a yam vine. "Good day, little Nyoka," she called to him. "You are welcome here. You will keep away any creatures who might spoil my vegetables." She bent forward, gave the little snake a loving pat on the head, and then returned to her work.

From that day on, Nyoka was always at Nyasha's side when she tended her garden. It was said that she sang all the more sweetly when he was there.

Mufaro knew nothing of how Manyara treated Nyasha. Nyasha was too considerate of her father's feelings to complain, and Manyara was always careful to behave herself when Mufaro was around.

Early one morning, a messenger from the city arrived. The Great King wanted a wife. "The Most Worthy and Beautiful Daughters in the Land are invited to appear before the King, and he will choose one to become Queen!" the messenger proclaimed.

Mufaro called Manyara and Nyasha to him. "It would be a great honor to have one of you chosen," he said. "Prepare yourselves to journey to the city. I will call together all our friends to make a wedding party. We will leave tomorrow as the sun rises."

"But, my father," Manyara said sweetly, "it would be painful for either of us to leave you, even to be wife to the king. I know Nyasha would grieve to death if she were parted from you. I am strong. Send me to the city, and let poor Nyasha be happy here with you."

Mufaro beamed with pride. "The king has asked for the most worthy and the most beautiful. No, Manyara, I cannot send you alone. Only a king can choose between two such worthy daughters. Both of you must go!"

That night, when everyone was asleep, Manyara stole quietly out of the village. She had never been in the forest at night before, and she was frightened, but her greed to be the first to appear before the king drove her on. In her hurry, she almost stumbled over a small boy who suddenly appeared, standing in the path.

"Please," said the boy. "I am hungry. Will you give me something to eat?"

"I have brought only enough for myself," Manyara replied.

"But, please!" said the boy. "I am so very hungry."

"Out of my way, boy! Tomorrow I will become your queen. How dare you stand in my path?"

After traveling for what seemed to be a great distance, Manyara came to a small clearing. There, silhouetted against the moonlight, was an old woman seated on a large stone.

The old woman spoke. "I will give you some advice, Manyara. Soon after you pass the place where two paths cross, you will see a grove of trees. They will laugh at you. You must not laugh in return. Later, you will meet a man with his head under his arm. You must be polite to him."

"How do you know my name? How dare you advise your future queen? Stand aside, you ugly old woman!" Manyara scolded, and then rushed on her way without looking back.

Just as the old woman had foretold, Manyara came to a grove of trees, and they did indeed seem to be laughing at her.

"I must be calm," Manyara thought. "I will not be frightened." She looked up at the trees and laughed out loud. "I laugh at you, trees!" she shouted, and she hurried on.

It was not yet dawn when Manyara heard the sound of rushing water. "The river must be up ahead," she thought. "The great city is just on the other side."

But there, on the rise, she saw a man with his head tucked under his arm. Manyara ran past him without speaking. "A queen acknowledges only those who please her," she said to herself. "I will be queen. I will be queen," she chanted, as she hurried on toward the city.

Nyasha woke at the first light of dawn. As she put on her finest garments, she thought how her life might be changed forever beyond this day. "I'd much prefer to live here," she admitted to herself. "I'd hate to leave this village and never see my father or sing to little Nyoka again."

Her thoughts were interrupted by loud shouts and a commotion from the wedding party assembled outside. Manyara was missing! Everyone bustled about, searching and calling for her. When they found her footprints on the path that led to the city, they decided to go on as planned.

As the wedding party moved through the forest, brightly

plumed birds darted about in the cool green shadows beneath the trees. Though anxious about her sister, Nyasha was soon filled with excitement about all there was to see.

They were deep in the forest when she saw the small boy standing by the side of the path.

"You must be hungry," she said, and handed him a yam she had brought for her lunch. The boy smiled and disappeared as quietly as he had come.

Later, as they were approaching the place where the two paths crossed, the old woman appeared and silently pointed the way to the city. Nyasha thanked her and gave her a small pouch filled with sunflower seeds.

The sun was high in the sky when the party came to the grove of towering trees. Their uppermost branches seemed to bow down to Nyasha as she passed beneath them.

At last, someone announced that they were near their destination.

Nyasha ran ahead and topped the rise before the others could catch up with her. She stood transfixed at her first sight of the city. "Oh, my father," she called. "A great spirit must stand guard here! Just look at what lies before us. I never in all my life dreamed there could be anything so beautiful!"

Arm in arm, Nyasha and her father descended the hill, crossed the river, and approached the city gate. Just as they entered through the great doors, the air was rent by piercing cries, and Manyara ran wildly out of a chamber at the center of the enclosure. When she saw Nyasha, she fell upon her, sobbing.

"Do not go to the king, my sister. Oh, please, Father, do not let her go!" she cried hysterically. "There's a great monster there, a snake with five heads! He said that he knew all my faults and that I displeased him. He would have swallowed me alive if I had not run. Oh, my sister, please do not go inside that place."

It frightened Nyasha to see her sister so upset. But, leaving her father to comfort Manyara, she bravely made her way to the chamber and opened the door.

On the seat of the great chief's stool lay the little garden snake. Nyasha laughed with relief and joy.

"My little friend!" she exclaimed. "It's such a pleasure to see you, but why are you here?"

"I am the king," Nyoka replied.

And there, before Nyasha's eyes, the garden snake changed shape.

"I am the king. I am also the hungry boy with whom you shared a yam in the forest and the old woman to whom you made a gift of sunflower seeds. But you know me best as Nyoka. Because I have been all of these, I know you to be the Most Worthy and Most Beautiful Daughter in the Land. It would make me very happy if you would be my wife."

And so it was that, a long time ago, Nyasha agreed to be married. The king's mother and sisters took Nyasha to their house, and the wedding preparations began. The best weavers in the land laid out their finest cloth for her wedding garments. Villagers from all around were invited to the celebration, and a great feast was held. Nyasha prepared the bread for the wedding feast from millet that had been brought from her village.

Mufaro proclaimed to all who would hear him that he was the happiest father in all the land, for he was blessed with two beautiful and worthy daughters—Nyasha, the queen; and Manyara, a servant in the queen's household.

Were you surprised by the ending of this story? Explain your answer.

Think about the things Manyara says and the things she does. If she had been chosen to become queen instead of her sister, do you think she would have been happy? Explain your answer.

Will Nyasha be a good queen? Why or why not?

WRITE   Nyasha is faced with many choices, and she always chooses to act kindly. Write a paragraph about a time when you made a choice to act kindly.

Words About the Author and Illustrator: John Steptoe

Which did you enjoy more about *Mufaro's Beautiful Daughters*—the story or the illustrations? John Steptoe spent more than two and a half years writing and illustrating this book. He worked at writing stories that African American children could relate to and that would encourage them to follow their dreams. The Cinderella theme came to Mr. Steptoe's mind, and he found that almost every culture has its own version of the classic tale. *Mufaro's Beautiful Daughters* was based on an African Cinderella tale. The story and the art were inspired by the people living near Zimbabwe in southern Africa.

John Steptoe was already an award-winning author and artist before *Mufaro's Beautiful Daughters* was published. He began drawing as a child and attended the High School of Art and Design in New York City for three years. John Steptoe wrote his first book, *Stevie,* at the age of sixteen.

Mr. Steptoe illustrated not only his own books but also stories written by other authors, including *Mother Crocodile,* another African tale. He received many awards for both his illustrations and his writing. John Steptoe died in 1989.

John Steptoe believed that there were many young people like himself who wanted to accomplish something important in their lives. It was his hope that he could help encourage children to seek opportunities, take pride in themselves, and achieve their dreams.

Dream Makers

The young people in the poem "Daydreamers" take the time to dream about their futures. Nyasha helps to create her own future. What have the selections in this theme taught you about dreams and goals?

WRITER'S WORKSHOP

Think about the message of "Mufaro's Beautiful Daughters." Write a folktale of your own with a message that is important to you. Remember that in a folktale animals and objects can act like people. Also, keep in mind that a folktale usually has a happy ending!

Writer's Choice

Folktales are stories that originally were not written down but were passed orally from one storyteller to another. You could plan a folktale and tell it orally, or you could choose another way to present a message that is important to you. For example, you might enjoy writing an original poem about dreaming.

THEME

Practice Makes Perfect

Setting and reaching goals is an exciting part of life. Do you dream of things you would like to accomplish? As you read the following selections, you may get some ideas on how to turn your dreams into reachable goals.

CONTENTS

SHORTSTOP FROM TOKYO

BY MATT CHRISTOPHER

ILLUSTRATED BY DENNIS ZIEMIENSKI

Stogie Crane wants to play starting shortstop for the Westport Mohawks. The problem is, so does Sam Suzuki, who has just moved to town from Japan. In this game, each boy is trying to prove he deserves the position.

Russ Russo led off in the top of the fourth with a looping single over second. The coach signaled Lee Cragg (pinch-hitting for Beak) to bunt, but Lee's first two tries resulted in fouls. He had to swing now. He took two balls, then lashed hard at the next pitch, sending it high into the air over short. The Copperhead shortstop grabbed it for the first out.

"Okay, Sam," said Fuzzy. "Show 'em how you do it in Tokyo."

"Tokyo?" Tony Francis frowned. "Is that where he's from?"

"Sure. Where did you think he's from—Mexico City?"

Sam whipped a couple of bats around a few times, then dropped one and stepped to the plate.

"He spreads his legs awful wide for a short guy," observed Dennis.

"And look at him wave that bat around," said Fuzzy. "Maybe he's chasing the bugs away."

Smack! Sam Suzuki connected with the first pitch. The ball sailed over the third baseman's head, curved outward, and struck the ground just inside the foul line. The entire Mohawk bench stood on their feet. "Go! Go!"

By the time the left fielder had relayed the ball in, Russ had scored and Sam was perched nicely on third base.

"A triple!" cried Fuzzy, clapping thunderously. "How

'bout that? And the first pitch, too!" He laughed at Stogie. "Looks like you've just lost your job, Stogie, ol' boy!"

Stogie grinned politely. He tried hard to hide a feeling that had been gnawing at him ever since Sam Suzuki had come upon the scene. That triple had magnified the feeling a hundred times over. Yet it was strange. He didn't know exactly what that feeling was. Was it envy? Was it jealousy? Maybe it was one or the other, or both. But he knew it wasn't right to be envious or

jealous of anyone. Envy and jealousy destroyed friendship, and made you feel sick inside, too.

Jim Albanese popped up to the catcher for the second out. Bob Sobus took a strike, then pitcher Larry Hill lost his control and walked him. Dennis Krupa batted for Fuzzy and grounded out to end the half inning.

"If I knew you were going to do that," grumbled Fuzzy, "I would've batted myself." As if he had anything to say about it.

The Mohawks trotted out to their positions and the Copperheads came to bat.

Coach Dirkus squeezed in between Stogie and Fuzzy on the bench. "Sam tell you guys about that glove of his?" he asked, grinning.

"Not me," said Stogie.

"Me, either," said Fuzzy. The other guys edged closer.

"He's really proud of it, you know," said the coach. "It seems a famous Japanese ball player, Shigeo Nagashima, signed his name on the glove. So it's worth a lot to Sam."

Russ fumbled a grounder, putting a man on first. The next hitter clobbered a long high fly that went clean over the left field fence for a homer. Stretch looked nervous on the mound after that, even though the infielders and outfielders chattered to cheer him up.

A grounder sizzled like a scared snake down to short. Stogie watched intently as Sam crouched, waiting for it. *Miss it! miss it!* Stogie couldn't help wishing silently.

Sam caught the wild grounder and pegged it to first.

His throw was like a tight string drawn across the diamond, incredible for a little guy.

"Look at that arm!" exclaimed Coach Dirkus. "The kid can really throw!"

Stretch chalked up a strikeout. Another hot grounder to Sam, which he caught easily and pegged to first for an out, ended the half inning. The scoreboard at the left of the left field foul line read:

Innings	1	2	3	4	5	6
MOHAWKS	2	0	3	1		
C HEADS	1	2	0	2		

Daren Holden singled for Bernie Drake in the top of the fifth. Tony Francis followed with another single. Then Stretch came through with a double, scoring Daren and advancing Tony to third. Russ popped up to the pitcher. Then Lee Cragg blasted a line drive to short and the shortstop picked off Stretch at second before he could tag up. Three away.

The Copperheads picked up a run in the bottom of the fifth. But the Mohawks, even though Sam Suzuki got his second hit of the game, a double, couldn't score. The Copperheads, at bat for their last chance, failed to hit. One of their outs was a pop fly on the grass far behind Sam. He ran back and caught the ball on the fingertips of his glove, drawing a tremendous cheer from the crowd. Mohawks 7, Copperheads 6.

"Sam certainly played a wonderful ball game," said Jill, Stogie's older sister. "I didn't know they played baseball in Japan."

"Huh!" Stogie snorted. "They probably play more baseball than we do. They draw bigger crowds, that's for sure. Haven't you ever heard about our big league teams going over there and playing their teams?"

"When I read the sports pages I read about our girls' softball team, not about big league teams playing in Japan," said Jill haughtily.

Dad chuckled. He and Mom were walking behind Stogie, Jill, Beak and Fuzzy. "Tell you one thing about Sam Suzuki," he said. "He's an all-around baseball player. He can hit, throw and field like nobody's business. And being among strangers his first day didn't seem to bother him a bit."

Fuzzy laughed. "Bother him? I guess not! I've never seen a kid like him in my life!"

What is your opinion of Stogie? Why?

The coach says that Sam's glove is worth a lot. What does he mean by this?

What do you predict might happen in the next game the Mohawks play? Use evidence from the selection to support your prediction.

WRITE   Give Stogie your advice. What can he do to be a better shortstop? What can he do to be a better team member? Write a list of tips for Stogie to follow.

587

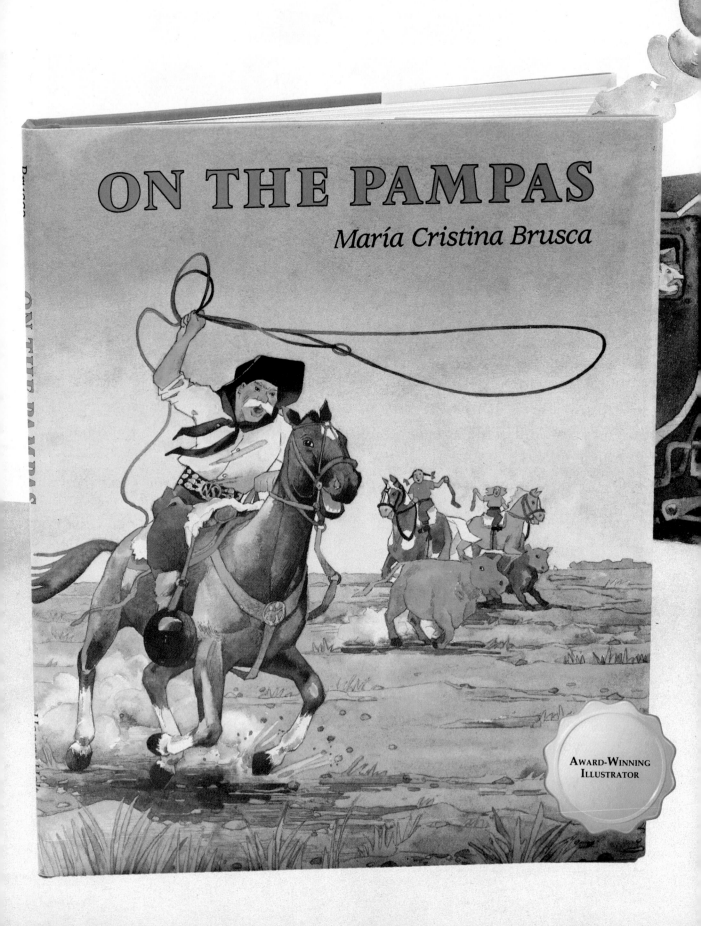

ON THE PAMPAS

María Cristina Brusca

AWARD-WINNING
ILLUSTRATOR

I grew up in Argentina, in South America. I lived with my family in the big city of Buenos Aires, but we spent our summers in the country, at my grandparents' *estancia*. One summer my parents and brother stayed in the city, so I went without them.

My grandmother met me at the station in Buenos Aires, and we had breakfast as we rode through miles and miles of the flattest land in the world—the pampas. All around us, as far as we could see, were fences, windmills, and millions of cattle grazing.

Our station, San Enrique, was at the end of the line, where the train tracks stopped. My grandfather was there to meet us in his pickup truck and take us the five miles to the estancia.

The ranch was called La Carlota, and the gates were made of iron bars from a fort that had been on that very spot a hundred years before. As we drove up to the gates, we were greeted by a cloud of dust and a thundering of hooves—it was my cousin Susanita, on her horse.

Susanita lived at the estancia all year round. She knew everything about horses, cows, and all the other animals that live on the pampas. Even though she was three years younger than me, she had her own horse, La Baya. Susanita was so tiny, she had to shimmy up La Baya's leg to get on her back. But she rode so well that the gauchos called her La Gauchita—"The Little Gaucho."

I didn't have a horse of my own, but old Salguero, the ranch foreman, brought me Pampita, a sweet-tempered mare, to ride. She wasn't very fast, but she certainly was my friend.

Susanita and I did everything together that summer. She was the one who showed me how to take care of the horses. We would brush their coats, trim their hooves, and braid their manes and tails.

Susanita was always ready for an adventure, no matter how scary. She used to swim in the creek holding on to La Baya's mane. At first I was afraid to follow her, but when she finally convinced me, it was a lot of fun.

I wanted to learn all the things a gaucho has to know. I wanted to ride out on the pampas every day, as Salguero did, and to wear a belt like his, with silver coins from all over the world and a buckle with my initials on

it. Salguero said I'd have to begin at the beginning, and he spent hours showing Susanita and me how to use the lasso.

It was going to take a while for me to become a gaucho. The first time I lassoed a calf, it dragged me halfway across the corral. But Salguero told me that even he had been dragged plenty of times, so I kept trying, until I got pretty good at it.

Whenever the gauchos were working with the cattle, Susanita was there, and before long I was too. Sometimes the herd had to be rounded up and moved from one pasture to another. I loved galloping behind hundreds of cattle, yelling to make them run. I never got to yell like that in the city!

One day we separated the calves from the cows, to vaccinate them and brand them with "the scissors," La Carlota's mark. That was more difficult—and more exciting, too. I tried to do what Salguero told me to, but sometimes I got lost in the middle of that sea of cattle.

At noon, everybody would sit down around one big table and eat together. I was always hungry. Grandma, Susanita's mother, and Maria the cook had been working hard all morning too. They would make soup, salad, and lamb stew or pot roast, or my favorite, *carbonada,* a thick stew made of corn and peaches.

After lunch the grown-ups took a *siesta,* but not us. We liked to stay outdoors. Some afternoons, when it was too hot to do anything else, we rode out to a eucalyptus grove that was nice and cool, and stayed there until it got dark, reading comic books or cowboy stories.

Other times we would gallop for two hours to the general store and buy ourselves an orange soda. Then, while we drank it, we'd look at all the saddles and bridles we planned to have when we were grown up and rich. Sometimes the storekeeper would take down a wonderful gaucho belt like Salguero's, and we would admire the silver coins and wonder where each one came from.

One day we rode far away from the house, to a field where Susanita thought we might find *ñandú* eggs. They

are so huge, you can bake a whole cake with just one
of them. After riding around all afternoon, we found a
nest, well hidden in the tall grass, with about twenty
pale-yellow eggs as big as coconuts.

Salguero had warned us to watch out for the ñandú,
and he was right! The father ñandú, who protects the
nest, saw us taking an egg. He was furious and chased
us out of the field.

The next day we used the ñandú egg to bake a birthday cake for my grandmother. We snuck into the kitchen while she was taking her siesta, so it would be a surprise. The cake had three layers, and in between them we put whipped cream and peaches from the trees on the ranch.

We had a wonderful party for my grandmother's birthday. The gauchos started the fire for the *asado* early in the evening, and soon the smell of the slowly cooking meat filled the air.

There was music, and dancing, too. We stayed up almost all night, and I learned to dance the *zamba,* taking little steps and hops, and twirling my handkerchief.

Most evenings were much quieter. There was just the hum of the generator that made electricity for the house. We liked to go out to the *mate* house, where the gauchos spent their evenings.

We listened to them tell ghost stories and tall tales while they sat around the fire, passing the gourd and sipping mate through the silver straw. We didn't like the hot, bitter tea, but we loved being frightened by their spooky stories.

The summer was drawing to a close, and soon I would be returning to Buenos Aires. The night before I was to leave, Salguero showed me how to find the Southern Cross. The generator had been turned off, and there was only the soft sound of the peepers. We could see the horses sleeping far off in the field.

The next morning, my last at the estancia, Susanita and I got up before dawn. Pampita and the other horses were still out in the field. Salguero handed me his own horse's reins. He told me he thought I was ready to bring

in the horses by myself. I wasn't sure I could do it, but Susanita encouraged me to try.

I remembered what I'd seen Salguero do. I tried to get the leading mare, with her bell, to go toward the corral, and the others would follow her. It wasn't easy. The foals were frisky and kept running away. But I stayed behind them until finally the little herd was all together, trotting in front of me.

I was so busy trying to keep the foals from running off that I didn't notice the whole household waiting in the corral with Salguero. Everyone cheered as I rode in, and before I knew it, my grandfather was helping me off the horse. "You've become quite a gaucho this summer," he said. My grandmother held out a wonderful gaucho belt like Salguero's, with silver coins from around the world—and my initials on the buckle!

"And," she added, "there's something else every gaucho needs. Next summer, when you come back, you'll have your very own horse waiting for you!" She pointed to the leading mare's foal, the friskiest and most beautiful of them all.

Before I could say a word, the foal pranced over to me, tossing his head. I would have the whole winter to decide what to name him, and to look forward to my next summer on the pampas.

Do you think you would like to visit Susanita and her family? Explain your answer.

The girls have a lot of fun during their summer together. Which of their activities would you enjoy the most?

What did you learn about the pampas that you did not know before?

WRITE It takes a lot of practice before María learns how to lasso a calf. Write about an activity that you needed to practice before you learned to do it well.

ALA
Notable Book
SLJ Best Books
Of The Year

Last Laugh

by Lee Bennett Hopkins · from *Surprises*

They all laughed when I told them
I wanted to be

A woman in space
Floating so free.

But they won't laugh at me
When they finally see
My feet up on Mars
And my face on TV.

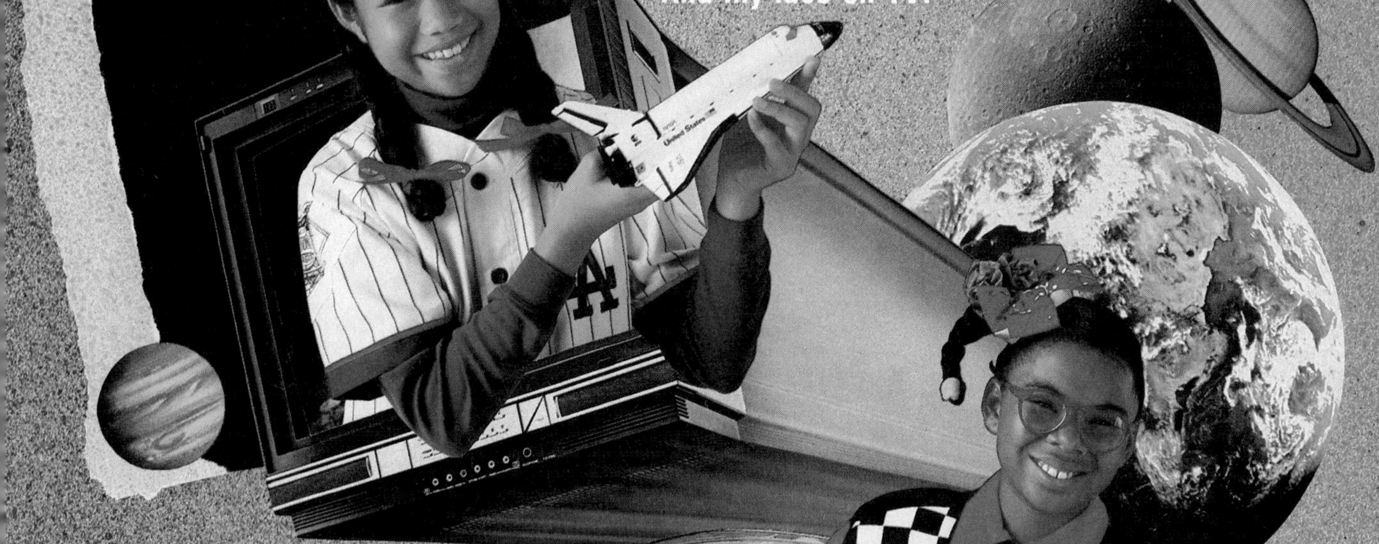

The Drum

by Nikki Giovanni

daddy says the world is
a drum tight and hard

and i told him

i'm gonna beat
out my own rhythm

Award-Winning
Author

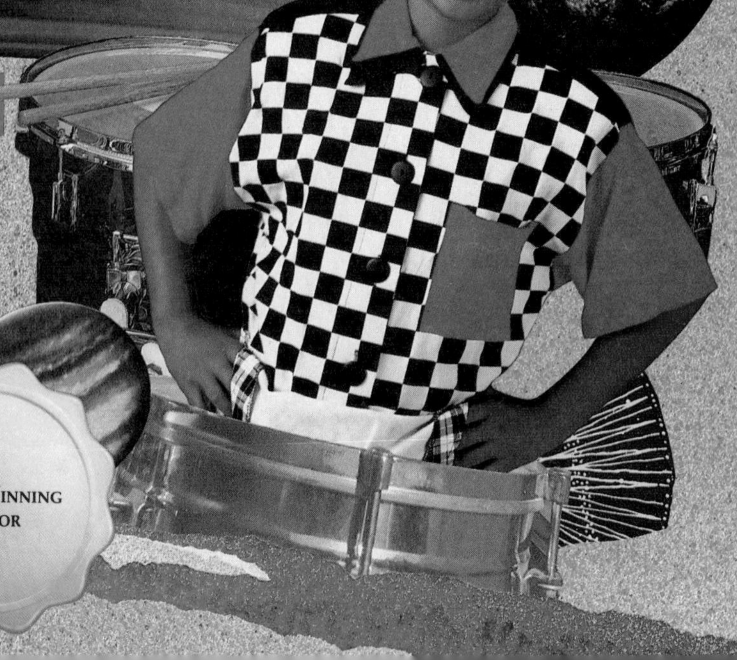

Practice Makes Perfect

How is practice important to Stogie, Sam, and María Cristina as they try to reach their goals? Give some examples from the selections to support your answer.

WRITER'S WORKSHOP

Use what you have learned about achieving dreams and goals to write a play. The characters, the setting, and the plot of your play can be realistic or fantastic—it's up to you.

Writer's Choice
Plan your own way to share your thoughts about achieving dreams and goals. You could tell a realistic story about something you or a family member has achieved, or you could decide on an idea of your own.

Connections

Multicultural Connection

Dream of a Better World

"I have a dream," said Dr. Martin Luther King, Jr., while standing in front of the Lincoln Memorial in 1963. Thousands of people listened to his historic speech.

Dr. King's dream was to live in a nation with equal rights and freedom for all. And he did more than just dream. He spent his life fighting for what he believed in. Thanks to Dr. Martin Luther King's hard work and the example he set, the dream is being achieved.

Many other African Americans, such as Rosa Parks and Thurgood Marshall, have taken part in the equal rights struggle. Find out more about the history of this struggle in America. Create a collage showing what you learned.

Social Studies Connection

American Dreamers

There have been many great dreamers like Martin Luther King, Jr., whose work has made our nation a better place. Read about other leaders, such as doctors, scientists, and soldiers, who improved the lives of others. Use what you learn to create a class bulletin board gallery of great Americans.

Art Connection

Your Own Dream

What is your own dream for a better world? With a small group, make a mural that shows some changes that you would like to see. Together, write a poem that tells how people can make a dream come true. Share your mural and poem with the rest of your classmates.

GLOSSARY

The **pronunciation** of each word in this glossary is shown by a phonetic respelling in brackets; for example, [ə•chēv′mənt]. An accent mark (′) follows the syllable with the most stress: [iks•klām′]. A secondary, or lighter, accent mark (′) follows a syllable with less stress: [ek′splə•nā′shən]. The key to other pronunciation symbols is below. You will find a shortened version of this key on alternate pages of the glossary.

Pronunciation Key*

a	add, map	m	move, seem	u	up, done
ā	ace, rate	n	nice, tin	û(r)	burn, term
â(r)	care, air	ng	ring, song	yo͞o	fuse, few
ä	palm, father	o	odd, hot	v	vain, eve
b	bat, rub	ō	open, so	w	win, away
ch	check, catch	ô	order, jaw	y	yet, yearn
d	dog, rod	oi	oil, boy	z	zest, muse
e	end, pet	ou	pout, now	zh	vision, pleasure
ē	equal, tree	o͝o	took, full	ə	the schwa,
f	fit, half	o͞o	pool, food		an unstressed
g	go, log	p	pit, stop		vowel representing
h	hope, hate	r	run, poor		the sound spelled
i	it, give	s	see, pass		a in *above*
ī	ice, write	sh	sure, rush		e in *sicken*
j	joy, ledge	t	talk, sit		i in *possible*
k	cool, take	th	thin, both		o in *melon*
l	look, rule	th	this, bathe		u in *circus*

*Adapted entries, the Pronunciation Key, and the Short Key that appear on the following pages are reprinted from *HBJ School Dictionary*. Copyright © 1990 by Harcourt Brace & Company. Reprinted by permission of Harcourt Brace & Company.

A

acrobat

ad lib *Ad lib* is a shortened form of the Latin phrase *ad libitum,* which means "at pleasure." So speakers and comedians who *ad lib* say whatever gives them pleasure instead of following a set script.

balance

a·chieve·ment [ə·chēv′mənt] *n.* Something that a person has done very well: **Learning to ride a horse was a special** *achievement* **for Felipe.**

ac·knowl·edge [ak·nol′ij] *v.* To look at someone and speak to him or her.

a·cre [ā′kər] *n.* A large amount of land.

ac·ro·bat [ak′rə·bat′] *n.* A person skilled in tumbling or in using the trapeze, rings, or other equipment: **The** *acrobats* **jump high when performing their stunts.**

ad lib [ad′lib′] *v.* To make up words or actions at the moment, not before.

ad·mis·sion [ad·mish′ən] *n.* The price charged to enter an event: *Admission* **to the baseball game is $1.00.**

ad·vise [ad·vīz′] *v.* To tell someone what to do. *syn.* recommend

a·gent [ā′jənt] *n.* A person who can act for someone else: **The actor's** *agent* **helped him get a role in a movie.**

a·nem·o·ne [ə·nem′ə·nē] *n.* A small sea animal with soft, flowing, armlike tubes that look like flower petals.

anx·ious [angk′shəs] *adj.* Worried or nervous: **Tom felt** *anxious* **and concerned about his sick uncle in the hospital.** *syn.* uneasy

as·ton·ish [ə·ston′ish] *v.* **as·ton·ished, as·ton·ish·ing** To amaze; to have a feeling of surprise: **Jim was** *astonished* **that Howie played the piano so well.**

at·ten·tive [ə·ten′tiv] *adj.* Careful to notice things and pay attention. *syn.* aware

av·a·lanche [av′ə·lanch′] *n.* The falling of objects suddenly in a heap.

a·void [ə·void′] *v.* **a·void·ed, a·void·ing** To stay away from something.

B

baf·fle [baf′əl] *v.* **baf·fled, baf·fling** To mix up. *syn.* confuse

bal·ance [bal′əns] *v.* **bal·anced, bal·anc·ing** To move or control the body without leaning or falling: **Juan stood on the diving board and** *balanced* **himself.**

bar·ri·er [bar′ē·ər] *n.* Something blocking the way: **The** *barrier* **prevented us from crossing the street.**

be·hav·ior [bi·hāv′yər] *n.* Manner of conducting oneself: **Your** *behavior* **in school is different from your** *behavior* **on the playground.**

be·wil·der·ment [bi·wil′dər·mənt] *n.* The feeling of not understanding something: **Oscar looked with** *bewilderment* **at the math problem because it did not make sense to him.** *syn.* confusion

bil·low [bil′ō] *v.* **bil·lowed, bil·low·ing** To rise or swell like a wave: **The forest fire created black clouds of smoke that were** *billowing* **in the wind.**

board [bôrd] *n.* A colorful flat piece of heavy paper or wood on which a game is played: **The** *board* **for checkers has squares of two colors.**

board·ing·house [bôr′ding·hous′] *n.* A house where a room and food are provided for an amount of money.

bored [bôrd] *adj.* Without interest or excitement: **The children were** *bored* **after the clown left the party.**

boun·ti·ful [boun′tə·fəl] *adj.* Plentiful; generous in size: **The crop was so** *bountiful* **that the farmer gave apples away.**

brand [brand] *v.* To make a permanent mark on an animal to identify it.

bunt [bunt] *v.* To hit a ball softly with a bat.

C

cam·paign [kam·pān′] *n.* Activities organized to gain or win something.

cam·pus [kam′pəs] *n.* The grounds and buildings of a school or an organization: **Our workplace is on a** *campus* **that has four buildings.**

can·di·date [kan′də·dāt′] *n.* A person being considered for a certain job or elected office.

can·vas [kan′vəs] *n.* A piece of heavy cloth stretched over a frame on which pictures are painted: **For his art project, Randy bought oil paints, special brushes, and a** *canvas* **to paint on.**

car·bon di·ox·ide [kär′bən dī·ok′sīd′] *n.* A gas that has no color or smell and that plants need.

car·ni·val [kär′nə·vəl] *n.* **1** A festival with parades and dancing. **2** (*written* **Carnival**) A special holiday that comes a few weeks before Easter: **Maria is happy about the beautiful costume she will wear during** *Carnival.*

candidate A candidate was originally someone dressed in white. To the ancient Romans, white symbolized purity and honesty. Our words *candid*, "honest," and *candor*, "honesty," go back to the same root, meaning "white."

canvas

a	add	o͝o	took
ā	ace	o͞o	pool
â	care	u	up
ä	palm	û	burn
e	end	yo͞o	fuse
ē	equal	oi	oil
i	it	ou	pout
ī	ice	ng	ring
o	odd	th	thin
ō	open	th	this
ô	order	zh	vision

ə = { a in *above* e in *sicken*
i in *possible*
o in *melon* u in *circus* }

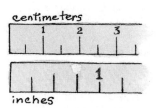

centimeter

chemical In the Middle Ages, the Arabs who invaded Europe brought with them practices they called *al-kimia*. The Europeans changed the Arab word to *alchemy*. From the name for the practices of working with metals and medicines came our scientific words *chemical, chemistry,* and *chemist.*

converse

cast [kast] *n.* The act of throwing a fishing line.

cen·ti·me·ter [sen′tə·mē′tər] *n.* A measure of length somewhat less than half an inch: **Luis learned that one *centimeter* equals almost half an inch.**

cer·e·mo·ny [ser′ə·mō′nē] *n.* Actions done for the purpose of celebrating something.

char·coal [chär′kōl′] *n.* A black substance that is made from wood burned in a special way, often used in drawing.

chem·i·cal [kem′i·kəl] *n.* One of many basic materials or elements found in nature and often combined by scientists to make medicines: **The students wear safety glasses when mixing *chemicals.***

chuck·le [chuk′əl] *v.* **chuck·led, chuck·ling** To laugh in a gentle manner.

clan [klan] *n.* A group of families who have the same ancestor.

com·mon [kom′ən] *adj.* Usual; widely available or found: **Chickens, pigs, and cows are *common* farm animals.**

con·cen·trate [kon′sən·trāt′] *v.* To think about one thing very hard.

con·cern [kən·sûrn′] *n.* Interest, caring: **Mike's *concern* only for himself left him with few friends.**

con·clude [kən·klo͞od′] *v.* **con·clud·ed, con·clud·ing** To form an idea or opinion after thinking about something: **Nora saw the dark clouds and *concluded* that it was going to rain.**

con·quer [kong′kər] *v.* To take control of by force.

con·sid·er·ate [kən·sid′ər·it] *adj.* Caring about another person's feelings. *syns.* kind, polite

con·tra·dict [kon′trə·dikt′] *v.* **con·tra·dict·ed, con·tra·dict·ing** To disagree or say the opposite. *syns.* deny, oppose

con·verse [kən·vûrs′] *v.* **con·versed, con·vers·ing** To talk: **Sometimes my mother and Mrs. Potter *converse* on the phone for an hour.** *syn.* speak

cor·al reef [kor′əl rēf] *n.* A hard ridge formed by the skeletons of tiny sea animals near the surface of seawater.

cor·ral [kə·ral′] *n.* A fenced area where animals are kept.

coun·ter·clock·wise [koun′tər·klok′wīz′] *adj.* In the direction of a clock running backward.

cow·er [kou′ər] *v.* **cow·ered, cow·er·ing** To curl up with fear. *syns.* tremble, cringe

crew [krōō] *n.* A group of people who work on a ship.

cur·rent [kûr′ənt] *n.* Water or air that flows in a definite direction.

cus·tom [kus′təm] *n.* A practice followed by most people in a group, often for many years: *Customs are different in Japan.*

cy·clist [sī′klist] *n.* A bicycle rider: **The *cyclists* were headed for camp after a long, hot day.**

D

dec·ade [dek′ād′] *n.* A time period of ten years: **It was many *decades* ago that my grandparents were born.**

deed [dēd] *n.* A written note proving that someone owns a piece of land.

de·gree [di·grē′] *n.* A unit used to measure temperature: **It was a hot summer, with daily temperatures above 90 *degrees.***

del·i·cate [del′ə·kit] *adj.* Very fine and not heavy: **The old curtains were made of very *delicate* lace.**

de·scen·dant [di·sen′dənt] *n.* A member of a younger generation of a family, such as a child or a grandchild.

des·ti·na·tion [des′tə·nā′shən] *n.* The place where one is going.

des·ti·ny [des′tə·nē] *n.* Something that seems certain to happen to someone. *syn.* fate

de·vice [di·vīs′] *n.* Something designed for a certain purpose. *syn.* tool

dis·cour·aged [dis·kûr′ijd] *adj.* Feeling bad about the way things happened. *syn.* disappointed

dis·guise [dis·gīz′] *n.* Something that changes the way someone usually looks. *syn.* costume

dis·may [dis·mā′] *n.* An uneasy feeling of alarm.

dis·solve [di·zolv′] *v.* **dis·solved, dis·solv·ing** To become a liquid or to melt: **The grease on the dirty pans will *dissolve* when Ray washes them with detergent.**

dis·tinct [dis·tingkt′] *adj.* Very clear: **The *distinct* smell of cookies filled the bakery.** *syn.* sharp

dou·ble [dub′əl] *n.* A two-base hit in baseball.

delicate This word is similar to the words *delicious* and *delight.* They describe things that give pleasure. Another related word is *delicacy,* which is a fine food that gives pleasure. In German, the plural of *delicacy* is *delicatessen,* which also names a place where fine foods are sold.

disguise

a	add	o͝o	took
ā	ace	o͞o	pool
â	care	u	up
ä	palm	û	burn
e	end	yo͞o	fuse
ē	equal	oi	oil
i	it	ou	pout
ī	ice	ng	ring
o	odd	th	thin
ō	open	t̶h̶	this
ô	order	zh	vision

ə = { a in *above* e in *sicken* i in *possible* o in *melon* u in *circus* }

dugout

echo   In Greek mythology, Echo fell in love with a young man who could love only himself. She was sad and hid in a cave. She faded away until only her voice was left. The story says that is why you hear an echo in a cave.

endangered

dug·out [dug′out′] *n.* A home built by digging out a living space in the side of a hill or river bank.

E

ech·o [ek′ō] *n.; pl.* **ech·oes** Sound reflected or bounced back: **The** *echoes* **in the empty room made it sound as if more than two people were talking.**

e·lec·tion [i·lek′shən] *n.* The choosing of a person for a position by voting.

e·merge [i·mûrj′] *v.* To come out or become visible.

en·dan·gered [in·dān′jərd] *adj.* In danger of no longer existing.

en·dur·ance [in·d(y)ŏŏr′əns] *n.* The ability to work hard for a long time.

en·vi·ron·ment [in·vī′rən·mənt] *n.* The place where something lives, or its surroundings: **Peaches grow best in a warm, sunny** *environment.*

en·vy [en′vē] *n.* Jealousy or resentment toward someone.

e·rupt [i·rupt′] *v.* To suddenly burst out.

e·vap·o·rate [i·vap′ə·rāt′] *v.* **e·vap·o·rat·ed, e·vap·o·rat·ing** To dry up: **The hot sun had** *evaporated* **the puddles on the sidewalk, so we didn't get wet feet.**

ex·claim [iks·klām′] *v.* **ex·claimed, ex·claim·ing** To speak with emotion, as in a surprised manner: **"What a beautiful painting!" he** *exclaimed.*

ex·er·tion [ig·zûr′shən] *n.* Hard work.

ex·haus·tion [ig·zôs′chən] *n.* The feeling of being very tired.

ex·ot·ic [ig·zot′ik] *adj.* Strange and interesting.

ex·pec·tant·ly [ik·spek′tənt·lē] *adv.* In anticipation of something; waiting for something to happen: **During the holidays, Paul watched** *expectantly* **for the delivery of the mail.**

ex·pla·na·tion [ek′splə·nā′shən] *n.* A reason given that makes something easier to understand: **The students learned from the teacher's** *explanation* **of the story.**

ex·qui·site [eks′kwi·zit *or* ik·skwiz′it] *adj.* Very beautiful: **Bright yellow, blue, and green feathers made the bird look** *exquisite.*

F

field [fēld] *v.* **field·ed,
field·ing** To catch or pick
up a batted baseball and
throw it to the proper
player.

fin [fin] *n.* A part of a fish
that sticks out, may be fan-
shaped, and is used for
steering or balance: **Sharks
can be spotted when their**
fins **move through the
water.**

flu·ent [flōō'ənt] *adj.* Spoken
smoothly and easily: **Carla
spoke such** *fluent* **French
that no one believed she
grew up in Chicago.**

fore·close [fôr·klōz'] *v.*
fore·closed, fore·clos·ing
To take away land from a
person who owes money
on it.

foul [foul] *n.* A ball hit
outside the first- or third-
base line: **After hitting
four** *fouls,* **he was out.**

fra·grant [frā'grənt] *adj.*
Having a sweet smell:
**Aurora's perfume smelled
like** *fragrant* **roses.**

frame [frām] *v.* **framed,
fram·ing** To cause
someone to appear guilty
of being involved in a
crime.

fur·nace [fûr'nis] *n.* A large
structure containing a very
hot fire: **It is hot working
in a factory where**
furnaces **are continually
burning.**

fur·row [fûr'ō] *n.* A groove
in the ground where seeds
are planted: **Andrew made
a** *furrow* **for the flower
seeds.**

fu·ry [fyŏŏr'ē] *n.* Great
anger.

fu·ture [fyōō'chər] *n.* Time to
come; time that hasn't
happened yet: **We don't
know yet what will
happen in the** *future.*

G

gape [gāp] *v.* **gaped, gap·ing**
To stare with an open
mouth: **Lani stopped in
the corridor,** *gaping* **at the
sight of a mother rabbit
and her babies.**

gar·ment [gär'mənt] *n.* A
piece of clothing: **Mr.
Sawado sells shirts,
jackets, suits, and other**
garments.

gau·cho [gou'chō] *n.* A
South American cowhand:
Gauchos **are workers who
ride horses and take care
of cattle.**

gen·er·a·tion [jen'ə·rā'shən]
n. A group of people born
around the same time.

fin This word may have
come from the word *pinna,*
which means "feather" or
"wing," or from the word
spina, which means
"thorn."

furrow

gaucho

a	add	ŏŏ	took
ā	ace	ōō	pool
â	care	u	up
ä	palm	û	burn
e	end	yōō	fuse
ē	equal	oi	oil
i	it	ou	pout
ī	ice	ng	ring
o	odd	th	thin
ō	open	th	this
ô	order	zh	vision

ə = { a in *above*   e in *sicken*
      i in *possible*
      o in *melon*   u in *circus* }

glimpse Originally *glimpse* meant "to shine faintly." It had a similar meaning to *gleam,* as of light. Eventually it came to mean a dim flash. The quickness of a flash allows only a brief look, or a *glimpse.*

herb

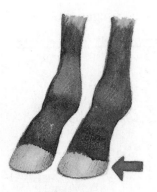

hoof

gill [gil] *n.* In fish, an organ used to take in oxygen from the water; the fish's breathing mechanism: **A fish uses its *gills* to breathe.**

glimpse [glimps] *n.* A quick look.

glis·ten [glis'(ə)n] *v.* **glis·tened, glis·ten·ing** To shine. *syns.* sparkle, shimmer

grieve [grēv] *v.* To be very sorry and upset about something lost: **Tony *grieved* over the death of his pet.** *syn.* mourn

ground·er [groun'dər] *n.* In baseball, a ball that hits the ground and rolls or bounces.

guard·i·an [gär'dē·ən] *n.* A person who takes care of and protects something or someone else.

H

haze [hāz] *n.* Dust particles in the air that prevent a clear view: **The *haze* prevented Dennis from seeing the stars.**

hearth [härth] *n.* The bottom of an industrial furnace, where metal being melted into a liquid collects: **When the *hearth* is filled, the hot liquid pours out.**

herb [(h)ûrb] *n.* A plant used for medicine or adding flavor to food.

hes·i·tate [hez'ə·tāt'] *v.* **hes·i·tat·ed, hes·i·tat·ing** To act slowly, as if in doubt. *syn.* pause

hoof [hŏof *or* hōof] *n.; pl.* **hoofs** or **hooves** The hard cover on the foot of an animal such as a horse: **You can hear the *hooves* of a running horse beat the ground.**

hov·er [huv'ər] *v.* **hov·ered, hov·er·ing** To stay around one area in the air with very little movement, as if held in place: **The bees were *hovering* over the honey-filled tree.**

hy·drant [hī'drənt] *n.* A large water pipe that is kept covered and is used in fighting fires: **When the firefighter connected the hose to the *hydrant,* water came pouring through.**

I

id·i·o·syn·cra·sy [id'ē·ō·sing'krə·sē] *n.* A way of acting that is odd or different.

im·me·di·ate·ly [i·mē'dē·it·lē] *adv.* Right away; without waiting; now.

im·mer·sion heat·er
[i·mûr′shən hē′tər *or*
i·mûr′zhən hē′tər] *n.* A
tool heated electrically and
put into liquid to warm it.

im·pa·tient [im·pā′shənt]
adj. Not wanting to wait:
**Tim was *impatient* for his
favorite television show
to begin.**

in·ning [in′ing] *n.* The time
it takes in a baseball game
for both teams to get three
outs: **After six *innings*, our
team was ahead, two to
one.**

in·no·cent [in′ə·sənt] *adj.*
Not to blame.

in·stinct [in′stingkt] *n.* A
natural force that makes
people or animals act in
certain ways: **The mother
duck's *instincts* were to
provide food for and
protect her babies.**

in·struc·tor [in·struk′tər] *n.*
A person who teaches.

in·su·lat·ed [in′sə·lāt′əd]
adj. Designed to keep
contents hot or cold:
**I have an *insulated*
container in my lunch box
that keeps my soup hot
all day.**

in·ten·si·ty [in·ten′sə·tē] *n.*
Great concentration.

in·ten·tion [in·ten′shən] *n.*
Plan or purpose: Because
she was too busy, **Carla
had no *intention* of going
to the party.**

in·ter·na·tion·al
[in′tər·nash′ən·əl] *adj.* In
nations all over the world.
syn. worldwide

in·ter·rupt [in′tə·rupt′] *v.*
in·ter·rupt·ed,
in·ter·rupt·ing To start
talking before someone
else has finished.

in·ter·view [in′tər·vyo͞o′] *n.*
A meeting in which two or
more people exchange
information.

J

jour·nal·ist [jûr′nəl·ist] *n.*
Someone who writes or
edits articles for
newspapers or magazines:
**The *journalist* wrote an
article about recycling for
the magazine.** *syn.*
reporter

K

ken·nel [ken′əl] *n.* A place to
keep and care for dogs.

kin·ship [kin′ship′] *n.* A
relationship or connection
like that between family
members.

instinct   *Instinct* comes
from the Latin word
instinguere, meaning "to
prod or force." Instincts
are inner forces that cause
animals to behave in
certain ways. *Instinct* is
also related to our word
stick. Think of an instinct
as something that sticks or
prods a rabbit, forcing it to
run away from danger.

insulated

journalist

a	add	o͝o	took
ā	ace	o͞o	pool
â	care	u	up
ä	palm	û	burn
e	end	yo͞o	fuse
ē	equal	oi	oil
i	it	ou	pout
ī	ice	ng	ring
o	odd	th	thin
ō	open	th	this
ô	order	zh	vision

ə = { a in *above*   e in *sicken*
i in *possible*
o in *melon*   u in *circus* }

lantern　This word first meant "a bunch of burning sticks." Later a lantern was something like a lamp inside a cover. At one time a lantern's cover was made of horn, and *lantern* was spelled *lanthorn.*

lasso

mane

L

la•dle [lād′(ə)l] *n.* A large cup-shaped spoon with a long handle, used for pouring liquids: **Using a** *ladle,* **Ben poured the soup from the pot into the bowl.**

lan•tern [lan′tərn] *n.* A kind of lamp used outdoors.

las•so [las′ō] *n.* A rope with a loop at the end, used for catching cattle.

laun•dry [lôn′drē] *n.* Clothes that need washing: **Donnie piled the family's** *laundry* **next to the washing machine.**

la•va [lä′və *or* lav′ə] *n.* Very hot melted rock that bursts out of a volcano.

log•i•cal [loj′ə•kəl] *adj.* In a way that is orderly and makes sense: **The plan was so** *logical* **that it was easy to carry out.**

loop•hole [lōōp′hōl′] *n.* A way of getting around a law or legal agreement.

lum•ber [lum′bər] *v.* **lum•bered, lum•ber•ing** To move along slowly and heavily. *syn.* plod

lu•nar [lōō′nər] *adj.* Having to do with the moon: **In the** *lunar* **calendar, one month equals the number of days from one full moon to the next.**

M

mag•nif•i•cent [mag•nif′ə•sənt] *adj.* Wonderful; impressive: **The king wore a** *magnificent* **jeweled crown that we all admired.** *syn.* splendid

mane [mān] *n.* The long hair on the neck of an animal, such as a horse.

mem•o•ry [mem′ər•ē] *n.; pl.* **mem•o•ries** Something a person remembers: **Mr. White has happy** *memories* **of the times he went fishing with his sons.**

mesh [mesh] *n.* A netlike device made from cords or wires that interlock with spaces between them, as in a screen.

mi•gra•tion [mī•grā′shən] *n.* Movement from one area to another with the changing of certain seasons: **In Pennsylvania, hawks begin their** *migration* **south every year from Hawk Mountain.**

mime [mīm] *n.* A performer who uses hand movements and facial expressions instead of words.

mis·chief [mis′chif] *n.*
Harmful or tricky acts.
mol·ten [mōl′tən] *adj.* Made
liquid by great heat.
mon·o·tone [mon′ə·tōn] *n.*
A voice that never changes
in highness or lowness.
mus·cle [mus′əl] *n.* A part
of the body that helps
produce movement:
**Bodybuilders develop
their *muscles* by
exercising and lifting
weights.**

N

na·tive [nā′tiv] *n.* A person
who is born in a certain
area.
nec·tar [nek′tər] *n.* A sweet
liquid made by flowers.
neu·tral [n(y)o͞o′trəl] *adj.* Not
on either side of an issue;
in the middle.

O

oc·cu·py [ok′yə·pī′] *v.*
oc·cu·pied, oc·cu·py·ing
To live in a place.
of·fi·cial [ə·fish′əl] *adj.*
Having the right or
permission to do
something: **Rick was not
an *official* contestant in
the game.**
or·di·nar·y [ôr′də·ner′ē]
adj. Something usual.

o·ver·take [ō′vər′·tāk′] *v.*
o·ver·took, o·ver·tak·ing
To chase and catch up to:
**In the field, the fox
overtook the rabbit.**
ox·y·gen [ok′sə·jin] *n.* The
part of air that animals
and people need to stay
alive.

P

pas·try [pā′strē] *n.* Sweet
foods, such as cakes or
pies.
ped·al [ped′(ə)l] *v.* To push
with the feet when riding a
bicycle in order to get the
bicycle to move.
peer [pir] *v.* **peered, peer·ing**
To take a close look:
**Wilbur *peered* at the sky
to see if dark clouds were
forming.**
pelt [pelt] *n.* The furry skin
of an animal: **Daniel
Boone's hat was made
from raccoon *pelts*.**
pinch-hit [pinch′hit′] *v.*
pinch-hit, pinch-hit·ting
In baseball, to bat for
another baseball player.
pitch [pich] *v.* To throw a ball
to a batter.
pol·i·ti·cian [pol′ə·tish′ən]
n. A person who takes part
in or represents the
government: **Some
politicians in
Washington, D.C., are
meeting to discuss
subjects such as clean air.**

muscle

nectar The Greeks called
nectar the drink of the
gods. Eventually any
delicious drink became
known as *nectar*.

a	add	o͝o	took
ā	ace	o͞o	pool
â	care	u	up
ä	palm	û	burn
e	end	yo͞o	fuse
ē	equal	oi	oil
i	it	ou	pout
ī	ice	ng	ring
o	odd	th	thin
ō	open	th	this
ô	order	zh	vision

ə = { a in *above* e in *sicken* / i in *possible* / o in *melon* u in *circus*

pollen

property

rare There are two meanings for the word *rare*. The first comes from the Latin word *rarus*, or "loose in texture, separated." Eventually, *rare* came to mean "scarce" or "uncommon." The second meaning comes from *rear*, meaning "underdone" – as "*rear* eggs." We now apply this meaning to cooking, as in "*rare* steak."

pol·len [pol'ən] *n.* A powder made by flowers that enables new seeds to grow.

praise [prāz] *v.* To say nice things about someone or something. *syn.* compliment

pre·cious [presh'əs] *adj.* Very special or valuable.

pre·serve [pri·zûrv'] *v.* To keep from harm. *syn.* save

pre·tend [pri·tend'] *v.* **pre·tend·ed, pre·tend·ing** To fake or make believe: **Steve knew his sister was only** *pretending* **to be asleep so she could listen to him talk to his friends.**

prey [prā] *n.* An animal hunted by another animal for food.

probe [prōb] *v.* **probed, prob·ing** To explore with a pointed object or tool.

prop·er·ty [prop'ər·tē] *n.* Land belonging to someone: **Mr. Teng built a fence around his** *property* **to keep the neighbor's dog out.**

pro·té·gée [prō'tə·zhā'] (refers to a female) *n.* A young person learning a craft under the guidance of a more experienced person. (The male form of this word is *protégé*.)

pro·test [prə·test'] *v.* **pro·test·ed, pro·test·ing** To object: **Some people** *protested* **that a new airport would make their neighborhood too noisy.**

Q

qual·i·ty [kwol'ə·tē] *n.; pl.* **qualities** A person's special feature or characteristic: **Kindness, generosity, and helpfulness are some of Mia's good** *qualities.*

R

ra·di·ance [rā'dē·əns] *n.* A glow; brightness.

ran·sacked [ran'sakt'] *adj.* Torn apart during a search.

rare [râr] *adj.* Very uncommon; found in very few places.

ra·vine [rə·vēn'] *n.* A long, deep ditch in the earth with steep sides.

re·al·ize [rē'əl·īz'] *v.* **re·al·ized, re·al·iz·ing** To understand, become aware of, or know something: **When summer came, Sue** *realized* **that the fair would soon be in town.**

re·cov·er·y [ri·kuv′ər·ē] *n.*
A return to good health:
**Everyone hoped Alana
would make a quick
recovery from the flu and
return to school soon.**

reel [rēl] *n.* A spool that
turns, winding or
unwinding a fishing line.

re·flec·tion [ri·flek′shən] *n.*
Something seen because
its image is bounced back
from a shiny surface:
**Robert looked at his
reflection in the mirror.**

re·ply [ri·plī′] *n.* An answer
to a message or a question.

res·er·va·tion
[rez′ər·vā′shən] *n.* An area
of land set aside by the
government for a certain
group of people to live on.

re·spon·si·ble
[ri·spon′sə·bəl] *adj.*
Having the duty to take
care of something or
somebody: **Ron was
responsible for feeding
the cat.**

re·tired [ri·tīrd′] *adj.* Having
stopped working because
of age.

re·trieve [ri·trēv′] *v.* To go
after and bring back.

ri·dic·u·lous [ri·dik′yə·ləs]
adj. Funny: **The puppet's
green, fuzzy hair looked
ridiculous and made us
laugh.** *syns.* laughable,
silly

roam [rōm] *v.* To wander
around.

S

scoff [skof] *v.* **scoffed,
scoff·ing** To ridicule or
make fun of: **Rosa *scoffed*
unkindly because Kathy
did not catch the ball.**

se·nhor [si·nyō(ə)r′] *n.*
Portuguese title for a man,
the same as *Mr.* or *Sir:* **In
Brazil, where they speak
Portuguese, the people
Mr. Mason met called him
senhor.**

sen·si·ble [sen′sə·bəl] *adj.*
Smart; reasonable: **Mike
knew that eating all that
candy was not *sensible*
because eating too many
sweets is not healthy.** *syn.*
wise

shal·low [shal′ō] *adj.* Not
very deep.

sheep·ish·ly [shē′pish·lē]
adv. With a feeling of
shame.

shel·ter [shel′tər] *v.* To
provide a safe, covered
place.

short·stop [shôrt′stop′] *n.* A
baseball player whose
position is between second
and third base.

shriek [shrēk] *n.* A screech; a
high-pitched scream or
outcry: **The *shrieking*
sound of the chalk on the
board hurt my ears.**

shriv·eled [shriv′əld] *adj.*
Small and dried up. *syn.*
shrunken

reflection

senhor This Portuguese
word for "Mr." traces its
origins to the Latin word
senior, which means
"older." Only an adult
man was considered
worthy of this formal title.
The Spanish word *señor*
and the Italian *signor* have
the same origin and
meaning. Even our English
word *sir* can be traced to
senior.

a	add	o͝o	took
ā	ace	o͞o	pool
â	care	u	up
ä	palm	û	burn
e	end	yo͞o	fuse
ē	equal	oi	oil
i	it	ou	pout
ī	ice	ng	ring
o	odd	th	thin
ō	open	th	this
ô	order	zh	vision

ə = { a in *above* e in *sicken*
      i in *possible*
      o in *melon* u in *circus* }

smokestack

submerge

talent   *Talent* was first used to mean "a unit of money." Because of a story about a man who gave his servants talents and how the servants succeeded in increasing the value of the money, *talent* came to mean "a skill or an ability to do something well."

si·es·ta [sē·es′tə] *n.* A nap in the afternoon.

sig·nal [sig′nəl] *v.* **sig·naled, sig·nal·ing** To give a sign or bring notice to something: **Ella *signaled* the movers to start loading the van.**

sil·hou·ette [sil′o͞o·et′] *v.* **sil·hou·et·ted, sil·hou·et·ting** To make a dark outline of a person or thing against a light background.

sin·gle [sing′gəl] *n.* In baseball, a hit in which the batter reaches first base.

smoke·stack [smōk′stak′] *n.* A tall, chimneylike structure on a factory building, used to release smoke: **You could see the factory's *smokestacks* for miles.**

spe·cies [spē′shēz *or* spē′sēz] *n.; pl.* **species** A group of living things that are similar and can breed with each other.

stam·pede [stam·pēd′] *v.* To rush wildly in a group.

star·tling [stär′tling] *adj.* Surprising; shocking. *syn.* amazing

strike [strīk] *n.* In baseball, a good pitch that the batter misses or does not swing at.

stunned [stund] *adj.* Very surprised.

sub·merge [səb·mûrj′] *v.* **sub·merged, sub·merg·ing** To go or put underwater: **The divers were *submerged*.**

sub·stance [sub′stəns] *n.* Material that something is made of.

sug·ges·tion [sə(g)·jes′chən] *n.* A hint, an indication, or advice: *Suggestions* **about a new lunch menu are welcome.**

sur·vive [sər·vīv′] *v.* To stay alive.

sus·pend [sə·spend′] *v.* **sus·pend·ed, sus·pend·ing** To hang: **The swing was *suspended* from a tree branch.**

sus·pi·cious [sə·spish′əs] *adj.* Having a feeling that something is wrong. *syn.* untrusting

sym·pa·thy [sim′pə·thē] *n.* The understanding of another person's feelings: **Because Kendra was crying, Gloria hugged her in *sympathy*.**

T

tal·ent [tal′ənt] *n.* An ability or a skill that is a natural gift: **Pat demonstrated her artistic *talent* by painting a self-portrait.**

tan·gle [tang′gəl] *n.* A twisted mass: **The necklace was a *tangle* of knots.**

tem·per [tem′pər] *n.* Mood.

ten·ta·cle [ten′tə·kəl] *n.* A long armlike structure growing out of an animal's body, used for movement or catching food: **An octopus has eight *tentacles*.**

tes·ti·fy [tes′tə·fī] *v.* To speak under oath in a court of law.

thick·et [thik′it] *n.* A group of trees growing very close together. *syn.* grove

torch [tôrch] *n.* An instrument that gives off a very hot flame: **As we watched the men light the *torches*, big sparks were given off that chased us away.**

tra·di·tion [trə·dish′ən] *n.* An idea or a way of doing things that is passed down among people over many years.

trans·par·ent [trans·pâr′ənt] *adj.* Able to be seen through: **We could see the cat sleeping behind the *transparent* curtains.**

trim [trim] *v.* **trimmed, trim·ming** To decorate something: **We *trimmed* the tree with lights.**

tri·um·phant·ly [trī·um′fənt·lē] *adv.* With joy and pride.

trout [trout] *n.* A small freshwater fish.

tur·moil [tûr′moil] *n.* Great confusion: **The disappearance of the President left the country in *turmoil*.**

twi·light [twī′līt′] *n.* The light as the sun sets.

U

UFO [yoō′ef·ō′] *n.* *U*nidentified *F*lying *O*bject; something seen in the sky that seems too strange to be real.

un·doubt·ed·ly [un·dou′tid·lē] *adv.* Certainly: **The sun is *undoubtedly* important to growing plants.** *syn.* surely

ur·gent·ly [ûr′jənt·lē] *adv.* In a way calling for quick action.

u·su·al [yoō′zhoō·əl] *adj.* In the normal or regular course of events.

V

va·ca·tion [vā·kā′shən] *n.* Time away from work, spent in amusement or relaxation.

torch The Latin word *torquere*, meaning "twist," became *torca* – and then *torche*, in French. Pieces of straw were twisted together and dipped in a flammable liquid. Thus, a torch was made.

transparent

trout

a	add	ŏŏ	took
ā	ace	ōō	pool
â	care	u	up
ä	palm	û	burn
e	end	yōō	fuse
ē	equal	oi	oil
i	it	ou	pout
ī	ice	ng	ring
o	odd	th	thin
ō	ope	th	this
ô	ord	zh	vision

ə = { a *above* e in *sicken*
       i *possible*
       n *melon* u in *circus* }

violinist

volcano *Volcano* comes from the name Vulcan, the Roman god of fire and metalworking. The Romans believed that Vulcan's workshop and fiery furnace were buried under Mt. Etna, a volcano on the island of Sicily near Italy. When Vulcan and his helpers were heating and hammering, the mountain rumbled and shook, and sometimes fire and smoke came from the top.

yoke

vain [vān] *adj.* Too proud of the way one looks: **The *vain* beauty queen thought she was the prettiest woman in the world.**

vet·er·i·nar·i·an [vet′ər·ə·nâr′ē·ən *or* vet′rə·nâr′ē·ən] *n.* A doctor who treats animals.

vig·or·ous·ly [vig′ər·əs·lē] *adv.* With strength and energy: **The girls played basketball so *vigorously* that they were worn out after the game.**

vi·o·lin·ist [vī′ə·lin′ist] *n.* A person who plays a musical instrument called a violin: **The *violinist* broke a string on her instrument as she was playing it.**

vol·ca·no [vol·kā′nō] *n.* A kind of mountain from which melted rock, stones, and ashes sometimes explode.

vol·un·teer [vol′ən·tir′] *v.* **vol·un·teered, vol·un·teer·ing** To offer one's services without being made to: **Joan *volunteered* to work at the local hospital.**

W

wa·ver [wā′vər] *v.* **wa·vered, wa·ver·ing** To be unsteady and show signs of falling or giving way: **After climbing on the bicycle, the little boy began *wavering* and fell off.**

weight [wāt] *n.* The heaviness of an object or a person.

weird [wird] *adj.* Very strange.

wil·der·ness [wil′dər·nis] *n.* Land not developed for people to live on.

wound [wo͞ond] *v.* **wound·ed, wound·ing** To injure or hurt. *syn.* harm

wrin·kle [ring′kəl] *n.* A line on the skin: **The *wrinkles* on his face signaled that he was very old.**

writhe [rīt͟h] *v.* **writhed, writh·ing** To twist or move as in pain: **The caged snake was *writhing*.**

Y

yoke [yōk] *v.* **yoked, yok·ing** To join together by a wooden frame.

INDEX OF
TITLES AND AUTHORS

Page numbers in light print refer to biographical information.

Acknowledgments continued

Holiday House: From *Totem Pole* by Diane Hoyt-Goldsmith. Text copyright © 1990 by Diane Hoyt-Goldsmith. Cover photograph by Lawrence Migdale from *Pueblo Storyteller* by Diane Hoyt-Goldsmith. Photograph copyright © 1991 by Lawrence Migdale.

Henry Holt and Company, Inc.: *On the Pampas* by María Cristina Brusca. Copyright © 1991 by María Cristina Brusca.

Houghton Mifflin Company: *A River Dream* by Allen Say. Copyright © 1988 by Allen Say. *Jumanji* by Chris Van Allsburg. Copyright © 1981 by Chris Van Allsburg. *Just a Dream* by Chris Van Allsburg. Copyright © 1990 by Chris Van Allsburg.

Japan Foreign-Rights Centre, on behalf of Komine Shoten Publishing Company Ltd., Tokyo, Japan: Cover illustration by Yoshiharu Suzuki from *Smell of the Rain, Voices of the Stars* by Norihisa Akaza. Copyright © 1987 by Norihisa Akaza and Yoshiharu Suzuki. Originally published in Japan under the title *Ame No Nioi Hoshi No Koe*.

Alfred A. Knopf, Inc.: *No Star Nights* by Anna Egan Smucker, illustrated by Steve Johnson. Text copyright © 1989 by Anna Egan Smucker; illustrations copyright © 1989 by Steve Johnson.

Lerner Publications Company, 241 First Avenue, Minneapolis, MN 55401: From *Carnivorous Plants* by Cynthia Overbeck. Text copyright © 1982 by Lerner Publications Company.

Little, Brown and Company: "Philippe and the Blue Parrot" from *Light: Stories of a Small Kindness* by Nancy White Carlstrom. Text copyright © 1990 by Nancy White Carlstrom. From *Shortstop from Tokyo* by Matt Christopher, cover illustration by Glenn Harrington. Copyright © 1970 by Matthew F. Christopher.

Lodestar Books, an affiliate of Dutton Children's Books, a division of Penguin USA Inc.: Cover photograph by Richard Hewett from *Getting Elected: The Diary of a Campaign* by Joan Hewett. Photograph copyright © 1989 by Richard Hewett. "The Case of the Million Pesos" from *Encyclopedia Brown Gets His Man* by Donald J. Sobol. Text copyright © 1967 by Donald J. Sobol.

Lothrop, Lee & Shepard Books, a division of William Morrow & Company, Inc.: *Supergrandpa* by David M. Schwartz, illustrated by Bert Dodson. Text copyright © 1991 by David M. Schwartz; illustrations copyright © 1991 by Bert Dodson. *Mufaro's Beautiful Daughters* by John Steptoe. Copyright © 1987 by John Steptoe. Used with the approval of the Estate of John Steptoe.

Macmillan Publishing Company: From *Down Under, Down Under; Diving Adventures on the Great Barrier Reef* by Ann McGovern. Text copyright © 1989 by Ann McGovern. Cover illustration by Karl Swanson from *Carver* by Ruth Yaffe Radin. Illustration copyright © 1990 by Karl Swanson. Cover illustration by Diane deGroat from *Jace the Ace* by Joanne Rocklin. Illustration copyright © 1990 by Diane deGroat. Cover illustration by Jerry Pinkney from *Turtle in July* by Marilyn Singer. Illustration copyright © 1989 by Jerry Pinkney.

Viqui Maggio: Cover illustration from *Ellis Island* by William Jay Jacobs. Illustration copyright © 1990 by Viqui Maggio.

McIntosh and Otis, Inc.: "The Case of the Locked Room" from *Two-Minute Mysteries* by Donald J. Sobol. Text copyright © 1967 by Donald J. Sobol. Published by Scholastic Book Services.

Morrow Junior Books, a division of William Morrow & Company, Inc.: Cover illustration by David Wiesner from *Man from the Sky* by Avi. Illustration © 1992 by David Wiesner. From *Class President* by Johanna Hurwitz, cover illustration by Sheila Hamanaka. Text copyright © 1990 by Johanna Hurwitz; cover illustration copyright © 1990 by Sheila Hamanaka.

National Geographic Society: "Running With the Pack" from *National Geographic World* Magazine, February 1987. Text copyright © 1987 by National Geographic Society.

Plays, Inc.: "Close Encounter of a Weird Kind" by A. F. Bauman from *Space and Science Fiction Plays for Young People*, edited by Sylvia E. Kamerman. Text copyright © 1981 by Plays, Inc.

G. P. Putnam's Sons: *Mirette on the High Wire* by Emily Arnold McCully. Copyright © 1992 by Emily Arnold McCully.

Random House, Inc: Cover illustration by Sheila Hamanaka from *The Skates of Uncle Richard* by Carol Fenner. Illustration copyright © 1990 by Sheila Hamanaka.

Roberts Rinehart Publishers, Post Office Box 666, Niwot, CO 80544: Cover illustration by Birgitta Säflund from *The People Who Hugged the Trees* by Deborah Lee Rose. Illustration copyright © 1990 by Birgitta Säflund.

Scholastic, Inc.: "How Many Spots Does A Leopard Have?" from *How Many Spots Does A Leopard Have? and Other Tales* by Julius Lester, illustrated by David Shannon. Text copyright © 1989 by Julius Lester; illustrations copyright © 1989 by David Shannon.

Charles Scribner's Sons, an imprint of Macmillan Publishing Company: From *The Best Town in the World* by Byrd Baylor, illustrated by Ronald Himler. Text copyright © 1982 by Byrd Baylor; illustrations copyright © 1983 by Ronald Himler.

Simon & Schuster Books for Young Readers, New York: From *Alexander the Grape: Fruit and Vegetable Jokes* by Charles Keller. Text © 1982 by Charles Keller.

George Swede: "The yellow tulip" by George Swede from *Time Flies*. Copyright © 1984 by George Swede. Published by Three Trees Press.

Viking Penguin, a division of Penguin Books USA Inc.: From *The Midnight Fox* by Betsy Byars. Text copyright © 1968 by Betsy Byars.

Walker and Company: Cover illustration by Barbara Lavallee from *This Place is Wet* by Vicki Cobb. Illustration © 1989 by Barbara Lavallee.

Photograph Credits

Key: (t) top, (b) bottom, (l) left, (c) center, (r) right.

Unit 1

133(t) AP/Wide World Photos, (b) John Biever/Sports Illustrated

Unit 2

228, © SOUTHERN LIVING, INC. March 1991. Photo by Dianne Young; 228–229 M&E Bernstein/Woodfin Camp & Assoc.

Unit 3

326(b) Rochester Museum & Science Center; 326–327, Horticultural Photography, Corvallis, Oregon

Unit 4

416, D. Donne Bryant; 417, Wilbur E. Garrett © National Geographic Society

Unit 5

512(t) Sovfoto/Eastphoto; 513(t) Susan Greenwood for Insight/Gamma-Liason, (b) Bill Gentile for Newsweek/SIPA

Illustration Credits

Key: (t) top, (b) bottom, (l) left, (c) center, (r) right.

Theme Opening Art

Vincent Chiaramonte, 168–169, 580–581; Pat & Robin DeWitt, 274–275; Joe DiNicola, 138–139; Jennifer Hewitson, 422–423; Linda Kelen, 460–461; Armen Kojoyian, 20–21; Richard Murdock, 556–557; Ruben Ramos, 332–333, 490–491; Larry Raymond, 60–61, 396–397; S.D. Schindler, 198–199; Steve Shock, 382–383; Troy Thomas, 518–519; Jean & Mou-Sien Tseng, 234–235; David Wenzel, 302–303; Dean Williams, 88–89

Connections Art

Gil Ashby, 229; Mouli Marur, 326–327; William Maughan, 600–601; Pat DeWitt, 416–417; Steve Shock, 132–133, 512–513(b)

Unit Opener, Bookshelf, & Connections Border Art (4/c)

Brian Battles, 132–133; Christopher Boyce, 12–13, 418–419, 420–421, 512–513; Mary Jones, 4–5, 16–17, 18–19; Doug Schneider, 8–9, 230–231(t), 232–233, 326–327; Troy Thomas, 14–15, 514–515